A
Half
Step
Behind

9th Century Poet
Ono No Komachi

A
Half
Step
Behind

·

Japanese Women
of the '80s

·

JANE
CONDON

Dodd, Mead & Company

New York

Published by Dodd, Mead & Company, Inc.
79 Madison Avenue, New York, N.Y. 10016
Distributed in Canada by
McClelland and Stewart Limited, Toronto
Manufactured in the United States of America
Text design and title page drawing by Kay Lee
Title page and modern style calligraphy by Rev. Jomyo Tanaka
First Edition

Library of Congress Cataloging in Publication Data

Condon, Jane.
A half step behind.

Bibliography: p.
Includes index.
1. Feminism — Japan.   2. Women — Japan — Social
conditions.   3. Women — Employment — Japan.   4. Women —
Japan — Attitudes.   I. Title.
HQ1763.C66 1986   305.4'0952   85-10147
ISBN 0-396-08665-9

To Mom

Contents

them out of their customary *tatemae,* and they often responded with a rush of *honne* that surprised them as much as it gratified me.

In some areas, I tried to follow Japanese custom as closely as possible. I never called a potential subject without an introduction; occasionally a single interview took weeks of polite letters and phone calls. At the outset, my biggest hurdle appeared to be whiskey. A Japanese friend told me that a gift of Scotch—preferably Chivas Regal—would be expected by everyone I interviewed. The Japanese even have a bastardized-English word for this: "nomunication," or communication plus the verb *nomu* (to drink). Fortunately, I found that six-dollar boxes of Godiva chocolates provided ample proof of my good intentions, and contrary to my original fears, it proved unnecessary to stockpile hundreds of bottles of nomunication Scotch.

Japanese women are wonderful hostesses. During the course of my interviews, I consumed hundreds of cups of green tea and hundreds of bean-paste sweets, which I hated before I moved to Japan, but for which I soon developed a taste. For chatting and socializing, I used my own fairly serviceable Japanese. But in the interest of accuracy, for the interviews themselves, I always used an interpreter, who was often the person who had provided the introduction. Since my interpreters, unlike myself, were not exempt from the rules of Japanese propriety, they were often more nervous than either I or my subject. This was the case when I visited a famous geisha in the old-fashioned town of Kanazawa, on the west coast of Japan. "Now remember," cautioned my interpreter, a conservative, middle-aged housewife. "Michiyakko is the greatest traditional dancer outside Tokyo. Please be respectful."

And I was. But as the afternoon progressed, and I ran out of polite questions about her background and her art, I started asking about the flirtatious games geisha play with their customers. The geisha herself was perfectly open and comfortable—we laughed uproariously together as she taught me how to bow correctly and how to look coy—but the interpreter began to look more and more distressed. I later reflected that Japanese women endure the double standard by remaining deliberately ignorant of whatever things might upset them. No wonder my interpreter, whose husband surely patronized geisha houses himself, had little appetite for the details of what went on inside.

When I interviewed a Kagoshima bar hostess, my contact and introducer was a Japanese businessman. Before we arrived, he told me, "Okay now, no questions about whether the hostesses are divorced, and don't ask if they sleep with their customers."

We took the elevator up to the third floor, knocked, passed the peephole test, and were invited in. The *mama-san* and I got along very well. I was particularly charmed when, despite the fact that I was five-and-a-half-months pregnant, she said that I was welcome to be a "pinch hitter" bar girl any time. Finally, she told me to ask her anything I wanted. "Anything?" I repeated. "Anything," she said. So I asked her if hostesses sleep with their customers, at which point my interpreter spilled his Scotch and water on his pants.

By the end of the interview, he looked as if he needed several good stiff drinks, so I wasn't surprised when he asked his assistant to take me back to my hotel while he stayed at the bar. The next day at his office, I noticed he looked a little rumpled. He even had on the same suit and tie! Now the pieces of the puzzle suddenly slipped into place. Yes, it seems as if hostesses sleep with their customers.

More than a year later, when I was in the northern city of Sendai talking to a clerk in a soy sauce factory, I myself had the experience of being interviewed. The local paper's only female reporter arrived at the factory in a chauffeur-driven car complete with company flag—leading me to think that being a Japanese woman journalist might have some compensations after all. Her questions were, as I had expected, uniformly polite. But I did feel somewhat embarrassed, when her article appeared, to read the final sentence: "Condon-san said with a smile that her eleven-month-old boy was looking forward to her returning home to Tokyo." Then I realized that the desire to be seen only in professional terms is both very American and very narrow. That quotation succeeded in capturing the readers' sympathy as well as reflecting how much the Japanese, both male and female, prize their children.

The Sendai reporter did not ask me anything very searching, but occasionally the women I interviewed did. After my questions were finished, they would often fetch me another cup of tea, settle themselves gracefully on the floor, and shyly ask me about my marriage, my family, and my work. They also asked how other Japanese women had responded to the questions they would never have the courage to ask themselves. If their husbands came into the room, they would immediately retreat to the inconsequential civilities of *tatemae*, but their eyes still shone with the excitement of having, for a few minutes at least, made *honne* a two-way street.

Jane Condon
Tokyo, 1985

Acknowledgments

To my mother, Doris Condon, who made me think anything was possible.

To Shinsaku Sogo, a prince among men, and his colleagues at Japan External Trade Organization (JETRO), who so generously gave of their time and provided so many introductions, as did Sonoko Matsuda of Kanazawa.

To my good friends, Anne Fadiman and Lou Ann Walker, who never stopped believing in me and this project.

And to my support team in Japan—my husband Ken Bartels, my son Todd Condon Bartels, Estela Sanchez, my colleagues at Time-Life News Service (Tokyo), and to all of my friends.

Most of all, my respect, admiration, and thanks go to those women all over Japan who were so kind and patient, spending hour after hour talking with me. I sincerely apologize for any errors.

A
Half
Step
Behind

Introduction

For centuries Japanese women, wrapped in silk kimonos, their black hair swept up with lacquered combs, minced along three steps behind their husbands. Heads bowed, they had a reputation for being devoted, demure, gracious, thoughtful, and self-sacrificing. They still do.

But now most Japanese women prefer to wear Calvin Klein jeans or an Yves St. Laurent suit, saving the delicate but restrictive kimonos for special occasions. Today, stylish young women, dressed in the most up-to-date Japanese fashions, walk beside their boyfriends as they promenade along upbeat Omotesando or through fashionable Roppongi. Yet the same modern girls, once inside a chic little French restaurant, will still pour their boyfriends' tea and debone their fish, much as their mothers did for their fathers. In their minds, the majority of Japanese women still follow their men—not three steps any longer but a half step behind.

Like the *kuroko* (black-clad figures) in kabuki, Japanese women do all the backstage work. Many women use the words "support" or "behind-the-scenes" to describe themselves and women's contribution to Japan's spectacular growth. They are the other half—the quiet, invisible half—of the economic miracle.

They run the home and house so that their husbands can apply themselves wholeheartedly to their work. Indeed, the Japanese word for wife means "inside person." She takes care of the children and their education. She is never included in the outside world of business entertaining, nor does she know much about her husband's work.

1

And if a woman's husband doesn't make enough money to support the family, it is not his fault but hers—for not living within her budget.

Women take care of the elderly, too. Nursing homes are few in Japan, as are "senior citizen" communities. Responsibility for the old and sick belongs to the first son (in theory) and to his wife (in practice). It is the wife's obligation to care for her husband's parents even more than for her own, because, as in feudal days, once she marries, she joins her husband's family register.

All this caretaking may be onerous, but in Japan it is a woman's duty. If she works in a factory or office, then the menial, repetitive tasks that are part of her job are her duty as well. To the Japanese, "duty," "honor," and "obligation" are not hollow words. Confucian philosophy teaches them that they are born into a world of obligations. Indeed, the very moment of birth creates an obligation to one's parents that can never be fully repaid. However, in Japan carrying a burden is an honorable act. Women are encouraged to be patient, persevering, and self-sacrificing. The person who endures is considered morally superior to the person who makes her endure.

There was a time in the early days of Japan when women did enjoy high status in society. In contrast to today's custom, a man joined his wife's family. Japan's most ancient deity, from whom the royal family proudly claims direct descent, was the sun goddess Amaterasu. Queen Himiko sent envoys to China. And more than a few empresses led the land.

The Empress Jingo (who reigned from A.D. 200–269) led her troops when they invaded Korea; Empress Suiko (592–628) encouraged the importation of Chinese ideas and the spread of Buddhism; Empress Jito (687–697) arranged the collection of the first code of laws which became the Taiho Code of 701; Empress Gemmyo (707–715) established in Nara the first permanent capital of Japan; Empress Shotoku (764–770), who also ruled as Em-

2

press Koken (749–758), was a great patroness of the arts under whom one of the treasures of Japanese literature, the *Manyoshu*, was gathered. Thanks to the interest of other preceding empresses, the two histories of Japan, the *Kojiki* and *Nihon shoki* were also compiled. But Empress Shotoku, due to amorous entanglements with a Buddhist priest who wanted to be emperor, outraged the nobility, who never again supported a powerful female sovereign. Although two other women, Meisho and Gosakuramachi, became empresses during the seventeenth and eighteenth centuries, they were only figureheads. The era of empresses had effectively ended.[1]

As early as the sixth century, Confucianism and its views of women as inferior beings were first introduced to Japan, but it was not until the Tokugawa period (1615–1868) that neo-Confucianism took firm hold and the idea of women's inferiority was reinforced. Confucian tracts asserted that a woman should obey her father until marriage, then her husband, then her sons. She was admonished to be humble and hardworking. Although adultery on her part was punishable by death, a wealthy man could have a second wife. A woman could be divorced with a flourish of an ink brush, on such grounds as talking too much or failing to produce an heir. And if a couple divorced, the husband's family kept the children. A proverb best expresses the prevalent feeling at that time: "The womb is a borrowed thing."

Compared to Tokugawa days, the woman's lot in life has improved greatly. There's no more *mabiki* (weeding out), the euphemism for infanticide, which was most commonly practiced with girls and occurred as late as the nineteenth century. And now women can own property. Still, traditional roots run very deep.

For example, although families no longer choose their children's spouses, as they did until World War II, many traditional notions about marriage do persist. A Japanese girl is not a woman until she marries. From earliest child-

3

hood, she imbibes this message from the posters of blissful, just-married couples and wistful brides-to-be that abound in magazine ads for wedding halls. At least one in four marriages is still arranged. Once married, Japanese men and women live in separate worlds. If the husband has an occasional affair, the wife is trained to look the other way. (At least she no longer has to live under the same roof with the husband's second wife or mistress, as she often did until the late nineteenth century.)

Today, women who want to divorce—and more and more of them do—are often discouraged by a society that tells them to *gaman* (bear up, endure). Since divorced women get little, if any, alimony and piddling amounts of child support and public aid, many of them indeed spend their lives enduring.

But the majority of Japanese women hardly feel downtrodden. They enjoy spending time with their friends, often old school chums or neighbors. They derive happiness from what a Westerner would consider minor pleasures—a once-a-week tea ceremony, a sixty-minute English lesson, or a luncheon with the girls. Today, droves of women attend education classes at local culture centers. As one woman told me, "The centers are a good place to meet people and to kill time."

Killing time is a relatively new luxury. The fruits of Japan's economic success are a materially rich society with affordable labor-saving household appliances and increased leisure time. In 1940, the average Japanese woman died at age fifty, only a few years after sending her youngest of five children off to elementary school. But in recent years, Japanese women have averaged only two children, and the younger one enters school when the mother is only thirty-five. Since the average Japanese woman lives until age eighty—the longest life expectancy in the world—that leaves her a long forty-five years to fill.

While some women remain mired in indecision about

what to do when the youngest child is packed off to school, many others return to work. Today 40 percent of the Japanese labor force is made up of women, and 59 percent of these are married. The number of married women returning to work has quadrupled in the last twenty years.[2] Many of these returnees are the wives of "salarymen" (white-collar employees paid by salary). However, the work the wives are usually able to get is menial in nature.

The salarymen's wives are joining the many women who have worked all along. They are the blue-collar factory employees who work to make ends meet, the wives of farmers, the moms of the mom-and-pop stores that dot the paved-over neighborhoods of Japan. Typically, however, the woman does the lower status work. Today, a mere 6.2 percent are managers or officials.[3]

Why don't women protest their lower station in the workplace? A few tried in the late nineteenth century, as part of the popular rights movement, and feminist stirrings began in the early twentieth century, but talk of suffrage and equal rights was quickly suppressed by the militaristic movement of the 1930s. The women's movement gathered momentum again in the 1970s, as in many countries around the world, but the Japanese media portrayed feminists as ugly and frustrated women and mocked them by focusing on an extremist pink-helmeted group who raided the offices of unfaithful men. Today only the skeleton of a women's movement exists.

Ironically, thanks to Japanese feminists and female American Occupation staff officers, Japanese women have an Equal Rights Amendment in their 1947 Constitution. But their ERA is seldom enforced and has yet to be absorbed into the nation's consciousness.

It is not surprising, therefore, that most of the influence for change comes from outside the country. The greatest pressure today comes from the U.N. Convention on the Elimination of All Forms of Discrimination Against

Women. Due partly to support from women's groups, but also to the extreme sensitivity of the Japanese to their image in other countries, Japan signed the Convention in 1980. But it was not until 1985 that it was ratified by the Diet, where it met great resistance.

Three areas of Japanese law had to change before Japan could ratify the Convention. The first related to defining Japanese nationality. Under the old law, a child born of a Japanese woman and a foreign man, even if living in Japan, retained only the father's nationality. However, the new Nationality Law, which took effect in January 1985, allows mothers for the first time to pass on their nationality to their children. The second problem area related to education. Only girls studied home economics, while boys took physical education. Although the subject is still under discussion, in the future, home economics will, most likely, be an elective for both sexes. The third problem area was the focus of the most heated debate, a bill known as the Equal Employment Opportunity Law governing the workplace, through which women will lose some protective legislation limiting overtime and night work. In turn, they gain a better (that is, equal) chance at training and promotion. However, the watered-down draft of the law that eventually passed the Diet does not punish offenders but only "encourages" employers to conform to equal opportunity guidelines. Once again, *tatemae* (that is, that women will have equal employment opportunities) has won out over *honne* (that women will not). And this is the real point. The status of women in Japan is a function not of law, but of the deeply ingrained cultural patterns. Radical change will come slowly, if at all.

Though Japan is only the size of Montana, it has the second largest gross national product in the world, a feat accomplished with a population only half that of the United States. Japan's surge to the forefront of the world economy certainly is due to management practices, hardworking businessmen, and the strong relationship between business

6

and government, but not to these factors alone. Japan's hidden asset is its women, who—largely unnoticed and un-heralded—graciously and quietly make the economic miracle possible.

Part I

FAMILY

Today, the average Japanese family calls itself middle-class. The Western-dressed husband and wife live with their two children—often taller than their parents—in a smallish, two- or three-bedroom urban apartment or house crammed chockablock with appliances. Twenty years ago, housewives longed for the three Cs—car, color TV, and cooler (air conditioner). Now the typical family has these and more—a Toshiba refrigerator, Yamaha stereo, National rice cooker. Nevertheless, the housewife still usually waits for hot water, uses space heaters rather than central heating, and hangs out her laundry to dry. (Japanese can afford dryers, but the "good" mother still dries her family's clothes in the fresh air.) Although houses tend to have at least one *tatami* (straw mat) room, layers of *futon* (bedding on the floor) are giving way to beds and low-lying tables to tables and chairs. The family rises early and sits down to a breakfast of ham and eggs, toast, and salad or more traditional Japanese fare—fish, seaweed, soup, and rice.

The Japanese father commutes an hour to an hour and a half, packed into the crowded morning rush-hour train, while the mother fixes a box lunch of rice, vegetables, and meat for the children. Once the children are off to school, the mother washes, dusts, and cleans, a job made considerably easier by all the famed Japanese labor-saving consumer products. She can walk or bicycle to the neighborhood stores, if she shops locally. She might take the train—trains are everywhere—or the family compact car to a larger supermarket or department store. But now that the majority of married women work, most mothers do these chores and errands after work or on their day or days off. (Most Japanese work five and a half days a week.) Father is not expected to help her because he spends so little time at home. If he's not working overtime, he's out with clients, colleagues, or buddies, having a drink after work or playing mah-jongg, while his wife stays home to feed the children and help with their homework. After the children take their nightly bath and go to bed, the wife waits up for her husband. She watches TV or reads, unless she's a working mother who needs this time to catch up on household chores. When her husband arrives home, she has a full meal or light snack waiting for him before he takes his bath.

So the week goes until Sunday (family day), when parks, zoos, and department stores fill up with fathers and their families. (Men call this time spent with the wife and children "family service.") Although interest is growing in "my-homeism," meaning men want to spend more time at home with their families, so far it's just a catchy phrase and far from a full-fledged trend.

Most families eat out at least once a month and vacation for a few days at a hot spring, the company vacation house in the mountains, or the beach, but the majority of employees take only half the vacation time allotted them. Summer usually includes a trip to the family home in the country to pay respect to the ancestors.

Japan is well-known worldwide for its family ties, which, although loosening, are still strong by American standards. The extended family is bound together by a tradition with its roots in Confucian concepts of filial piety and duty toward others and Buddhist concepts of reverence for the ancestors. As has been done for centuries, the *butsudan*, a small but ornate altar in which a small statue of Buddha (*butsuzo*) and wooden tablets (*ihai*) with the ancestors' posthumous Buddhist names on them are worshiped, is kept in the first son's home, where it is highly venerated.

12

Despite the rising numbers of nuclear families and increased urbanization, 65 percent of the aged live with one of their children.[1] One out of five families still lives with the husband's parents. This is down from twenty-five years ago, when one-third did, but still high compared to any other industrialized country.[2]

What makes Japan unique, at least among advanced industrial nations, is the clear differentiation in roles that characterize the Japanese husband and wife. As early as they learn to speak, boys and girls learn they are different. For instance, men can add a syllable at the end of a sentence (*zo* or *ze*) to indicate their definite opinion, whereas women add *wa ne* or *wa yo*, to soften what they say and to indicate hesitation or deference. Japanese women are trained to be shy and to defer to others, particularly men. Several well-known proverbs pervade their thinking. "Resignation is the first lesson in life." "A woman's thinking is shallow."

So do Japanese women regard themselves as inferior? "No," says author and feminist Atsuko Chiba. "Women don't think of themselves as number two. They just think they are totally different from men and that they have different roles."

The word "equality" has been readily adopted into the Japanese language but "equal" in Japan, as applied to the sexes, means "separate but equal." "Oh, yes, my wife and I are equal," insisted a male wood-carver in Sapporo. His wife huddled in the corner of the *tatami* mat room after serving us tea, while we sat in the center and talked. Then why did his wife sit in the corner and not say anything? "Well, our roles are different," he explained.

Historically, the woman's focus, both by choice and by societal pressure, has been the family. A woman's most important work is taking care of the children, the home, and her husband, in that order. In this highly literate country, the women use their education and intelligence to raise the next generation, the human resources that are any nation's greatest asset. Their other role is freeing their husbands from all worries concerning home and family.

The husband-wife relationship strikes the outsider as a vertical relationship with an "inside man" (the wife) and an "outside man" (the husband) or a chief operating officer, who handles the gritty day-to-day details, and the chief executive officer, who handles big-picture decisions and outsiders. Husband and wife have separate spheres of influence. As one housewife said, "My husband and I live on two different islands." The only bridge between them is the children.

As soon as a woman gives birth, the pivotal relation in the family shifts from husband-and-wife to mother-and-child. As social anthropologist Chie Nakane writes in her classic book *Japanese Society*: "The structure of the family is based on a central core, mother and children, to which the husband (father) attaches. . . . The core of the Japanese family, ancient and modern, is the parent-child relationship, not that between husband and wife."[3]

From the moment of conception, ideas about babies and child-rearing differ from those prevalent in the States. For instance, Japanese women say they are pregnant for ten months and ten days (*totsuki toka*) instead of just nine months. A month or two before birth, the mother-to-be returns to her family's home to be taken care of by her own mother, who instructs her in the age-old way of taking care of babies. Few women use any anaesthetic during childbirth, and most have such self-control that they do not cry out. When I screamed during my natural childbirth in a Tokyo hospital, I was told politely but firmly, "Please be quiet."

Some women save the umbilical cord, a symbol of how closely the child was once attached to its mother. But an imaginary umbilical cord exists, and the dependency continues, indeed, is fostered by a constant physical closeness—sucking milk at mama's breast, sleeping in the parents' bed, taking a bath with mama (or often father), and sitting or sleeping on mama's back while she's out shop-

1 4

ping. Japanese call this *skin-ship*—what American psychologists call "comfort contact."

As the children get older, the mother—not the father—is the disciplinarian. There is little scolding or corporal punishment. Instead, misbehaving children are excluded from family activities or, as they get older, are simply made to feel guilty because they have disappointed their mothers. Children are indulged (we might say "spoiled") until they enter school, where the noose of discipline tightens. Anthropologist Ruth Benedict calls Japanese life "a great, shallow U-curve," in which children at the beginning of the curve and the aged at the end are catered to.[4] Japanese look back on their early childhoods nostalgically, as the best days of their lives, when they had unbridled freedom and unquestioning love.

Stories of motherly love abound in every society but are particularly numerous in Japanese literature and drama. One film tells the tale of thoughtless children who all desert their devoted mother. Years later, when one son returns to care for her, he scornfully criticizes the others, and she begs him not to, insisting that all her children are equally sweet.[5]

Small wonder then that most men want their wives to act like mothers. Anthropologist Chie Nakane notes that this is one traditional pattern little affected by postwar change. She says, "Most Japanese wives adopt the role of mother rather than wife to their husbands."[6] Anthropologist Takie Sugiyama Lebra backs up this idea with the picture she paints of the Japanese wife rushing around to take care of her husband. ("He takes more time than the children in the morning.") The wife arranges her husband's clothing and makes sure he has his cigarettes, handkerchief, and pocket money. And when he returns in the evening, she quickly responds to whatever her husband commands. "It's just a series of nouns," says Lebra, "newspaper," "ashtray," "supper," "bath," "towel." This is known as *mi no mawari*, around-the-body care.[7]

15

Are men really still coddled and pampered? Compared to American men, definitely. Compared to their Japanese grandfathers, less so. But even if around-the-body care is on the decline, men in Japan are hardly to be pitied. At home and in restaurants, they continue to be served first. At home, a woman fills her own rice bowl last, after serving everyone else. She's last in the bath and last to bed and usually first up in the morning.

Once I heard Japanese men being likened to thoroughbreds and women to their coaches, trainers, and stablehands. Feminists say the economic miracle was made on the backs of women, who have not received the recognition they've earned. But recognition is not a sought-after goal in Japan. All school girls and boys quickly absorb the saying, "The nail that stands up is hammered down."

It is commonly said that a woman's power comes from holding the purse strings and doling out her husband's allowance, not to mention doing research and making decisions about major household purchases like the refrigerator or family car. The home is the woman's castle—so much so that she is sometimes jokingly referred to as "the inn-keeper," while her husband is known as "the boarder."

In public a Japanese wife would never shame her husband by scolding him or disagreeing with anything he says. But behind closed doors in her own bailiwick (although never so loud so that the neighbors might hear), he might get an earful. Every night, TV audiences laugh uproariously at scenes of henpecked husbands in the evening soap operas, known as "home drama." I suspect it's the laughter of recognition, because more than one Japanese woman spoke to me of "controlling" her husband. As one housewife put it, "You just have to know which string to pull."

Controlling the husband, home, and bank account may sound like a lot of power—and the standard male argument is that it is—but such female power is in part illusory, because if she is divorced, the woman has next to nothing. And without her husband's income, she does not control anything. Only when she has substantial earning ability of her own will she be able to make choices.

The urge is strong to date the situation in Western terms. A common analogy is that Japanese women are like American women in the 1950s. American housewives had high status in those days. They were well-respected, as housewives in Japan are now. But if this is the 50s, it is the 50s with a twist, and that difference can be summed up in three words—*wa, meiwaku*, and *amae*. Americans, men and women, have a history of being independent and pioneers. We believe in change and the future. We value confrontation. But Japanese people, not only women, more highly value harmony, a simple little word in Japanese—*wa*—that has shaped Japanese thought and action since before Prince Shotoku made it the first article in the first constitution of Japan in 604. "In your society," explains a Japanese journalist, "truth is of the utmost importance. But in our society, harmony is. We can't rock the boat. It's a small island with too many people who must live together and get along. At whatever cost, we must have harmony." The second word—*meiwaku*—refers to the importance of not bothering others. Lastly, unlike most Westerners, the Japanese value the group more than the individual, and in such a society dependency or *amae* is not a bad word. (In fact, one of the classic books on Japanese behavior is Takeo Doi's *The Anatomy of Dependence*.) This passive, yielding behavior is encouraged from babyhood through adulthood. So the urge to maintain the status quo is stronger than in most societies.

In Japan, there are many happy couples, fine men, and caring families that would be the envy of any American. The country has been enormously successful economically. But at what price for the women? On the other hand, many others argue equally forcefully, why tinker with success?

The chapter that follows examines the Japanese woman's role in the family: why, whom, and when she marries; and her attitudes toward love, divorce, feminism, sex, pornography, birth control, abortion, and aging.

Marriage

Marriage in Japan is the building block of society, the brass ring, the pot of gold at the end of the rainbow, beyond which most young women rarely think. The Japanese are the most marrying people in the world: only 4 percent are still single in their late forties.[1] There is even an expression, *tekireiki*, which means the appropriate age for marriage (twenty-five and under for women, twenty-five and older for men—a three-year difference in ages is considered ideal). In conservative Kyushu in southern Japan, they mince no words over this idea. Everyone there knows the saying: "Women are like a Christmas cake—no good after the twenty-fifth." Women grow up like little Cinderellas, each eagerly awaiting her prince, preferably a blue-suited salaryman in a large and secure company.

She finds him at school or the company where they work. They date, fall in love, and marry. That's the ideal for most young people today. But realistically speaking, contacts between the two sexes are more limited than in the West, compounded by the fact that Japanese tend to be shy, especially with the opposite sex. Fortunately, even if no Prince Charming appears, a safety net exists, to insure that every woman will find fulfillment in family life and every man will have a wife to take care of him. The safety net is arranged marriage or *omiai* (literally, "look and meet").

Surprisingly enough, in a country known for high-tech hardware, the feudalistic practice persists—albeit in the updated form of an arranged meeting or introduction. No longer is the decision made solely by the head of the household. The young man and woman both have veto power, which they feel free to exercise. However, a person can get a reputation for being too picky or aiming too high if he or she rejects all candidates. And there is some slight reluctance to put the uncle, aunt, or boss who introduced you in a bad position by saying no. These days, even many educated young women prefer *omiai*, knowing that it's "safe" to fall in love with the selected person, because her parents already approve of him.

Most girls and boys live at home with their parents until they marry, for both practical and traditional reasons. Foremost is the lack of space. The majority of college grads cannot afford to rent an apartment on their own. (Big companies have to offer subsidized dormitory space to entice young applicants to sign up with them.) So instead of rent, the young people (often called *dokushin kizoku*, single aristocrats) spend their money on clothes, entertainment, and travel, while also setting aside some yen for their wedding and future housing. The second reason for staying home is custom. As I have mentioned, being dependent is normal, even encouraged, especially for girls. The chances for marriage can actually be reduced by having lived in a dormitory away from home—if, for example, a girl from Sapporo comes to university in Tokyo. (Some job notices specify that girls not living with parents or relatives need not apply.) The common fear is that, despite concerned housemothers and strict rules (if one girl in the dormitory gets back late, all are grounded for a week), the young ladies might get tainted—a euphemistic way of saying she might have sex. Prewar, that would have ruined her prospects for marriage. But then, prewar girls rarely went away to school.

Only recently did the Japanese do their first survey of sexual attitudes, in which, interestingly enough, 33 percent of married women indicated that they just "put up with sex." Two generations ago, a wife's objective—or, more accurately, her family's objective—was not passion but practicality and security. Since her status in life was through her husband's status in society, she wanted to marry the best she could. "Best" meant best income, education, earning potential, and family background. Until the years after World War II—the great turning point in the history of Japanese women—marriage was used to cement alliances between families. The idea of an individual marrying an individual did not yet exist. Women were more like property than partners and were considered legally "incompetent." And they accepted their fate, because it was their duty.

OMIAI (OLD-FASHIONED)

One grandmother who runs a stationery store remembers well how she, eyes down, served tea to her future husband. That was their only contact before they were betrothed. When sixty-five-year-old Ayako Tanabe was a girl, *omiai* was still an arranged marriage and not just an arranged meeting. If love came later, all well and good. If it didn't, it didn't. In any case, the purpose of marriage—the continuity and strengthening of two families—had been accomplished.

I met shopkeeper Tanabe-san one snowy, frigid afternoon in the conservative, coastal town of Kanazawa. We knelt facing each other on the floor of a drafty *tatami* mat

20

room in her home behind the shop, where she lives with her son, daughter-in-law, and their two children. "Living with your children is the happiest way, don't you think?" she said as she thoughtfully turned the lone space heater in my direction. The cold didn't seem to bother her. We were occasionally interrupted by the buzzing of her shop bell and her welcoming cry of *"Irrashaimase"* (Welcome, come in). While she took care of the customers, I gratefully sipped the hot but bitter green tea.

This small, sturdy lady in her fresh white apron and drab green kimono was a no-nonsense woman who had always worked. She had no time for introspection (the American fascination) or gossip (the Japanese fascination). She had difficulty reaching back in her mind for some memories—I wondered how often, if ever, anyone had asked her opinion—but on the subject of her late husband her mind was perfectly clear.

AYAKO TANABE:

Did I do *omiai?* Oh, I'm so embarrassed. Why, yes. It was my aunt who acted as the go-between. She lived in my husband's neighborhood.

It wasn't a formal arranged meeting. One day he just appeared in my house. Actually, I knew he was coming. First, I heard his footsteps on the stairs. I was sewing, and he appeared. We didn't talk at all. I didn't even look up. (If I had, he would have thought I wasn't going to be an obedient wife.) He just came to have a look at me. In those days we didn't date. The man just looked.

Later my brother's wife said, "Isn't he a nice man?"

I really had no impression, so I said, "Well, I think so."

Nowadays, my niece says, "What an adventure. What a chance you took."

When I was a girl, parents decided what was good for their daughters. I was already twenty-five, and all my

2 1

friends were married and had children, so my mother wanted me to marry as soon as possible. Almost any man would have been acceptable. Things have changed now. Personality is the most important thing.

But I think arranged marriages are better. In love marriages these days, the young people only think about what their boyfriend or girlfriend looks like or how much they love them or how much they are loved. In a word, they only think of the present.

They seldom think of the future or the other person's background, like how wealthy the family is. If the parents find a wealthy family, the young couple may be able to have a house. But a young love-match couple usually ends up in a small apartment. Parents think of the future, not just the present.

After my husband-to-be left the house, he must have told my aunt that I was O.K. because a few days later she came over to tell us the news. Then we had an engagement ceremony. My aunt brought engagement money from my husband plus ceremonial gifts of various foods like dried seaweed and cuttlefish, sake and other presents— all symbolizing good luck.

We got married about six months later. I wasn't scared of marriage, but the idea itself was very vague to me. It was so long ago. How things change.

At first I was just the daughter-in-law in the family. I had to say *"Hai, hai"* [Yes, yes] to everything my mother-in-law said until my son was born. My son never met his father because my husband had been sent to the front a month before the baby was born. In those days almost all men were sent to the front. It was considered a shame for a man to stay at home at such a critical time for the nation. At least, he died an honorable death, in action, on Tinian Island. He didn't die from an illness or in prison. How did I feel? Well, there were a lot of war widows in my neighborhood. War is just part of the passage of time. People can't do anything about it. Things just turned out that way. And since I was living with his parents and three sisters, I didn't feel particularly lonely. You see, I don't know how deeply I knew him. He went to the front after we'd been married for a year. But my husband was a stranger to me, even after a year of marriage. He was not so talkative. We had nothing special to talk about, really. So I don't have any memory of having a nice time. Did we have a happy marriage? I don't know. What's a happy marriage?

Not knowing whether one had a happy marriage or not may sound sad to us, and *omiai*, on first glance, may therefore seem cold and mechanical. But Japanese women do not wake up every morning and ask themselves, "Am I happy today?" Of course, the Japanese want to be as happy as anyone else, but they seem to lack the obsession we have with the "pursuit of happiness." They are far more concerned with the pursuit of security. And that's the attraction of *omiai*.

OMIAI (MODERN-DAY)

Omiai today differs in several significant ways from the days when the Kanazawa stationery store owner met her match. It's more of an arranged meeting, an introduction, an honorable look-see. Many times the girls and boys do fall in love after several dates and before they marry. These days, girls are no longer *hako iri musume*, an expression meaning "a daughter kept in a box," whose association with the other sex is restricted to her father and brothers. No longer are her eyes downcast. She enters the process with eyes wide open, looking over her parents' shoulders as they examine the boys' résumés, detailing education, job, salary, and hobbies. The veto power that young women (and men) can exercise at any stage in the process exists thanks to Article 24 of the 1947 Constitution, which dictates that marriage must be based on "mutual consent." Although so many laws changed for the Japanese woman since World War II—they got the vote, coeducation, equal rights—an even greater number of cultural attitudes and traditions like *omiai* persist, which tend to offset these legal changes.

The Aokis, an upwardly mobile, prosperous young couple (the Japanese equivalent of our Yuppies) frankly discussed with me why and how they did *omiai*. Ten minutes spent with Noriko Aoki, a thirty-six-year-old Japanese teacher who could easily pass for twenty-five, instantly dispelled any lingering suspicion I had about *omiai* being for losers. Her only fault (at least to American eyes) was that she is painfully shy. I had to ask her several times before she would agree to be interviewed. Once she took me to a company baseball game to avoid conversation. She made sure to ask her husband if it was all right for her to talk with me. He answered, "Why does she want to talk with you? Why doesn't she interview me instead?" I did talk to him, but only after interviewing his wife first and agreeing not to use their real name.

The Aokis live in Tokyo in a ferroconcrete, one-bedroom, Western-style condominium. They have no children, but not from lack of trying—a disappointment they have learned to live with. Noriko Aoki tries to joke about it: "I already have one baby to take care of—my husband." (Newcomers soon learn that Japanese laugh to break the tension when they are nervous.)

The autumn day that I first visited their home, I jumped a bit when the thick, steel door of her apartment clanged shut behind me. (Before I moved to Tokyo, I'd always had an image of Japanese houses having warm, wooden sliding doors.) As I shed my street shoes and put on a pair of slippers, I looked around. All the inside doors of the apartment were shut, and the curtains were partially drawn— reminders, it seemed, that Japan is a closed society. But I felt lucky, perhaps a bit special, to have been invited at all into her home. (Japanese are sensitive about their cramped living conditions and usually refer to their homes apologetically as "rabbit hutches.") Except for the smaller size, their apartment looked like any American home, complete with refrigerator, TV, and stereo (all, of course, big-name brands such as Hitachi, Sony, and Matsushita). Aoki-san's prize possession, a black upright piano, fit snugly in the corner.

NORIKO AOKI:

In the *omiai* ceremony, a person called *nakodo* (go-between or matchmaker) introduces the two families. First, the families exchange photos and documents, which tell such things as which university the boy or girl attended, birthdate, background, and hobbies. Then the *nakodo* sets up the place where the boy and the girl and their families will meet. These days, people use hotel lobbies, restaurants, or theater lobbies like the one at the kabuki. If the couple has any marital trouble later, they go to the *nakodo* for advice.

My parents did *omiai* too, but the first time my mother saw my father was the *omiai* ceremony, and the second time was her wedding day. Things have certainly changed since then. My husband and I were engaged for two months before we married and we saw each other many times.

I was still studying in Tokyo at that time. I was twenty-two years old and a senior at Tokyo Women's College. I only did an *omiai* because my friends did. He was twenty-five and three years out of Tokyo University. It was his seventh or eighth *omiai* and my first. One of his relatives told me that he had refused every girl, but no one turned him down. I don't know if that's true. In fact, I don't know why he picked me.

We first met in my parents' house in Gifu, rather than at a hotel or theater. He's from Gifu originally, too. He was very mild and looked outgoing. Most of my friends say that I am quiet, and it's true, so I wanted someone

2 5

who was outgoing. That was more important to me than the fact that he had gone to Tokyo University. So I had a good first impression of him. And I had a good first impression of his parents, too.

It's not uncommon in Japan for each family to want to check out the other family, as we did. A detective makes sure that the spouse-to-be has no lovers at the time and that there are no criminals among the family or relatives. The detective usually asks the neighbors what kind of people the family are. The neighbors don't mind. It's normal. Then the detective gives a written report to the family who hired him. All in all, it's expensive, but it's worth it.

What Aoki-san was too polite to say about the detective was that in addition to his checking up on whether the family had any mental or physical handicaps, he also makes sure that the family has no *burakumin*, Korean or Hiroshima blood. Japanese consider that one of their great strengths comes from being a pure race, which would be diminished by the addition of genes that were possibly defective (Hiroshima victims) or from an inferior and disliked race (Koreans) or class (*burakumin*, the untouchables).

Happily, Yoshio Aoki and his family checked out quite well. He was graduated from the best school in the country, Tokyo University (Todai, for short), and works for one of Japan's most prestigious companies.

Many of the large companies work an elite five-day week, instead of the normal six days, but those five days usually include work or entertaining for five evenings as well. Yoshio Aoki agreed to give up his Saturday round of golf so we could talk, which we did from after breakfast until dinner time. Without interrupting us, Noriko Aoki served sandwiches at lunch time and kept our glasses continuously filled with one beverage or another.

Unlike his wife, Yoshio Aoki was hardly shy at all. Having received the Todai imprimatur, he knew he was a catch in the world of *omiai*. Most of his friends were married—"I was feeling left behind," he said—so he started looking for "a high-class, pretty girl who was a four-year university graduate." I believe this attractive, clean-cut fellow would have had little trouble getting dates if he didn't work such long hours and if he'd been looking for a love match. Aoki-san turned to *omiai* as a kind of high-quality dating service.

A woman professor friend of mine put it a little more bluntly. She said, "Whatever reason people give for doing *omiai*, what they are really looking for is money, brains, or a well-known family."

Yoshio and Noriko met at her family's home under the watchful eye of her father, mother, and sister. Having done several *omiai* in six months, the young man wasn't very nervous, but willingly acknowledged that he did have one defect—he was too skinny. As for his wife-to-be, he noted, "She received very few bad marks." He explained, "In *omiai*, you judge by how few defects or faults there are.

"To my mind, *omiai* is just a first clue for *ren'ai* (love marriage) really. After our first meeting, we went to movies and restaurants a lot together. Then the *nakodo* began pressing us to make a decision. So two months later we held our engagement ceremony."

Estimates of the percentage of *omiai* marriages range from as low as 25 percent to a high of 60 percent, precisely because of what Aoki-san said about an arranged meeting turning into a love marriage. Many young people who do *omiai* call their marriage *ren'ai* or even *omiai/ren'ai* because they fall in love after they meet. A love match these days is considerably more fashionable—although definitely more risky. It's common knowledge that more love matches than arranged marriages result in divorce.

In the olden days, only commoners could indulge in love marriages, but they gradually began to follow the Confucian example of the upper classes in which a boy and girl in love risked ostracism from the village if they wanted to marry against the objections of the heads of their households. (Some of those who were forbidden from marrying committed a double love-suicide instead, a popular theme in Japanese drama.) More love marriages occurred in Meiji days (1868–1912), following contact with the West, and even more in the liberal Taisho period (1912–1926). But the flood gates for love marriage did not truly open until after World War II, with the emulation of all things Western and abolishment of the *ie* (family) system in which the head of the household made all important decisions for family members.

Kenju Kaneko, forty-seven, a publisher in Kanazawa, who married in his early twenties proudly notes, "No question, my wife and I have a love marriage. Hey, love's a many splendored thing, right?"

At one time, I assumed that the majority of young Japanese today had stars in their eyes when they married. Then I read a 1982 survey of 700 young women, of whom 40.9 percent stated that to them "love" and "marriage" are two separate things. Only 37.6 percent insisted on marrying a man they love.[2]

Then it dawned on me that I had not learned to say "I love you" (*Aishite iru*) until more than a year after I'd been studying Japanese. How could this be, I asked Noriko Aoki, when in French and Spanish "I love you" was one of the first expressions any student was taught?

"But we don't say it," she explained. "We don't have to. Without saying it, we understand. You know that, historically, Japanese don't express their inner feelings."

"Not even boyfriends and girlfriends say it?" I asked.

"Well, maybe some of them do."

"Doesn't your husband tell you?"

"No," she answered, surprised. "He doesn't need to, because we're married. It's understood."

"But did he ever say it?"

"Oh, yes, sure."

"When?"

She paused. "Once . . . ahh, when he decided to marry me."

"When was that?"

"I don't remember exactly . . ." Aoki-san looked perplexed. She put two fingers to her forehead; her brown eyes stared into space. After much thought, she shrugged her shoulders. "Maybe he's too shy. But you know we hear that, if American husbands don't say it all the time, their wives become anxious. Is that true? Japanese husbands say, 'Oh, those poor American men. They have to say "I love you" over and over again.' Aren't the wives confident in America?"

I didn't have a good answer.

Two days later, we met again at my house, and Aoki-san pulled a *Nikkei Shimbun* (Japan's *Wall Street Journal*) article out of her Louis Vuitton handbag. "Did you see this? The story is called 'Wives Please Keep Quiet.' The reporter begins by comparing American and European films. In the latter he observed that the European stars tend to keep quiet. Catherine Deneuve, for example, expresses her deep feelings in a few words. Now this is pleasing to Japanese. Whereas in American films and TV, like the recently shown *Glenn Miller Story*, Americans are always certifying their love with words. Sure they say 'I love you' to their partners, but if this is good, the writer asks, then why is their divorce rate five times that of Japanese?

"It used to be that the typical Japanese husband needed to use only three words at home: *meshi* (rice), *furo* (bath), and *neru* (sleep). Those words were enough. But now housewives want their husbands to talk with them more. [A study showed that the average Japanese couple talks only thirty-eight minutes a day.] But this reporter feels that Japanese housewives have been unduly influenced by American films and drama. That's why he called his article, 'Wives Please Keep Quiet.' "

"Well what do you think, Aoki-san?" I asked.

"Well, it's true a lot of Japanese women would like their husbands to spend more time talking with them. After the war, we were educated by American democracy to think that men and women are equal. So we do want a little more. But Jane-san . . . it doesn't have to be the words, 'I love you.'

"Once an older student of mine, an American, asked me to translate into Japanese the speech he was going to give at the wedding of a Japanese friend. The words were: 'My wife and I have loved each other for thirty-five years, and we hope you will have the same happiness.' Now a Japanese would never say that. But no one at the reception laughed at his speech because they knew he was American."

Perhaps I shouldn't have been surprised at this discussion with Aoki-san about love. Although the Japanese have a long tradition of love poetry, Japan has no tradition of chivalry toward women. Samurai had the idea that sex might sap their vitality. And, as former ambassador to Japan Edwin Reischauer notes, Confucianism teaches that love is a weakness, and sex is for the purpose of continuing the family line, period.[3]

In any case, it is a widely held, though seldom voiced, notion that Americans are too loud and talk too much. Whether or not the Aokis voice their love for each other, I believe they have a very strong marriage. Before I first met them, they had lived for two years in Abu Dhabi and two years in Dubai—hardly plum assignments by an American wife's standards. But Noriko Aoki says she loved those years. Her reasons are that she had no family obligations, her husband had a month off each summer (much more than he would take in Japan), which they always spent in Europe, and she could take English lessons and play tennis at the local Sheraton.

Now her husband has a new four-year assignment to Tehran, where she will again have to cover up in public.

This time there will be food shortages to face and no Sheraton to visit. But Japanese employees do not turn down transfers. The wife's only choice is whether to join her husband or not. (Many of the wives who have children in the all-important preexamination years from fifth grade to senior high school do not. The children's education comes first.) Now, I can easily imagine my own emotional reaction to the prospect of going with my husband to Tehran—as a Japanese friend Japanized one of my expressions: "Fat-o chance-u"—but there wasn't a speck of self-pity in Aoki-san's voice when she told me about the impending change. Sounding like a Biblical Ruth, all she said was simply, confidently: "Where my husband is, I am."

MUKOYOSHI (ADOPTED SON AND HUSBAND)

Noriko Aoki's best friend is thirty-five-year-old housewife Miwako Yamakawa. Yamakawa-san comes from a noble family, though she says, "No one pays any attention to that anymore" (after the war, nobility was essentially abolished). Aside from her pedigree, she is a typical Japanese housewife with a mix of modern clothes and traditional values. Her parents did *omiai*, as did most of their generation, and she has a love marriage, as do most of her generation.

Since Yamakawa-san's maternal grandparents had no sons and three daughters, I wasn't surprised to learn that her father had been a *mukoyoshi*, a man who not only marries into the woman's family but is also adopted by the wife's parents in order to carry on their family name. Many *mukoyoshi* take on the family business as well.

This refined, birdlike woman is the wife of an oil company salaryman and the mother of a round-faced, first-grade girl. Despite her aristocratic roots, try as I might, I could imagine neither her nor her ancestors as Heian court ladies with layered and flowing robes, long black hair, blackened teeth and shaved eyebrows. Yamakawa-san looks as if she'd be more comfortable with a Chanel suit and Christian Dior bag, although like most housewives she wears an apron around the house. Her hair is short and probably permed. Everything is neat, clean, and in its place in her Western-style condominium, where a stereo cassette of Rachmaninoff plays in the background as we talk.

She uses very proper Japanese and is totally confident that her most important mission in life is as a housewife. She makes sure she's home to greet her daughter in the afternoon and her husband in the evening, no matter what time he returns. She takes care of her father-in-law when her mother-in-law is sick, noting that he doesn't know how to do anything but work ("He can't even go to the bank," she says). And once a year she helps her in-laws with their annual New Year's housecleaning. It is a time when house-wives all across Japan, whether of aristocratic ancestry or not, scrub the floors and clean the house from top to bot-tom.

MIWAKO YAMAKAWA:

My mother's marriage was *omiai*, but a little differ-ent from most because my father came to live with her family and took her family name. Not only did she marry him but her parents adopted him as their son. So my maiden name comes from my mother's family and not my father's family, as is the custom.

Usually the *mukoyoshi* is selected for the eldest daughter. But my mother's older sister refused and mar-ried a man whom she loved. Since her marriage was a love match, the family disowned her. Neither she nor her hus-band was ever allowed to mix with the family, because she was supposed to have married a man chosen by her par-ents. Since my mother was the second oldest girl, her parents found her husband instead.

I'm not sure how my father felt about taking my mother's name. He wasn't a merchant, you know, but an

employee of a big company, so he might have been embarrassed. I'm not sure. He didn't say. Anyway, he came
to live with my mother's family in Kobe. Although many
families share the same name in that city, our family was
honke, the head group.

As for my mother, she couldn't show her true feelings about whether she liked him or not because he had
been chosen by her parents. But she used to say that if
she had really hated her husband, she could have killed
herself. And she didn't do that, so she either liked him or
she didn't hate him. I don't know. She was obliged to receive her fate. She told me, "Whatever happens to you,
you have to take responsibility because you chose that
way."

Another *mukoyoshi* I know of—a tatami-mat maker—was
only too happy to inherit his father-in-law's tatami-mat
business. Being one of eight children and not the oldest,
he had no chance of inheriting the family farm. And besides he was eager to trade the long hard hours on the farm
for the bright lights of the city where his wife and in-laws
lived.

In general though, the position of *mukoyoshi* is considered somewhat unmanly. People always mention how
uncomfortable it must be for a man to live with a stranger's
family. Interestingly enough, no mention is made of the
similar discomfort women must feel when they join their
husband's family.

LOVE MARRIAGE

Like most Japanese women, Yamakawa-san worked
before she married. She describes those days and tells more
about her family and the events that led up to her own
love marriage.

MIWAKO YAMAKAWA:

During my last year at Seijo University, where I majored in Japanese art, I worked part-time at Dentsu, the big advertising agency. When I applied, I told the director I couldn't type fast, and I wasn't good at writing letters. I told him that I couldn't do anything at all, and he said that was all right, it didn't matter.

After I started work, I typed, and of course I served tea. I was supposed to read documents written in English, but I couldn't do that then, and I can't do it now, either.

I worked from after my graduation in March until the end of the year. Then my mother became seriously ill with cancer. At the same time, my sister was preparing to get married. She was making clothes and choosing a house and furniture. So I quit my job to help them both.

A few months later, after my mother's death, my father was supposed to become head of the family. But after mother's funeral, all my aunts, uncles, and other relatives sent their condolences to me and ignored my father. My maiden name, Miwako Kojima, was on the envelope, and not his name, Osamu Kojima. My eldest sister was in the convent at the time, and the second oldest girl had married the eldest son of another family. So that meant that I, Miwako Kojima, became the center of the family. I hated that, though, because I thought of myself as the daughter of both my father and mother, and not only of my mother.

So when it came time for me to marry, I didn't consult with my relatives beforehand at all. They would have been upset to learn I was marrying the eldest son of another family who couldn't possibly take our family name.

My father knew and approved of my upcoming marriage, and he thought it was not so necessary to keep the family name going anymore. His feeling was that times have changed.

3 4

But the relatives were offended, especially since we had the reception in Tokyo. I had sent invitations to all of them in Kobe, but only a few came. They recommended that we have another reception in the Osaka-Kobe area, where they live, so we did.

Now another family has the *butsudan* [family altar]. I remember how embarrassed all the relatives had been years ago when my mother was first baptized a Catholic. Her family, like most Japanese, are Buddhist and the biggest supporters of the biggest temple in Kobe. Anyway, they were afraid that she would burn down the altar. But my mother took good care of it. She never stopped worshiping our ancestors. We keep her bones and ashes in a church near here, where we were married. The funny thing is that her bones are kept together with the ancestors' memorial tablet. Of course, the church doesn't know this.

My sister is married to a Mitsui Trading Company man, and they lived in Houston for five years, although actually her husband was there for six years. Her husband went to the States one year earlier than she did. She was pregnant when he left and stayed home alone to have the baby in Japan. At that time the rule was that you couldn't take your wife for the first six months. I guess the bosses think that a man needs time to settle in and get accustomed to the new country. If the man took his family with him, they would just bother him. Even now a Mitsui wife has to wait three months before she can join her husband.

I met my husband through my sister and her husband who knew him when he worked in Houston. When he returned to Japan, they asked him to bring back a small present from them. So I received a call from him in January. He said, "I have a gift for you from your brother-in-law." That was the first I knew of Yamakawa-san. My brother-in-law had never mentioned him before.

At that time I lived with my father. (My mother had

3 5

died about two years earlier.) Well, my father kindly agreed to drive me to the Okura Hotel where I met Yamakawa-san.

He had so much money then. It was extra money from going to Houston, so he was very rich at that time. But only at that time. We had lunch together, and he gave me my present from my sister and brother-in-law, which was a necklace.

The next night Yamakawa-san called again and said, "I'm dining with my friends. Won't you join us for a drink?" So I did.

After that, he visited me every day. At that time, he had just started thinking about marriage and finally he decided to marry me. So by the end of February we were engaged.

I had had many boyfriends in my university days, but I hadn't really wanted to marry any of them. I knew what sort of man my parents would want, and my husband knew what his family expected of him. You see, if there's a big gap between the families' ranks, the parents are afraid that the children won't have a happy marriage. So you want to marry someone from relatively the same background.

My parents had never said anything against my college boyfriends. They said the boys were all very good, very nice people. But they didn't think Seijo University graduates were good enough for me. They had in mind someone from Tokyo University, Keio, Waseda, Hitotsubashi, or Kyoto University. Those schools were good enough. Fortunately, my husband graduated from Waseda. His father is a professor there, and his younger brother went there, too. His mother and sister both graduated from Japan Women's College, which is also a prestigious school.

So we encountered no opposition to our marriage. Now I'm very happy to have married him. My husband and I agree that my most important job is to keep the house clean. I take care of the home, which means taking care of my daughter, too. My husband goes out any time he likes, but he thinks that his wife should always be home. I think he's right. You see, if a mother goes outside for a walk, there might be a phone call or a problem, and she wouldn't be there. I want to be home when my daughter comes home from school, and her school advised me to do so. I stay home because I don't want to disturb any other member of the family.

If they can meet a suitable young man, young women in their twenties vastly prefer love marriages. But it's not enough that the two of them get along. Parents still have a strong say in their children's choice of partner. Even though more and more young people choose their own partner, they still can't choose their in-laws. It's a package deal with much more potential for discord than in the United States, especially if the girl might live with the boy's family.

The problems of Miki Suzuki (not her real name) with her future husband and in-laws boil down to differing expectations between generations and between the sexes. As in the West, women have changed faster than men. Meanwhile, Miki's boyfriend had erroneously harbored a few "she'll get used to it" expectations. Young and old alike agree that Japanese women are not nearly so obedient as they used to be. A frequently heard male lament is, "Since the war, women and nylons have become stronger." Conflict is often avoided when, due to the young man's job, the couple lives in an urban area away from his parents. Then they start their own nuclear family. Living with the young man's parents is not what the increasing numbers of postwar, university-educated, urban women like Miki Suzuki want out of life.

An American would call twenty-five-year-old Miki a girl with a head on her shoulders—the total opposite of the empty-headed, giggling young girls known as *burikko*, the *Ah-so-desu-ka* ("Is that so?") type many young men find attractive. She and her fiancé met at their university volleyball club. She was a pretty good player—not surprising since she'd been an avid player since her junior high school days. And both she and her fiancé graduated from Keio, one of Japan's elite universities. "But," she confides, "this is not necessarily a plus for a girl who wants to marry. Some boys prefer to be served by a dumb girl."

Miki Suzuki completed a rigorous interpreters' school and now works full-time as a professional translator. (We got to know each other by working together on several magazine stories.) Having spent her senior year at a high school in the Midwestern United States, she doesn't mind if I call her by her first name—Miki—rather than Suzuki-san.

Like most young working women, she wears preppy, conservative clothes—today, a navy-and-white striped French boat sweater over a navy blue skirt and low black heels.

When I met her at the train station, Miki was all flustered because she was late. She had another bigger reason to be upset too. "How are the wedding plans going?" I asked in all innocence, as we walked to my house. "Not so well," she said. "I'm having second thoughts."

We walked along in silence. "Want to tell me what's happening?" I asked. She did want to talk and did so, although several times with a dry throat or on the verge of tears. She never permitted herself to break down in front of me, however. Though the Japanese consider themselves an emotional people, they believe in controlling their emotions in public.

MIKI SUZUKI:

I never knew his parents until last Saturday. Well, I'd met them before, but I never really knew them. They want my parents to give them lots and lots of money for our new household. I know the new bride usually contributes some money but they are asking a really outrageous amount. And his parents told me not to bother to bring any furniture that's even been slightly used. Newlyweds should have all new furniture, they say. Well, my parents were insulted.

His parents are so conservative and so money-oriented. And they keep telling their son how important money is in life. His mother says, "First comes health. Then comes money." Always money, money, money, which worries me because I wasn't raised that way. What about the importance of love, education, and peace?

The worst part is that they started the conversation by saying that maybe we should go back to the starting point. That means that the wedding should be stopped. What an insult. But I am beginning to have serious doubts myself. His mother! Ohhh! We talked about what I would do when my boyfriend goes to business school in the States. He's been accepted at Northwestern, and his bank's policy is not to let the wife go until the second year. I don't know why they won't let me go the first year, but he feels he must do what the company says or he'll ruin his chances in the bank. Well, his family is going to help support him when he is in the States. (His company pays only for the schooling.) But his parents said that my family should help pay our household expenses once I move to Chicago in the second year, because they weren't going to support me, too. My parents were upset by their attitude and the way they said it, but my mother just calmly pointed out that I had this skill in translating so I could support myself. And do you know what his mother said? I couldn't believe it! His mother answered that all his family really wants in a wife for him is a healthy, obedient girl who could produce a baby boy—that is, a family heir! And listen to this. During the first year that he is away they insist that I move from my home in Tokyo to Osaka to live with them, so they can train me! Train me? These people are really old-fashioned. Their ideas seem to come from a time before Meiji. They are positively feudal.

39

At least my boyfriend is not the first son, so he doesn't have to take over the family lumber business some day. Thank goodness. That duty belongs to my boyfriend's older brother. He lives next door to the parents now. My boyfriend and I had often talked about this, and he promised me that he would always work for the bank. But just in the last few weeks he's begun to say that someday maybe he will work for the family business!

Another thing that worried me was that his mother told him—in front of all of us—that he can't do anything without her. Every important decision that he's ever had to make she has made for him. And he didn't defend himself! He doesn't defend me nor does he defend himself. What kind of marriage is this going to be? I thought I was marrying just him. All he says is that after thirty years he's used to her, and it doesn't bother him any more. I should have realized something might go wrong when I heard a few months ago that his thirty-three-year-old sister had to cancel her marriage plans because his mother and father disapproved of the boy. It turns out that they don't approve of me either. (For one thing, I do a lot of translating for foreigners, and they think the foreigners have been a bad influence on me.) But they didn't want to tell their son how they really felt about me until after he heard from business schools in the U.S., because they didn't want to put extra pressure on him. Well, my parents don't exactly approve of him and his family either—especially after last weekend. But they will support me if I still choose to marry him.

Do I really love him? Well, we've dated each other for the past six years. That's a long time, isn't it? And I know how he thinks. I almost always know how he will react in any situation. You know, all I ever wanted to do was to help him in whatever he wants to do.

But I am really worried about his parents' influence. About a month ago my boyfriend and I went looking for an engagement ring. I really wanted a Tiffany diamond, and we found one. Oh, it was very small—not nearly as big as yours—but it was from Tiffany's. So simple and so classic-looking. Not a ring with a lot of metal on the side. And not so high a setting that it will catch on everything—the perfect ring for wearing every day. It was small, but I loved it. But when my boyfriend's father heard about this ring, he said, "My son can't walk in public beside a woman with such a small diamond!" So his father went out to a department store and bought a huge one, more than a carat. And it's yellow! Yellow! I wouldn't mind the size if I were older. Big rings look good on an older woman. But I liked the small one. And now I have this huge, yellow diamond! His father said it had to be big, because I'll only wear it on special occasions. But I wanted to wear my ring every day. I didn't care about the size. I wonder if maybe I should have spoken up, but my boyfriend said, "If you do, he'll think you're aggressive."

Worst of all, his mother makes no bones about telling him, "All I want from you now is obedience. We have poured millions of yen into your education, and I've devoted my life to you. What use will my life have been if you don't obey me now?" This woman is a monster. And he has given in to her on every little detail of our wedding—even down to which wedding hall to hold it in. So what will happen to us in the future? He had always said we just have to put up with this until we get married. And then we will be free. Then things will be different. But I'm not so sure anymore. I used to believe him. Choosing me was the first decision he's ever made for himself. But can he make others? I don't know.

Right now my wedding dress is waiting for me at the dressmaker's. I was supposed to go pick it up yesterday, but I couldn't. I should be packing my clothes for the honeymoon now too, but I'm not. Oh, I'm so confused, and there are no guidelines about what to do. For the first time in my life, no one and nothing is telling me what I should do.

I spoke with a priest about my problem. (I'm not Catholic yet, but I went to a lot of Christian schools, and I may become one.) He advised me to postpone the wedding. I haven't really spoken about it with any of my friends. You know, it's embarrassing. But I'm so worried. I know many people get nervous before they marry, and I know you have to make compromises, but . . .

My boyfriend and I've been talking every night, but even he says I'm being selfish. Yet he's been changing so many things he says just this last month! And the wedding is just a week from Saturday, eight days away! The invitations have already gone out. Oh, what should I do? I'm so grateful you listened to me. I'm sorry to take so much of your valuable time. Sorry, Jane-san.

My advice to Miki after she poured her heart out was that she consider her whole life and not just the next few days. I was referring to the potential short-term embarrassment of not having the wedding compared to a lifetime spent with an unpleasant mother-in-law and a spineless husband, but I didn't out-and-out say those things. I've learned to be a little vague myself, like the Japanese. I told her to keep talking with her boyfriend so that everything is understood perfectly clearly between them, such as the fact that she had no intention of living with his parents. I also recommended that she think and think and think about what she wanted out of life. Miki had mentioned once that her boyfriend didn't mind if she worked, as long as she was home when he got home. Working the unpredictable hours of a translator, could she really promise that? But most important of all, did she really love him?

Eight days later, I was in the United States visiting my family, and I felt a sad twinge as I imagined Miki in her kabuki-white makeup, elaborate hairpiece, and elegant kimono standing at the Shinto shrine sipping sake from nuptial cups with her husband-to-be. It was supposed to be the day little girls dream of. I wondered how she felt.

When I returned to Japan, the first letter I opened was from her. It read, "As you can see on the envelope, my family name is still Suzuki. I did not get married as planned . . . Love, Miki."

I was more than a little shocked, mostly pleased, a little sad, and very admiring. I wonder if I would have had the courage to make a decision like that so close to the wedding day. How strong Miki was, particularly in the face of enormous societal pressure to marry. (At twenty-five, nearly twenty-six, she's considered almost over the hill.) No matter how meek, mild, and subservient Japanese women may seem, I am continually surprised at the real strength that lies beneath their polite facades. Curiously enough, Japanese men wouldn't be. Most freely admit that women (although inferior in most ways) are stronger psychologically.

The next time I saw Miki, she looked great. She had a new haircut (some things don't change cross-culturally) and had dropped five pounds thanks to the currently fashionable all-the-rice-you-can-eat diet.

She was so relieved that she had finally made a decision. So was I. Miki hadn't enjoyed complaining about her boyfriend or his parents. "I hated myself for having done that so much," she said. "The worst part is that I still care for him . . . but I believe it was a wise decision."

What would happen next? I asked, and teased her, "I know omiai's too old-fashioned for someone like you, but how about computerized matchmaking?" (Mitsubishi, the most prestigious group of companies, has their Family Heart Club; the largest private operator, Altmann, claims more than 6,000 matches out of 60,000 clients; even the Tokyo municipal government tries to line up lonely hearts. This country really wants people to get married!) But Miki only laughed. She had no interest in state-of-the-art, electronic omiai.

"I guess you'll want to fall in love," I said.

"Well, I don't know," she answered and paused. "I used

to think that *omiai* was an awful system—just cold and cal- culating. It doesn't look at the man's personality, just how much money does he make and what's his educational background and career possibilities and how easy will my life be.

"But about half my friends have found their husbands through *omiai*, and they've met really good people. They have happy marriages. I couldn't believe it at first. But once I met their husbands I decided that maybe *omiai* isn't such a bad system after all. I might try it myself, now that my love marriage didn't work out. But this time I think I'll try to find someone with nice parents."

Ahh, the safety net.

As teacher Noriko Aoki says, "People say there is less *omiai* these days. But *omiai* will never die out completely. *Omiai* will always be a safe and secure way to meet people."

Divorce

In feudal days, divorce was an option for men only. A husband could easily divorce his wife for any of seven reasons: if she was unable to bear children, immoral, argumentative with her in-laws, too talkative, dishonest, jealous, or diseased.[1] All he had to do was write a letter that said, "You are incompatible with the customs in my family. So you are no longer needed and are free to seek happiness elsewhere."[2]

If a woman wished to leave her husband, her only option was to run to a Buddhist temple or nunnery known as *kakekomidera*, literally "a temple to flee to." As long as she threw her shoes over the fence before her husband arrived, she was admitted and after two years considered officially divorced. Most husbands would not take such an affront to their dignity lightly however, so they usually assembled a chase party, which celebrated at a local restaurant if the wife was successfully captured. The runaway wife was left bound on the dirt floor during the festivities.[3]

Although most women's rights have been gained since World War II, women were given the right to divorce by the Meiji Civil Code of 1898. Many women did. But for most there were two big catches. First, the divorced woman had to support herself—a difficult feat now but nearly impossible back then. Second, the husband's family got the children. So most women continued to *gaman*. They had no choice.

Today the tables have turned. Now 74 percent of all Family Court petitions for divorce are initiated by women. Tokyo has divorce go-betweens, a divorce hotline and a divorce magazine called *Start*. Health and Welfare Ministry statistics show that divorces occur at twice the rate of fifteen years ago, but this is still low compared to United States figures (1.5 per 1,000 in Japan compared with 5.3 per 1,000 population in the United States). On a world scale, Japan's divorce rate of 20 percent is one of the lowest.[4]

Both children and economics keep the family together. Most mothers who have considered divorce feel that the children's need for a father both socially and financially outweighs their own needs. And women worry about how they will support themselves and their children.

One thirty-nine-year-old housewife says, "If we ever

divorce, it could really damage his career. And I wouldn't dare destroy a man's future. His company feels that, if a man can't handle his own affairs at home, he can't handle the company's affairs."

Hiroshi Ishikawa, twenty-eight, a staff officer at the Foreign Press Center says, "I know that in the States you can get a divorce like this. (He snaps his fingers.) But we Japanese are brought up to believe in patience.

"Maybe it has something to do with our shame-conscious society. We don't want to be shamed in front of our neighbors. I mean, what would the neighbors think if we got a divorce? That thought makes you pause.

"Besides," he half jokes, "how can you say good-bye to your wife when everyone in your neighborhood, everyone you know, came to your wedding?" Ishikawa also cites the tremendous cost. The average wedding (in Japan the figure includes the cost of furniture in the newlywed's home as well as the honeymoon) cost 6.68 million yen ($26,720) according to a Sanwa Bank survey. Although more and more young people have less and less patience—"If they don't like the situation, they say good-bye"—he adds that, if you divorce, "People still look at you as if there's something wrong with you."

The fact remains that divorce is still a social stigma in this country where patience and perseverance are highly valued. The idea still holds that through divorce you have dirtied the family name.

So Miki Suzuki, the young woman in the previous chapter who didn't go through with her planned wedding, was smart to get out of a potentially bad situation with her mother-in-law now rather than later. The tyrannical mother-in-law bossing around her son's young bride (as she was ordered about by her mother-in-law) is a well-known stereotype of Japanese stage and screen. No son-in-law jokes exist in Japan, but combine the words for "bride" (yome) and "mother-in-law" (shutome), and the first image that leaps to mind is struggle (yome–shutome). Even though fewer couples live with the husband's family these days, as one woman says, "Many husbands still belong mentally to their mothers." The Japanese call this *maza con* (mother complex).

A twenty-eight-year-old English teacher in Hiroshima tells how *maza con* destroyed her marriage to a government civil servant.

"My husband is a very conservative person. He's the first son and the only son. A lot of women these days don't want to marry the first son because of all the family responsibilities he has, like organizing family gatherings during New Year's and *Obon* (the summer holidays in which we return to our family home to pay our respects to our ancestors) and also funerals and weddings. Although the law says all children are supposed to take care of the parents in their old age, custom still dictates that the first son (that is, the first son's wife) take care of them when they are old and sick.

"My husband's mother came over to our house every day—to make sure I was taking proper care of him, I guess. And my husband was always talking about how good a cook his mother was. He said things like, 'But my mother cooks curry rice this way' or 'You use too many canned foods. My mother makes her own soup stock.' And he didn't like the way I dressed. He said, 'My mother likes red and she wears feminine clothes. So why do you always wear pants instead of dresses?' His biggest complaint was about my working outside the home. He didn't want me to. 'My mother never did,' he said.

"You know there's a book that's selling very well now called *How to Get Along With an Only Son*. This is a serious problem for Japanese women."

Ninety percent of all divorces are through mutual agreement, according to Todai-trained lawyer Kurumi Nakamura, a divorced mother who writes a bimonthly column on divorce for a popular women's magazine. If the husband and wife both agree to the divorce, amount of settlement, child support and custody, then all they have to do is visit their local ward office with two witnesses, fill out a one-page form, sign, and seal it. That's it. Nothing more. "The easiest divorce in the world," says lawyer Nakamura. And fortunately, the Japanese, in their wisdom, have included "in-law trouble" as one of the thirteen allowable reasons for divorce by mutual agreement. Most couples don't 'fess up to other reasons like extramarital affairs or wife-beating. They just circle "incompatibility," the most frequently named reason.

The second way to divorce is through the Family Court, a route taken by only 10 percent of all those divorced. And the 10 percent of those cases that can't be resolved in Family Court—a mere 1 percent of all divorces—end up in the regular Japanese courts. The numbers show that in divorce as in everything else legal, the harmony-oriented Japanese tend to avoid lawsuits and confrontation.

The Hiroshima English teacher had to go through the Family Court because her husband initially opposed the divorce. "He was afraid of losing face at his company, but fortunately he worked for the government and had guaranteed lifetime employment. So it didn't affect his chances for promotion, as it might have at a bank or some other kind of private company.

"When we went to Family Court, I cried in front of the mediators and begged them to give me a divorce. And I kept saying to my husband, 'Please let me go. Please let me go.' But the mediators told me, 'You have no good reason for divorce. So you should *gaman.*'

"Most of these people are older. The Court consists of one male mediator, one female mediator, and a judge. These people usually have very old-fashioned ideas about women, and they always tell the wives to bear up and endure, to be patient and reconsider. The traditional education of women requires that we be modest and obedient to men.

"So my husband and I went home. But my husband

relented and said he would give me a divorce on one condition—that I give him three million yen [$12,500] cash. Of course I didn't have that kind of money, so I told him, 'That's impossible.' But then I realized maybe I could give him all the furniture and electrical appliances that my parents had given us. That was worth three million yen.

"He accepted, and in that way I got his seal, and we were divorced."

Most divorces occur among those married less than three years, and the Hiroshima couple fit this pattern, having been married for two years. Besides the problem of *maza con*, their marriage and subsequent divorce is a good illustration of the risky side of *omiai*. These two young people had met about six times and spent a grand total of twelve hours together before marrying. The young woman finally admitted that her parents pushed her into it. "They felt I was getting old," she said. "I was already twenty-six."

Fortunately for her, she has a salable skill—her English ability. Most divorcées, having little or no work experience before they marry, have few options other than minimum-wage jobs as a supermarket cashier, department store clerk, or waitress. The only big, fast money is in working as a bar hostess. Prestigious, large companies tend not to hire divorcées, although smaller companies often do want them because they work hard and tend not to leave. (The majority of divorced women do not remarry.)

The divorce agreement includes only one lump-sum settlement payment which averages 1 to 5 million yen ($4,176–$20,833).[5] (One Japanese woman called it "severance pay.") There is usually no alimony in Japan, although the settlement is occasionally paid out monthly, but not indefinitely, only until a fixed sum is reached. One reason settlements are small is that in the old days a divorcée returned to her family. Indeed the word for "divorcée" (*demodori*) means someone who *de* (goes out) and *modori* (comes back). Child support is minimal, and 78 percent of men do not keep up the payments anyway.[6] And there's no system of attaching wages. Single mothers tend to count on the monthly child support from the government—32,700 yen ($136) per child. Ironically enough, single fathers do not receive any state child support, and a movement is on to change this inequity.

So how does a single mother make ends meet? Like most American single mothers, usually she doesn't. Her average annual income is 2 million yen ($8,333), less than half the national average for heads of households in Japan.[7]

Yuko Sugai, thirty-five, a hard-bitten insurance saleswoman in the northern town of Sendai, describes her experiences post-divorce. We spoke in a coffee shop, where she downed several cups of coffee between what seemed like an endless series of cigarettes. Dressed in a fashionable brown tweed suit, she was so good-looking that, as my translator said, she's the kind of woman you want to keep your husband away from. I wondered if she had always had an edge to her or if her divorce had made her that way.

YUKO SUGAI:

I went to junior college because both my mother and I thought that girls didn't need a four-year university education. And I wanted to work for at least two to three years before marriage, because I wanted to get married at age twenty-four or twenty-five—like everyone else.

After junior college, I got a food nutrition license. That was my major. The other majors at my school were English literature, childcare, and home economics. It was an all-girls school.

Then I started to work as a clerk at a construction company. Meanwhile, I went to professional cooking school at night for one and a half years. I wanted to have my own restaurant or *snakku* [snack bar], but I didn't have enough money. Besides, my mother didn't want me to, because she is prejudiced against those kind of people in the entertainment business.

So I spent two years at the construction company, and that's where I met my husband, an engineer. That's called *shokuba kekkon* [a company marriage]. Two months before we married, I quit my job because my husband didn't want me to work.

So I stayed home for the three years we were married. Our little girl was a honeymoon baby. We spent our honeymoon at a *ryokan* [Japanese inn] in Kyoto. Then we got divorced eight years ago.

Even though we got divorced, I still think love marriage is better than *omiai*. But now that I have my own child, I think that *omiai* would not be so bad. About three years after the divorce, a few people interested in setting up *omiai* with me visited my mother. But I couldn't think of remarrying then. I was too busy supporting my child. And my mother thought I didn't want to remarry so she turned them all away.

I've changed a lot since the divorce. I hadn't really liked staying at home, but being divorced was worse, much worse—I had a really hard time economically at first. Now that I have a higher position, I'm happy I'm working. I can have my own life. I enjoy working. But if I hadn't divorced, I'd probably be quite a different person today. I'd still be at home. And who knows? I might have been happy that way.

My mother opposed the divorce. She was very ashamed of me. In fact, she was so angry with me that I didn't see her for six months after the divorce. It was *Obon* time. I had gone home to visit her and see the relatives. But I wanted to hide myself, I was so ashamed.

My father opposed the divorce too, but he was more understanding. He said, "It's better to get a divorce than to live with a man you don't like."

We divorced for two reasons. One was money. I saved

the money for our wedding ceremony and everything. I had been taught by my parents to live independently without being economically dependent on anyone. I thought that was the natural way of living. But my husband pretended to have a high standard of living. He must have told his parents in Hokkaido that he lived a luxurious life, because they depended on him financially. They often asked him to send money. The last straw came when they asked him to send a lot of money to build their new house. Yet here we were struggling to get by on just his salary ourselves!

I didn't like his attitude either. He believed his wife should obey whatever his parents said. He was the *chonan* [first son]. So three years later we got a divorce. I myself might be to blame. Maybe I was too young. If I were older, I wouldn't have divorced him. (I was twenty-three when we married and he was twenty-six.)

It's easy to get a divorce, though. All you need is two witnesses. We didn't even have to go to Family Court. We just talked and decided that a divorce was best for us. So we filled out a form at the city office, and I changed my family register, because my mother worried that people in the countryside where she lived would find out. We changed the place of residence from where she lives (ten kilometers away) to here. Only then did we remove my husband's name from the register. That way people wouldn't know. Of course, everyone knows now. But I don't care. Even my mother has changed her mind. She sees TV dramas about divorce all the time now. So she knows that divorce is nothing special. In the old days, people thought it was a crime. But it doesn't surprise people anymore.

After the divorce, I tried working in a snack bar for a week to see what it was like. I chose a job with a cosmetics company instead though, because they had their own childcare center. The salary was very low—just enough to feed us. Our apartment rent alone cost half my salary. So I volunteered to do cosmetics sales as well as my clerical work. But even working both jobs didn't bring in enough money. I also delivered lunch boxes in the morning and saved all that money.

I had long wanted to have my own shop, so I started a sake snack bar [*snakku*]. But I continued the delivery work, because it was so profitable. My biggest problem right up until the day before I opened my *snakku* was that I couldn't find anyone to take care of my little girl. Fortunately my elder sister rescued me. She came up from Ibaraki Prefecture to care for my daughter for a week. And best of all, she persuaded my mother to take care of her. At that time, my mother taught kindergarten. I went to her, bowed deeply and said, "Please take care of my child. I can't do anything with her around." So she let my daughter join her kindergarten.

The *snakku* I opened was a big success. It was big enough to hold twenty people, plus the two young hostesses and one young boy who worked for me, so I made a lot of money. I don't know why my shop prospered, but it may have been because I didn't know anything about the snack bar business. I just treated the customers naturally. I didn't flatter them. I never went out with the customers. And I gave strict instructions to my employees not to.

After two years of running a *snakku,* though, I decided it was time to close down, because my little girl was about to enter elementary school, and I thought it wouldn't look good to have her mother be a *mama-san.* (Maybe I'm prejudiced.) You see, parents have to fill out a form at the school saying what company the father belongs to and what the mother does. Since I didn't even have a husband, I thought that at least I should have a more respectable job.

Besides, I just couldn't bear to be apart from my little girl any longer. She was living with my mother most of the week. I often cried when I thought about her. Every Sunday she came to my apartment to stay overnight, and

I kept her out of kindergarten on Monday morning so we could spend more time together before I dropped her off in the afternoon when I went to work.

Many divorced women are hostesses because it's an easy way to make money. My father and my mother gave me some land across the street from their house. So I built my own house with my own money there. I should be able to pay off the loan in five more years. Then I'll buy a condo in the center of the city and give the house to my daughter.

My next job, in sales for an insurance company, has lasted four years now. I was attracted to this company because they aren't prejudiced against divorced women. Insurance saleswomen have more free time. I can attend the PTA if need be or if my child is sick, I can take care of her myself or take her to a doctor.

I work on a commission basis. I'd say I make an average of 380,000 yen [$1,583] a month. I made about 700,000 yen [$2,916] a month at the snack bar, but that was unstable work.

Most people selling insurance are women—I'd say 90 percent. The other 10 percent are men who enter the company fresh from university. They will become the executives and future elite. I've heard that insurance agents are well-respected in other countries, but that's not so in Japan. People here tend to look down on insurance agents.

I am head of one sales division. Five women work for me now, and if I recruit three more women, I can have my own office. I'd like to be director of a branch building. Right now there are thirty branches in Sendai. Becoming one of the directors of a branch building is the highest a woman can get.

When my little girl grows up, I want her to go to junior college—university if she wants to. I want her to decide for herself what to do with her life. Of course, I want her to be liked by everyone and to be thoughtful. But I don't want her to sell insurance. It's too hard. And being a hostess is out of the question.

Sometimes I wonder what will happen to me when my child grows up? Maybe I'll get lonely. But for now I think it's better to stay unmarried. You know, men remarry very quickly after a divorce, although my own husband didn't remarry until four years later. Sometimes my daughter and I need a pair of man's hands to repair something around the house. But I don't need anyone to cook and clean for me. A divorced woman just needs to make enough money to put food on the table. I know my child would like to have a father. But she doesn't say anything. Other friends of hers don't have fathers either.

I think the Japanese woman has changed a lot. Look at me, how much I've changed. But Japanese men—I'm not so sure.

On the other hand, I can't say that I'm really thoroughly modernized, even though I may look that way. I tend to think of other people's feelings first, not business first. I'm certainly not what you call the me-generation, like some of the young people.

Inside my mind, I approve of the old way of thinking. I always thought men should wear the pants in the family. Even now I think men are superior to women. And a woman should do what a woman should do—cook well and keep the house clean. Men should be the ones who can be relied on by women. I want to rely on men, but men tend to rely on me.

I have no one definite type whom I'd like to meet someday. Whomever I fall in love with is the best type.

Wives generally take care of the children after a divorce. Custody goes to the mother in about 80 percent of the cases, according to lawyer Nakamura. The judge makes his decision according to two factors—age and economic condition. If the child is under ten years of age, mothers tend to get custody. But if the child is older than ten, and especially if the child expresses a preference, sometimes the father is given custody. Also, if the wife is not capable of supporting the child, the father gets custody. Statistics show that 167,300 families have a single father compared to 718,100 families with a single mother. It appears that children are no longer the metal piece that holds the fan together, as an old saying goes. In 1983, for the first time, more children lost their father through divorce (49 percent) than through death (36 percent), creating headlines in the newspapers.

Fatherless children born to women out of wedlock are very few. Single unwed mothers constitute less than 1 percent of all women.

When statistics say children "lost" their father, it's sadly accurate. There are no legal visitation rights in Japan. "I envy your system in the States where the father picks up the children for the weekend," lawyer-columnist Nakamura says. "That's not so in Japan."

"My husband and I divorced when our son was three months old. I had to be in the hospital for three months because of the damage my husband did to my left eye. He'd always been very nervous, but once the baby came, he wasn't the center of the family anymore, and he didn't like that. We quarreled a lot, and he got violent.

"I've finally decided that, next year, I'm going to explain everything to our son and insist that he see his father."

Nakamura-san's son is fourteen now, and since his parents' divorce he's never seen his father. His situation is typical. Even in amicable divorces—with very, very few exceptions—once custody is decided, the child no longer sees the other parent. "We believe you can't divide the child in two. Splitting custody might emotionally damage the child," she explains. "And remember in Japan a couple is not only the husband and wife but also the family. This custom prevents the two families from quarreling as well.

"I've heard about the idea of the husband and wife

remaining friends. But that's an American idea. It's a good one, and some Japanese like artists and actors can do it. But most Japanese couples tend to break off completely after the divorce. After all, if we could be friends, we wouldn't need to divorce."

"Higher education for women, that's the root cause of divorce today," moaned an engineering consultant and company president. Certainly it's true that more education means more of an opportunity to get a job, not a great one, but at least some economic support, and that can make the difference between *gaman*-ing and not.

The rising rate of divorce is also indicative of a small but widening gap in expectations between what men want— a wife in the kitchen—and what women want—a chance to experience life in the outside world. The biggest divorce headlines in 1984 were made by singer Shinichi Mori and his wife, actress Reiko Ohara. He wanted her to stay at home. Although she agreed that her work did "impose" on him, she said she could not stop. "Both of us working was like having two men in the house," she added. [8]

Children have always been the biggest deterrent preventing women from divorcing. "But," lawyer Nakamura has noticed, "year by year women are beginning to think more and more about their own life and and own happiness." Nakamura-san has begun to get more clients in their forties and fifties, the fastest growing age group of divorced women. "These are the women whose children have grown up and who don't want to take care of their husbands anymore," she says.

Professor Sadako Ogata of Sophia University elaborates further, "A middle-aged woman has endured for a long time—given all her energy, love, and service—but without receiving much companionship, much anything in return. She is more patient than women in other cultures, but there is a limit to endurance." [9] With perhaps a second lifetime of a second forty years in front of her, she is beginning to wonder if there isn't something more to life.

There are other, less appealing alternatives to divorce too—running away or suicide. Unfortunately, the numbers are growing.

A manager of a house-painting business explained. "This is a confusing time for men. Imagine the shock of a man when he comes home and his wife says she wants a divorce or, worse yet, she is gone," he says. "She's tired of being subjugated and subservient. She doesn't know that male and female roles are different. She doesn't know what her role is." Adds a high-level corporate executive, "I've seen morning TV programs when the husband brings the children to the studio and goes on air to beg his wife to return. Can you imagine? It's so sad."

The greater sadness comes from the second alternative—the suicide of those women who don't have the energy or will to divorce. On August 4, 1984, two articles on suicide appeared in the *Japan Times*. The first detailed the death of a thirty-six-year-old Osaka housewife who jumped several stories from her condominium and died instantly. She and her husband had argued the night before over his transfer. She begged him to move back home, saying she was lonely. He told her she should be more patient. The second housewife, forty-one, set her Yokohama house on fire and died in the blaze. The Kyodo news report said, "Her action was apparently motivated by loneliness, because her husband was too busy working to be with her."

Even worse are the family suicides, such as the one that happened a week later, again in Yokohama. An unhappy thirty-nine-year-old wife was not getting along with her husband, said the story in the *Japan Times*, so she jumped from their eighth-floor condominium, "taking her daughter, Maiko, with her."

Now why would anyone force her innocent six-year-old child to die with her? Well, the Japanese feel that to be an orphan is a fate, quite literally, worse than death.

Japanese tend only to adopt the child of a relative, someone whose bloodline is known to them. A mother would
wonder who would take care of her children and fear that
they would be a burden on others.

It's little wonder that most people do *gaman* and remain married. Lawyer Nakamura believes that "More than
50 percent of married women are unhappy, but they tell
themselves 'Be patient. Be patient.' "

Feminism

There is no Gloria Steinem in Japan. The feminist movement is so limited that even the word *feminist-o*
refers not to women but to men who say, "Ladies first."

Probably the first real *feminist-o* (in the Japanese sense)
was the founder of prestigious Keio University, Yukichi
Fukuzawa who opposed traditional Confucian expectations
of women. His 1872 book recommended .that mistresses
not have the same rights as a wife, and in 1880 the law
did change.

A handful of Meiji women tried to elevate the status
of women through the popular rights, socialist, and labor
movements. Some upper-class women campaigned against
prostitution, concubines, and drinking. But women were

59

still not accepted in the political arena. The government made it known that female contribution to modernization was not needed or welcomed; their proper role was still in the home as good wives and wise mothers, pillars of tradition and stability in a time of great social upheaval.

These women set the stage for the first feminists—in the sense we use the term—and the "big three" in the history of the Japanese women's movement are Raicho Hiratsuka, Shizue Kato, and Fusae Ichikawa.

Any history of feminism usually starts with the *Seitosha* (Blue Stocking Society) founded by Raicho Hiratsuka in 1911. This literary organization encouraged women writers, but their increasing interest in writing about social concerns and women's problems led to the banning of several issues of their magazine, *Seito*, and the group's eventual dissolution in 1916.

In 1920, Raicho Hiratsuka joined forces with Fusae Ichikawa and Mumeo Oku to start the New Women's Association, which eventually won women the right to hold political meetings and give speeches. But government repression and internal bickering led to the dissolution of the association in 1922. Hiratsuka retired. Ichikawa left to study in the United States and returned to found the Women's Suffrage League in 1924. Although all men, regardless of income, won the right to vote in 1925, Japanese women were again left out in the cold. (American women won that right in 1920.)

Ichikawa was increasingly criticized by other feminists for continuing to emphasize the need for enfranchisement. They felt improving the conditions of working women should take priority; left-wingers stressed the need for a whole new social order, built along socialist lines. A women's civil rights bill came closest to becoming law in 1931 when it passed the House of Representatives, but was soundly defeated in the upper house, the House of Councillors.

The third of the "big three," Shizue Kato, was the

pioneer of birth control. Then known as Baroness Ishi-moto, she made speech after speech arguing the necessity for family planning. But following the Manchurian Invasion of 1931, when it became clear to military authorities that they would need more soldiers, the government suppressed the birth-control movement.

Any movement for women's rights at this time was considered selfish—by women as well as men. Immediately before and during the war, the nation's needs came first, and all women were encouraged to join national patriotic societies that saw the boys off to war, wrote them encouraging letters, and set up neighborhood teams that organized air raid drills and distributed rations and government directives. "None willingly sent their sons to war," says one Tokyo woman. "Mothers are mothers at any time, but they couldn't speak up for fear of being labeled *hikokumin* [unpatriotic, traitors]."

After the war, thanks to General Douglas MacArthur, American female staffers, and the groundwork laid by prewar feminists, women were finally given the right to vote, a right they actively use today. (In every election since 1968, more women than men have turned out at the polls.)[1] And Shizue Kato reemerged in April 1946 as one of thirty-nine women elected to the House of Representatives, a high number that has not been equaled since. (In 1985, only eight women belong to the House of Representatives, and nineteen to the House of Councillors.)[2] One of the most illustrious members of the postwar House of Councillors was the grand old lady of women's rights, Fusae Ichikawa.

In the late '60s, the women's rights movement gained momentum once again, under the influence of young female student activists and feminists in other countries. Japanese feminists were inspired by the writings of Betty Friedan and Gloria Steinem. Most importantly, the Japanese mass media began to report on the women's movement. In the seventies, they focused particularly on the activities of two women: Fusae Ichikawa and Misako Enoki. Most people assumed that when Fusae Ichikawa turned seventy-five, she would stop being effective. Yet after the International Decade of Women started in 1975, it was Ichikawa-san—and many say only Ichikawa-san could have done this—who brought together forty-eight women's organizations in order to pressure the government into ratifying the U.N. Convention on Elimination of Discrimination Against Women. (Despite her death in 1981 this group remains very active.)

The other woman, a pharmacist, Misako Enoki, led the movement to liberalize abortion and set the pill free. (Since the Ministry of Health and Welfare banned its use, women cannot buy the pill in Japan unless their doctor prescribes it to regulate their periods.) She and the pink-helmeted members of her group (*Chupiren*) decided to attack the double standard too, by raiding the offices of unfaithful men. Very quickly, *Chupiren's* pink helmets came to symbolize the whole women's movement. The media paid scant heed to feminists who tried to effect change on the day-to-day level, like Mitsu Tanaka who opened the Shinjuku Lib Center, a rescue house for battered or abused women. The press vastly preferred the antics of hysterical pink-helmeted women. Women's lib began to look ridiculous.

Meanwhile, publicity propelled Misako Enoki into the national consciousness. In the 1977 election to the Diet, she backed ten female candidates from her newly formed Japan Women's Party, promising that if they were not elected she would go home and be a good housewife. Although the women garnered thousands of sympathetic votes, each and every one lost, so, true to her word, Misako Enoki went home, but her statement set back the women's lib movement fifteen years.

On a quieter scale, many other small women's groups started in the seventies are still active: Agora Asian Women's Society (*Ajia No Onnatachi No Kai*), and the Japan

Women's Conference (*Nihon Fujin Kaigi*). In the eighties, all of these groups have been concerned with the ratification of the U.N. Convention on the Elimination of Discrimination Against Women, the passage of the Equal Employment Opportunity Law, and blocking periodic antiabortion bills.

Japanese women are more conscious than women in other countries that the years 1975 to 1985 have been the U.N. Decade of Women and that 1975 was International Women's Year. Says *Yomiuri Shimbun* senior editor Tokiko Fukao, fifty-two, "International Women's Year probably didn't mean much to American women because America had already changed a lot. But it had quite an impact on us. Once Japanese women realized that the U.N. supported the idea that women should be treated equally, women felt they could speak up and say discrimination is not fair."

Today, the largest feminist organization is the International Women's Year Action Group, begun in 1975. Although initial interest was high and members of the Action Group numbered as many as 10,000, ten years later the group had condensed into a group of about 500 activists.

One of the prominent members of the group is Yumiko Jansson, forty, both a devoted mother and an ardent feminist who, as we sat at the dining-room table of her Western-style home, constantly fielded phone calls from feminists, friends, and newspaper editors. She leads a life of interruptions, of organized chaos ("Please don't look at my messy kitchen," she said). We talked several times, my interview usually being sandwiched in between others. The arrival of a reporter from the *Women's Democratic Newspaper*, coming to ask this feminist's opinion about abortion, ended our first interview, just as my arrival had signaled the departure of a woman interviewing Jansson about international marriage. "I think she wanted to hear how difficult it is to be married to a foreigner," laughed Jansson, who is married to a Swedish businessman, Staffan Jansson. Yumiko Jansson transformed her experiences of marriage and living in Sweden into two books: *Kokusai Kekkon (International Marriage)*, and *Nagai Sampo (A Long Walk)*. Jansson has also coedited several books on education, labor, and reproductive freedom.

Jansson speculates that she is much in demand for interviews because, in addition to being a feminist, she is the mother of two. (Most feminists in Japan are single women in their twenties and thirties.) "I can show that it's normal to be married and have children, yet still want to change society," she says.

When Jansson is busiest, she wears her hair pulled back in a single, thick, functional braid. Her two children Mattias, twelve, and Sara, eight, run in and out of the house, always checking in first with "Mummy." Though Jansson is as devoted and loving as any Japanese *okasan* (mother), even an outsider can tell that she doesn't play by all the rules of Japanese society anymore. Not only is she married to a foreigner, but at an age when most mothers are still wearing aprons around the house, Jansson also sports clothing by the playful, high-fashion designers of Japan—a Jurgen Lehl blue blouse over blue jeans or a black sweater over Comme des Garçons black pants. There is a joie de vivre about her, an "it's great to be alive" and "I've lots to do" feeling that I haven't found in many Japanese women. Jansson is more emotionally open than many, but she has her more subdued side too. She feels a tremendous burden and a responsibility to effect change. And the secondary position of women in this society makes her angry.

YUMIKO JANSSON:

I was born in November 1943, so I'm exactly forty years old. I was raised in the countryside in a very traditional, very feudalistic family, where I was a troublemaker; I don't know why. Once a foreign interviewer asked me, "Why did you become like that?" And I couldn't answer. My sister is very traditional and very obedient, and my brother never raised questions either. But I have been this way since I was a child. Both my mother and father saw me as a problem. They didn't know what to do with me.

My maiden name is Yanagisawa, which is also my mother's family name. You see, my father married into her family. He was *yoshi,* the adopted son of my mother's father. My grandfather was very rich. He had a soy sauce and miso production company, and he didn't want to give his daughter away because he thought she was ill and weak. Yes, he had a son, but the son (my uncle) was kind of an enemy of my mother. He was jealous and envious of her. Grandfather asked my mother what kind of man she'd like to marry. Well, at that time, my mother was learning flower arranging, tea ceremony, and all the things a good Japanese girl would—even now—do. She also played *shamisen* [a stringed instrument] and sang traditional songs, so my mother wanted a husband who was a professor of these arts. As it turns out, my grandfather had some connections in Tokyo, where my father was. Anyway, that's how he was selected. Grandfather and mother both agreed on him, I assume, and mother and father got married.

Officially, my father's occupation is music teacher. He's an artist. His earnings were not so important to their marriage since my grandfather supported our family. But when grandfather died, harsh times started for my mother. Her brother took his revenge by not sharing the inheritance—even though the postwar constitution dictates that all children are supposed to share the inheritance equally from their parents. But a woman, daughter, or a sister must follow the family law. That's what counts more than national law. Living law is stronger than legislation, we say. That's what I learned in my house.

So my uncle's family became *honke* [the head family], and my grandmother lived with them. My uncle assumed ultimate power over the relatives, and my mother and father became subordinate to this family. It was so humiliating. And not just for my mother, either. The situation changed for her uncle and aunt, too. Her aunt's position became very low. She wasn't even allowed to sit inside the room on the tatami. She had to sit in the hall on the wooden floor. All these things I saw were normal in those days, although now I think they're disappearing.

But I saw the rigid and original form of discrimination against women in my childhood, and I couldn't bear it. I was constantly angry. My mother, for example, never went out of the house alone before she was married. She always went with someone. Even now, she still hates to go out alone. When she visits us in Tokyo, I tell her to go out and enjoy herself. I say, "Mother, you speak Japanese. Every sign in Tokyo is in Japanese, or you can ask someone, so why don't you go out to Takashimaya [a department store] or to an exhibition?" But she can't. She's sixty-five, yet she still uses excuses, saying that's the way she was raised. But that was forty to fifty years ago. Such behavior is so deeply rooted in her character that she can't break free.

Another remnant of her old-fashioned education is the high little voice she uses with strangers or newcomers. She talks normally when she's with people she knows like me or my sister, but with people she doesn't know so well, she changes her tone totally. Her voice seems to come from the top of her head. The words change. There's more politeness, more smiles, more bowing. Everything is totally different—even on the phone. She thinks that by doing this she shows more respect and reverence. She puts a respectful distance [enryo] between herself and the other person. It's a woman's way of saying, "You are better than me. You show me the way." This little high voice always reminds me that the Japanese woman's position is lower. It drives me crazy.

I've had a very difficult time with my mother, because she is from an older generation, from an old world where she was taught that women should stay at home to take care of their children, husband, and neighborhood. In a way she was a kind of servant. And it was really humiliating to see when I was growing up. Of course, this is true not only of my mother but also of the other women in the rural area where I was raised. They were always so subdued. It never occurred to them to take the initiative. Never, never. They were so afraid of men. They always obeyed men and followed their orders. Of course subconsciously they knew that if they revolted, they'd be treated very badly. They'd be thrown out of the family or rumors would start that the wife was a strong woman.

As my mother was trained to do, she obeyed her brother, and when he told her to come to his house with her seal, after grandfather died, she did. She never ever thought he would cheat her. He gave her a piece of paper with nothing written on it and told her to sign it. He assured her, *"Warui yo ni shinai"* [I won't do anything bad to you]. Well, since she had the kind of education that trained her not to ask questions, she did as she was told. Later she learned the paper said, "I hereby give up all my rights to the inheritance." That was what started the twenty-year cold war between them. Neither invited the other to their children's wedding ceremonies. It was only on the occasion of my grandmother's death three years ago, when they were both more than sixty years old, that they finally reconciled.

I know this kind of world where women endure and don't speak up. They just listen to others and worry about how the man feels. They concentrate on observing the man's face. In Japanese we say, *"Otoko no kao no iro o ukagau."* That means the woman observes and reacts to the color of the man's face. The woman thinks, "I'm ready to do anything. If he wants this, I'll do this. If he wants that, I'll do that." They are so constantly afraid of misbehaving, of not fitting in, of not being able to accommodate his demands. This man can be a brother, father, uncle, husband, any man. That is the root of my anger.

Everyone knew I was *namaiki* [cheeky, strong-willed, show-off]. And I just took it as my character. And I was strong enough to say, "It's okay, that's me." But I was so lonely. I can't tell you how lonely. No, there was no one like me when I was growing up. All the girls tried to act a little stupid because they knew that boys couldn't stand intelligent girls. If a girl were smart, the boys would say, "She's not feminine. She's not girlish. She's not popular." For a girl at that age to be told she was not popular among the boys was the worst thing that could happen. So I closed myself off in order to protect myself and not become just like the others. Maybe I had only a couple of friends, and they were really just superficial friendships.

Anyway, after graduating from high school in Iwate, I came to Tokyo to study at Sophia University. Coming here to study was just an excuse to leave my hometown. Otherwise I never would have been able to, as I was a girl. Because our family had no financial difficulties, all the young people, both the boys and the girls, went on to higher education, but most of the girls went to two-year schools to study nutrition. A few went to four-year women's colleges. I think I was the only one to go to a four-year coed school.

Even at Sophia, I didn't make many friends. After a half year there, I realized I was in the wrong university. It's a good university, but everyone felt that girls should get married and be good mothers. However, I was very interested in politics in those days [1962–1966]. But Sophia prohibited any students (boys or girls) from being involved in any political movements. This was just after the demonstrations opposing the Japan-American Security Treaty, and the political climate was very touchy. The university wanted to protect their academic peace. I understood their viewpoint, but I was too wild, so I did not feel at home at that university.

I have to admit the lack of communication was also my fault. I didn't let myself act like one of the girls. I was not confident, so I didn't take my strength as a good thing. I thought I wasn't a good girl. I didn't value myself highly. So that was my fighting period.

I felt something was wrong with the idea that girls take for granted that they will marry, have children, and take care of the home and family. This is the unwritten curse we have in us—the longing for marriage. Marriage is the utmost important thing in a woman's life. Women will do anything to get married. Because if you are married, you are first regarded as a woman. You have no worth if you are single in this society. Marriage is everything.

I didn't share that particular religion. On the contrary, I wanted to work, and I wanted to continue to work, too. Actually, marriage was the last thing on my mind, but oddly enough, I was one of the first in my class to get married.

It was in my fourth year of university that I met Staffan, a Swedish student studying Japanese on a government fellowship at Tokyo Foreign Language University. He was the first person and only person who said, "You are O.K." That gave me a lot of confidence, which I really wanted. We dated for two years and married in 1967.

My family didn't object at all to the marriage, not at all. I think that may have been for two reasons. First of all, Staffan is a good person. And he could speak Japanese, so they could tell he was a good person, too. And second, I think they thought I was too strong and didn't think I'd ever get married in Japan. Not that they'd ever thought I'd marry a foreigner. It was just that for my own happiness they might have thought I'd never marry a rigid, traditional, fixed Japanese man.

We were married in a church in Tokyo in a small ceremony.

After graduation and before marriage I worked at a Korean bank. That was my first experience of racial discrimination. I'm from the North of Japan where we don't have many Koreans or *Dowa (burakumin)* people, so my experience with them was very limited. I knew from books that, during the war and throughout history, there'd been discrimination against them, but I didn't know the reality firsthand. Once I started working there, people would say in hushed tones, "Are you working at a Korean bank? Are you possibly Korean?" Well, they didn't actually ask if I were Korean, but I could tell by the look on their faces that that's what they were thinking. But I didn't care if they did take me for Korean. I had no objections to working for the Koreans. They took me at face value, so I liked working there. They were very straight, very fair people. There was no problem inside the bank. But outside the bank, in Japanese society, they are discriminated against. Koreans are very open and frank. Japanese are more complicated. They are not so clear in taking a stand on one side or the other. So that was the first time I had my eyes opened to racial discrimination. I was not married during that time, and people at the bank knew I had a foreign boyfriend. But that was nothing special to the Koreans. After all, they were foreigners too.

I worked at the Korean bank for one and a half years until March 1968, when we moved to Sweden. In that country, I felt like a fish in water. It was a very positive experience. I immediately started learning Swedish, which I spoke for three to four years. So many people speak English that I could have spoken English all the time, if I'd wanted to. But I studied at the University of Stockholm for one and a half years. Then I worked for Scandinavian Airlines, where I did anything and everything—check-in, reservations. I spoke English, Swedish, and Japanese, but mostly Swedish and Japanese. That period at SAS was the best school in Swedish that I had. And I really enjoyed working with the people. I was not treated as a foreigner. I was treated equally. In Sweden, if you stand on your own two feet and say what you believe, it's okay. But in Japan, people judge you as a woman. They say, "You can't say that. You're just a girl. You're young and inexperienced." So you are always in an inferior position, and I don't like that.

The years in Sweden were the most intense years in feminism everywhere [1968–1971]. During that time, women gained more rights, they had more say, and more of them went out to work. Laws in Sweden were changing, and all this had a strong influence on me.

It was near the end of our stay there that I became pregnant with Mattias. We moved back to Japan when he was two and a half months old (in late 1971) and had only been back a few days when I thought, "Oh, no. Nothing has changed." I felt I was physically here and mentally in Sweden. And I longed to go back. I didn't have friends with whom I could communicate about my new experiences. The impact of feminism was so important and so real to me, but I couldn't share it with anyone. It was very frustrating. I could only talk to one or two people, but only partially. But maybe the fault was on my side, too. I still thought that my family and marriage should come first, so I didn't go out in the evening to meetings or get to know other women.

Staffan was a researcher at an institute then, and I translated and interpreted Swedish to Japanese. For three years, I was always reading the Scandinavian newspapers and writing the Scandinavian news into Japanese. Then I sold my first article to Kyodo News Service. It was a story comparing women's working conditions in Sweden and Japan. I wrote about the father's right to take care of the children. And if a man and a woman separated, how they shared custody of the child. I believe both men and women should be responsible for raising their children. I have no problem with my husband, though. He really does a lot with the children.

While I was writing about women and family and politics, Sara was born, in August of 1975. That was International Women's Year, so I was really glad I had a girl. I thought, "I'll do something. I want to fight for my daughter." I decided to become actively involved and take positive steps. I thought, I'll actually join the movement. Just writing was no longer enough.

Thus, I became involved with the International Women's Year Action Group, which had 10,000 members. We took action whenever we found sex discrimination. For example, there was a *ramen* [noodle] ad on TV, in which the girl said, "I am the one who cooks," and the boy said, "I am the one who eats." We protested and it was taken off.

We have been very strong on the abortion issue and recently stopped the presentation of the revised bill to the Parliament. But the movement stopped there. My stance is that we shouldn't wait. We want a new law that allows abortion on demand, regardless of conditions. It's quite symbolic that the Japanese women's movement is not influencing Japanese politics on reproduction. Our feminist movement has never been in the mainstream. No one takes it seriously. But now is the time really, by demanding what we want and not just criticizing what we don't want.

You have to understand that feminism is very different from other Japanese social patterns. Feminism is considered a very antitraditional, destructive movement. It's like a timebomb because it would require total social change. It is not based on the traditional division of labor. Feminism wants both men and women to be open and to develop totally and equally. So it doesn't fit in with the existing social system. Hence it's regarded as very dangerous.

Before feminism, it was called women's lib, and it was ridiculed. Men made a joke out of the women's movement. The mass media projected an image of the feminist as an ugly and unloved woman who joins the movement out of desperation. They still use this propaganda, so this image is very strong, even today.

The Japanese system is patriarchal, so feminism is quite different from the behavior we learned as children. For a woman to stand up and show she's a feminist creates an uproar. It's so final, so dangerous. Women think they will lose so many things; that's why there are so many closet feminists in Japan. The women worry that they will lose men's support and men's love because they aren't acting the way men want them to. Feminism is doing what you believe, and that's against the Japanese mores for women.

Many closet feminists read my articles and books, then they write me letters and say, "You are so right. But I am afraid." I write back to them and say, "Come and listen to my next lecture. Maybe we can talk during the question-and-answer time." And to a few I write a personal note saying, "You must love yourself. Take care of yourself first—before your husband, your child, your lover. You are the most important person for you." You know, women are so afraid of being lonely, of being different, of being an outsider. They don't want to be pointed to and called an old maid or a woman not charming enough to get a husband. They are so afraid of criticism. I say, "Don't worry. You can certainly have women friends." At this point, though, in the feminist movement, there is not a lot of solidarity between women and women.

The big problem, of course, for both men and women, is that there's no individualism in Japan. And feminism is the utmost individualistic idea, saying "You are an individual. You are a woman. You can be as you are. You are you. You say O.K. to yourself." That idea is not Japanese. This can be said for men, too. Many people think individualism comes from Western countries. Actually there are many individuals in Japan, but they just think they are special, that they are queer and different. Before

I came out of the mythology of myself, my vague self, I felt the same way. But they can speak out. If only they would say we don't have to observe the fixed idea of men's roles and women's roles, there's nothing to lose. But many women still live according to the standards set by men. The men sit on the power center, and they have nothing to lose by remaining there. But women have nothing to lose, either. If they'd just be strong.

But did you know that the word "strong" sometimes has bad connotations for women in Japan? Just yesterday I was talking to a good friend who was upset because someone told her that she is strong in crisis situations. I told her that to be called strong is a compliment. But to Japanese (men and women) the word strong is bad when it means only caring for one's self, being oppressive to others, and liking to be a leader. So she hates to be called strong. I told her not to take it negatively. But being strong in that way as a woman is not and never has been desirable in Japanese society. It's not considered a good trait.

Radical is a word that can never be good either. I'm often called a radical. I'm a radical to the average Japanese woman, because of my ideas on employment, pornography, birth control, and abortion.

A Swedish politician once told me there's a saying: "Don't wake the sleeping baby." But I believe the sleeping baby needs to be awakened. Now.

SEX AND PORNOGRAPHY

Japanese historically have had a much more casual attitude toward sex than Westerners. In Heian days (794–1185), court nobles like Prince Genji routinely slipped in and out of a lady's bedroom between sunset and sunrise. And mixed bathing was common right up until the Meiji Restoration in 1868. (Even today a few mixed baths exist, but for the most part women bathe only in their half of the public bath and are quite adept at averting their eyes from others or at modestly covering their private parts with the most minuscule towel.) In Meiji days, Japanese, being quite sensitive to the opinions of foreigners, soon got the message from the red-haired, blue-eyed barbarians that their coed bathing was considered "barbaric." So out came the towels and up went the walls splitting the bathhouses into single-sex sections.

Since then Japanese society has become an incredible mixture of flagrant openness and severe repression of sexual matters. Customs officers routinely confiscate all copies of Western "men's" magazines from travelers arriving at Tokyo International Airport. That doesn't mean that *Penthouse* and *Playboy* do not exist in Japan; far from it. But the Japanese editions have no pictures of pubic hair or genitals. (Actually a few wisps of pubic hair are slipping by the censors these days.) Anything goes in Japan as long as the publisher follows that one guideline, so imported American editions are allowed to circulate once the little ladies with their little knives have scratched out the offending portions of the pictures. (This was reportedly once a man's job until someone realized that women work faster.) Even art books with abstract Picasso nudes are subject to such scrutiny. One friend who'd been transferred to Tokyo told us about his photography book series that included *The Nude*, a slender volume that the ever-diligent and thorough customs officials found after painstakingly examining each item of his family's one-ton shipment of furniture, books, and personal effects. He was summoned to Narita, handed a pair of scissors, and given three choices: cut out the offending pages, ship the book back to the States, or add the book to customs' pile of pornography. (He shipped it back.)

The unfortunate result of the pubic hair guideline has been the frequent publication of what seems more kinky and more offensive to me—the prepubescent, Lolita-like pornography. (No pubic hair, so no problem.) The first photo book of this ilk, called *The Pretender*, graphically chronicled the growth of a little girl from ages six to nine.

So successful was the first printing in 1979 of 50,000 copies that a fifth edition is now available.[1]

Pornography in the States never used to bother me much. Probably because I chose not to go to porno bookstores. One trip to Boston's Combat Zone and New York's Forty-second Street were enough for me. And I no longer flip through copies of *Playboy* at the supermarket. But in Japan I'm surrounded, and I can't get away from it. It's not unusual to sit on the subway next to a perfectly respectable pinstriped businessman reading the latest *manga*—an adult comic book (available at every newsstand) some of which have graphic stories of sex and violence. The strap-hanging teenager has his sports newspaper complete with the daily photo of a naked lady. I see pinup posters in bookstores. An S&M club story in a weekly photo magazine. *Playboy* calendars of bunnies whose breasts nearly touch the desks of even the most reputable businessmen whom I otherwise admire and respect. Rapes on Saturday night primetime TV. (It's rip-open-the-kimono-time again.) Late-night shows where the fully clad host merrily hops into bed with two giggling, naked girls, holds the microphone to one of their mouths and cheerfully inquires *"Do desu ka?"* (How's business?)

What is going on here?

What do Japanese women think about pornography? Or do they think about it? After all, they've been surrounded by photos of bare breasts and bikinis all their lives. Do they consider it degrading? And is there a difference between how feminist Jansson feels and how the average Japanese woman feels toward porn?

YUMIKO JANSSON:

"There's no sex education in the schools, so the children pick up what they know out on the street, which is easy to do. There's so much commercialized sex all around them. Japanese advertisements sell things as different as Scotch whiskey and refrigerators and cars with a woman's body. And it's not just a smiling face but an open-legged body. These days an ad for Haig scotch shows a totally naked woman lying on a rug with a glass of scotch in her hand. She says, "You can have a glass of whiskey with me in my room."

I have another poster that I've stolen from a train—one of the newest ads. It shows a woman from the waist down. Five centimeters under the navel, she's wearing tight pink pants in the shape of a man's shirt with a tie flapping in the breeze. And what are they advertising for? Students! Students for a design school, which trains fashion designers, makeup artists, fashion coordinators, and stylists. Do these people think it's art to show the woman's body like this, or are people just perplexed and don't know what to do?

As you know, many of the models in ads are foreign women. Perhaps that's why they have a reputation for being loose. I don't really know why. But one night I was with a Swedish girlfriend, and we were walking just two steps behind our husbands, when a Japanese man came up to her and said, "How much?" She was so mad. She said, "That sort of thing happens a lot to me."

"That's because *gaijin* [foreign] prostitutes do solicit men here," countered a Japanese female TV director. "One approached a friend of mine just the other night. 'Only 30,000 yen [$120]' she said, but he had to get back to work. It's a good market for them here."

And on television it does tend to be female foreigners who do the underwear ads or any advertisements that require sexy overtones. For a whole series of ads for jewelry, we had lots of bosomy jiggle (lots more than in "Charlie's Angels") and flowing blond hair, first from Farrah, then from Susan Anton.

Japanese have heard about the sexual revolution in the States. Being very well-informed, they have read about wife-swapping and the singles bars. They see American movies where everyone is jumping into bed with everyone else. And they believe it—all of it. Living in Japan they have no way of putting it in perspective. When I asked one young translator in Sapporo why American women have such a bad reputation, she explained, "Well, we've seen *Emmanuelle* [a steamy x-rated movie showing Emmanuelle having sex with female as well as male lovers], so we know what Americans are like."

"But *Emmanuelle* is French," I protested. "And most French don't do that either." No matter. Japanese lump together Europeans and Americans, the way Americans do Japanese and Chinese. A Caucasian is a Caucasian.

Prince Hiro of Japan's royal family could never marry a Japanese girl who'd been educated in the States, Noriko Aoki once informed me. "She wouldn't be a virgin," she said.

I don't know whether it was because of the foreign woman's "loose" reputation or whether I was just the nearest available female, but one night a drunkard grabbed me on the Ginza and planted a big sloppy kiss on my lips. I yelled ahead to my husband, and once he turned and realized what had happened, his fist was nearly as quick to form as mine. But when we looked to our Japanese host for a clue as to what we should do next, he just laughed. So we laughed too, and walked away, but I felt degraded. Our host, one of my favorites among my husband's clients, a very kind man, explained to us that all is forgiven in Japan if someone is drunk. We nodded, but I still felt somehow dirty or more accurately dirtied. *"Shikata ga nai"* (It can't be helped), most Japanese would shrug in this situation.

YUMIKO JANSSON:

I also get very irritated and very angry when I see the dirty kinds of *manga*. [Not all *manga* are sex comic books.

Some have science fiction, war, or romantic stories.] They are so revolting, yet they are everywhere—even in the barbershop where the children go, even at the pension where our family stays in the mountains. These dirty comic books give the impression that violence and sex go together. Sex is never enjoyable or good or part of a personal relationship, to show that you respect and love another person. The reader doesn't get that image at all. They just see masochism and women getting raped, women wanting to get laid.

And what's the message of these pictures? Women are always waiting; all women like sex combined with violence; you can take a woman whenever you want. As a consequence, boys believe in this illusion and really think of women as different human beings. The women have their own illusions, that men should take the lead, and women should wait. And a woman shouldn't act any other way, or it would look as if she were experienced.

Adolescents absorb this, and that's the only kind of information they get as sex education. Premarital sex is forbidden yet there's so much stimulus. The young people have no consistent guidance or knowledge. No serious effort is made to convey sex information. So many girls have made a mistake when their boyfriends have insisted on sex or when the girl believes the myth that it's a way to be liked by boys. It's a vicious circle.

Married couples have problems with sex, too. They don't know what to think because there are so many exaggerated stories in the mass media. There is no human consulting institute to turn to. No family therapist, no sex therapist. It's a very undeveloped field. It's nonexistent. Nor do we have state-licensing exams as you do in the States.

Both young and old alike get a double message that marriage is sacred, but you can do whatever you want. That is, it's a free world for men, but women should stay at home. Men can do anything—one-night love at a bar or go to a professional at a Turkish bath. In general, it's thought that men should be more experienced and women should be virginal. So men have no bad conscience about it. But I think it's insulting to women.

This double standard and fixed image of sex roles makes for a strange atmosphere, as you can imagine. People don't speak openly about sex or of sex as a good thing. As though a married couple didn't sleep in the same bed?! People have a puritanical way of regarding sex in official places such as schools. That part of society is sexless. Yet at the same time, the community is supporting Turkish baths, bars, entertainment quarters, and no-panty coffeeshops. I don't know what goes on there because I never go to those places.

Actually I can't really say that we are puritanical, because people are not religious here. But still we have a concept of shame, of dirtiness, and of a lack of respect.

Whenever I tell people that I am disturbed by pornography, they tell me I am immature, that my personality is not well-rounded. Even my sister says I'm naive and green. Both men and women say things have been that way for a long time. They say, "How do you expect to change it? Don't make a fuss. If you don't like it, don't look at it."

"Porno?" shrugged twenty-two-year-old coed, Yasuko Furuichi, "It's a man's thing. I don't really think about it.

Most Japanese women don't. The majority seem to dismiss it as something for men. And the handful who don't like it are reluctant to speak up. Again it's a question of harmony taking priority. Japanese women are not likely to bang a shoe on the table, although a few feminists belonging to the Action Group did rally together in May 1984. They insisted on the immediate removal of a subway ad showing a woman's breasts (beneath a sheer blouse) and a man's hand picking at one nipple with chopsticks. This advertisement for a new *manga* called *Morning* came down within five days, according to Jansson, so it can be done.

So many times did I hear women say, "Pornography can't be helped" and "It's just for men," that I decided to be more directive in my next interview.

"Aren't the *manga* awful," I said to one housewife.

"Awful," she agreed.

"And the rapes on TV, aren't they terrible?" I asked.

"Yes, terrible," she said.

"So how do you feel about sex and pornography?"

"I don't see it," she announced succinctly.

Is that the answer? Perhaps. It is true that the Japanese have an uncanny ability for seeing what they want to see and not seeing what they don't want to see. For example, from my study window, I can see a rusty water tower, train tracks, telephone wires, electricity lines, an old-style wooden Japanese home, and a cherry tree. If a Japanese woman looked out my window, she would see a cherry tree.

Meanwhile, whether Japanese women notice or not, every year seems to bring a new sexual fad. In sex as well as electronics, the Japanese are quick to spot a trend. When we first moved to Japan in 1981, the newspapers were full of stories about "sex tours" to the capitals of Asia. A sex tour to Bangkok supposedly cost less than a vacation trip to Hokkaido in the North. Under the guise of a golfing vacation and observing the well-known maxim that "the traveler knows no shame," thousands of men set out each year for Seoul and Manila from Narita Airport, where they conveniently park their clubs in lockers for the duration of the trip. But Asian women are beginning to protest, particularly the Filipinas, who let both Pope John Paul II and newly elected Prime Minister Nakasone know that they didn't appreciate being treated as Japan's bordello. So sex tours are on the wane but not totally wiped out. Last year we saw a group of Japanese businessmen in Taipei having a rollicking good time with their "dates" at the table next to ours. I doubt they planned to play golf later.

The next popular fad was the *no-pan kissa* of Japan. In these coffee shops, anyone willing to pay ten dollars for a cup of coffee could look as long as he liked at the waitresses who wore no panties (*no-pan*) under their aprons or miniskirts.

The current rage is considerably more costly to participate in—the lovers' banks (696, according to the National Police Agency's latest count). Although the Anti-Prostitution Law went into effect in 1958, what people do behind closed doors is their own business, so places like The Adam and Eve, which only "introduce" members to each other, are flourishing. One of the more exclusive clubs, The Adam and Eve even boasts that over sixty of its members belong to the Diet. (That is almost 8 percent of the Diet.) Whether doctor, dentist, or Diet member, the man pays $1,250 to join and about $2000 a month to his young friend. Often she is a college student, office lady, or housewife, since the amateur is much in demand these days.[2]

After the 1983 disclosure that members of our own Congress had sex with teenage pages, it is hard to wag a finger at Japanese politicians. But it does seem ironic that Diet members began a porno and prostitution crackdown in 1985, which included a new law that prohibited minors from entering or working in sex shops, established a midnight curfew, and required that all sex-oriented businesses—including lovers' banks—be located more than 200 yards away from schools and libraries. Several movie theaters in *Kabuki-cho* (the Forty-second Street of Japan) voluntarily removed their steamier billboards, hoping to head off any legislation in their direction. (Japan has a thriving porno film industry.)

The standard explanation for all the sex and pornography in Japan is the need for fantasy and an escape from Japan's repressive society. How harmful could reading *manga* or visiting a no-panty coffeeshop be when, after all, Japan does have an extremely low rate of rape—3.7 per 100,000 in Tokyo compared to 88 in Los Angeles and 54.6 in New

York, according to 1981 Metropolitan Police Department figures. But is the figure really so low or do Japanese women just not report rape?

One of the founders of Tokyo's only rape crisis center (*Tokyo Gokan Kyuen Center*), Tada Chiyuki, says that Japanese attitudes toward this crime are twenty years behind those in the United States. She estimates that the true number of rapes is ten to twenty times higher than official figures show. But women are reluctant to risk social disapproval, or worse, to be suspected of actually having seduced the man, when rapists rarely go to prison anyway. A victim can receive damages—from $1,000 to $10,000—but the size of the award varies according to her age, occupation, and whether she's a virgin or not![3]

Even if true rape figures were known, I suspect Japan has fewer rapes overall. In general, I feel physically safe in Tokyo, much safer than in New York. No gangs of threatening-looking toughs strut down the Tokyo streets. The men make no lascivious leers or whistles. Most impressive of all, the society is remarkably drug-free. (You can imagine that if the customs officers are good at ferreting out art nudes, they are even better at finding drugs.) When I walk the streets at night (clean streets, I might add), I feel no fear at all. Robbers, muggers, or murderers are the last thing on my mind.

Of course, needless to say, I do keep my distance from drunks. And occasionally I hear stories about the *chikan*, the pawing, pinching gropers who take advantage of the crowded, rush-hour subways for their own perverted reasons. Japanese women tend not to say anything when this kind of man not-so-accidentally rubs up against them (that would disturb the harmony and draw attention to themselves), which I think has only had the effect of encouraging these men. When I first heard about the *chikan*, I asked several Japanese what to do? They said, "Move." From my foreign friends, I got two pieces of more aggressive advice: Yell *"chikan"* or step on his foot. I tend to place my briefcase in between me and the sardine next to me. And I haven't been bothered yet. Nor in four years have I been bothered by the other common affliction of foreign women: the flasher.

If anyone ever tells you that Japanese aren't creative, I suggest that you pass along this story, which is admittedly second hand, but which I believe to be true nonetheless. A blond-haired, blue-eyed woman was walking along in the bustling business district of Marunouchi one morning at 9:00 A.M., while blue-suited businessmen and young office girls moved double-time around her. All of a sudden, a Japanese man in a raincoat walked straight up to her. Did he open up his raincoat and flash in broad daylight? Why, no, of course not. He whipped open his briefcase instead, which had a picture of him whipping open his raincoat and standing stark naked. He closed his briefcase, bowed, and continued on his way to work.

BIRTH CONTROL AND ABORTION

Whenever I take people sightseeing in the ancient capital of Kamakura (just an hour from Tokyo), first we visit the Great Buddha, a sixty-five-foot high bronze statue. Our second stop usually is the Goddess of Mercy statue at Hase Temple, just a five-minute walk away. The first time I visited this hillside temple, I was charmed by the thousands of miniature stone statues (mizuko jizo) with red crocheted hats, plastic bibs, and colorful pinwheels that line the steps leading to the famous wooden statue. "How cute," I thought. But now I get a chill when I see them, now that I know that each one stands for an abortion, a stillbirth, or a child who died in infancy. Most of the little stone gods (the traditional guardians of children) are bought in memory of abortions, and selling them has become big business at many temples.

Although Japanese women often feel guilty or ashamed, they have no religious reasons for opposing abortions. In

84

1983, Japan had more than 500,000 abortions, about one for every three births. [1]

Although the total number of abortions is declining, according to Japan's first sex survey, two out of three women have had at least one abortion. [2]

Married women have almost all the abortions in Japan, but Japanese have become alarmed by the doubling of teenage abortions in the past two decades (still less than 5 percent of the total). [3]

Single motherhood is a seldom exercised option (less than 1 percent of all women) for several reasons. Since even college graduates have difficulty getting a good job, what kind of work could an unwed or teenage mother expect to find? What would she do about daycare? Facilities are already oversubscribed. Most importantly though, an illegitmate child "dirties" the family register, and even if the child is adopted, the name of the natural mother must appear with the child's name in a document that follows this young person throughout life when he or she is applying for schools and jobs.

The high number of abortions is most likely due to the absence of both sex education and reliable contraception—the pill is effectively banned in Japan. According to a 1979 *Mainichi Shimbun* survey, eight out of ten Japanese couples use condoms. Two out of ten use the notoriously unreliable rhythm method (either alone or in combination with a condom). One in ten couples rely on the IUD, and the rest pin their hopes on withdrawal, the diaphragm, jelly, douche, or sterilization. A slim 3 percent have access to the pill, due to menstrual irregularity or other disorders if their doctor chooses to prescribe it.

The Ministry of Health and Welfare ostensibly decided against the pill years ago because of its possible harmful side effects, including cancer. One of the underlying reasons, though, is the fear of duplicating a United States-like sexual revolution.

At present there seems to be little movement to gain

the government's approval of the pill. Condoms remain the contraceptive of choice and are easily available in drug-stores, supermarkets, and sidewalk vending machines. Located next to the local sex magazine machine, our neighborhood condom machine offers three brands (Passion, Passion Rose Z, and Passion W—all are imprinted with "For Your Lovely Tonight"), which cost $1.67, $2.08, and $2.50 per half dozen. And the more shy housewife (women buy more than half of all condoms) needn't go out at all. She can buy privately from the "skin lady," who goes door-to-door.

The Japanese approval of birth control and abortion has often waxed and waned. Infanticide and abortion were societally-approved methods up until the end of the feudal period. But during the days of modernization and industrialization after the 1868 Meiji Restoration, both were banned. The country needed more workers for its factories. Yet despite the illegality, more women began to have abortions during the depression following World War I. Shizue Kato spearheaded Japan's first birth control movement. Momentum grew until the prewar government briefly arrested Kato and her followers. The military, needing able-bodied young men, drove through neighborhoods with sound trucks, exhorting women to "bear children, swell the population!" (*umeyo fuyaseyo*). But after the war, public opinion changed once again. Japan was devastated and could barely feed and house those who remained and those who were repatriated. The weak economy, a postwar baby boom, and the spectre of mixed children fathered by the Occupation troops, inspired the 1948 Eugenic Protection Law, which allowed an abortion for "economic" reasons.

Although Japan has lagged far behind the other advanced nations allowing the pill, it led the pack in legalizing abortion. (Britain legalized it in 1967, the United States and Denmark in 1973, Sweden and Australia in 1974, France in 1975, and even predominantly Catholic Italy followed suit in 1978.) And Japan became known internationally as an abortion haven.

Although the Japanese are far from poor today, 99 percent of all abortions are still given for economic reasons. So the word "economic" has become grist for the right-to-life mill, which is pouring out reasons to revise the law. Ever since 1965, the fundamentalist right-to-life group, *Seicho No Ie* (House of Growth) has been active. Their bills before the Diet in 1972 and 1973 were rejected, but ten years later in the spring of 1982, the group once again made headlines. Their champion, Masakuni Murakami, headed a group of 104 ruling party members also in favor of revising the law. Agitation reached a head by March 1983. By then, women's groups as disparate as housewives and feminists had banded together to form a united resistance. Gynecologists, doctors, family planners, and female politicians opposed any change as well. The usually quiescent Japanese women joined activists, and in Yoyogi Park 1,500 women protested. Five staged a hunger strike in front of the Ministry of Health and Welfare. It takes a lot to inspire Japanese women to act, but, as in our own country, the abortion issue hits close to home.

Due to the intensity and diversity of feelings, by the end of March 1983, the Ministry of Health and Welfare gave up its plan to submit to the Diet a bill to revise the current law. The ruling party itself was sharply divided. They could only agree to further study by a special research panel.

Yuri Watanabe (not her real name), thirty-six, vice-president of a rapidly growing small Japanese advertising company, has had two abortions. Outfitted in a fashionable but conservative red-and-black plaid suit, she gestures to make a point when she speaks. "I don't like the one-sided image of Japanese women as kind, gentle, quiet, and obedient," she insists. Certainly no one would describe this former student radical as "quiet and obedient." Confident and determined, she runs the six-person sales department and is unusual in her devotion to her work. Two months pregnant, she is also unusual in that she is not married, but living with her boyfriend. (They plan to marry next month.)

"No, I'm not the average Japanese woman," she readily admits. "But I'm no different when it comes to having an abortion." Her face saddens, and her flashing eyes suddenly drop and fix on her cup of coffee. "Every woman like me who's had an abortion shares the same sense of guilt."

YURI WATANABE:

I was born in Osaka on August 21, 1948. My father was an engineer and my mother a seamstress. She owned her own shop until she was fifty-five. She worked literally day and night. I didn't think it was right. Life was not easy for us. I didn't want to be like her when I grew up, although of course I admired her.

I have a brother who's two years younger. He's an engineer too, like my father.

I went to a public kindergarten, elementary school, and junior high. Then I went to a private all-girls high school. I took the exam for the public school, but I didn't make it.

I used to like theater when I was in junior high school, and I took ballet lessons. In high school I belonged to the theatrical arts club. So I took the exam for the theatrical arts division of Waseda and applied to Haiyuza, a drama school attached to a theater. I didn't make it into Waseda, so I studied at the drama school for three years. I took the acting course, although I really wanted to be a producer.

These were the days in the sixties when the student movement was very active. Most students at my school were involved in the protests.

At that time I was living with my boyfriend, and I was—so to speak—ignorant. I thought I was being careful about contraceptives, but I guess I wasn't careful enough. We used the condom-and-rhythm method, the most popular method. I tried to stick to the rules. At times I did, but at times I didn't. So I got pregnant. I was only twenty-one and not in a position to have a child myself. I had more things I wanted to do with my life. At that time I was trying to make big decisions in my life, such as whether to continue my involvement in the student movement or go abroad to study and work. If I had the child, I would have had to give up these options.

So I didn't consult my boyfriend. I made the decision myself, and I got an abortion. Actually my boyfriend was supposed to sign a paper giving his approval, but at some clinics they'll do the abortion without the boy's signature. You just get a friend to sign the paper or do it yourself. I signed it myself.

A friend of my friends had told me about this doctor, that he was the kind who'd do it without both signatures. He knew the signature wasn't really my boyfriend's, but he didn't investigate it any further.

I didn't think the pregnancy was an issue for both my boyfriend and me. I thought it was my problem. I never told him about it, and he never knew.

My doctor had me come to the clinic at odd hours, like Saturday afternoon, which most doctors take off, or after seven at night or early in the morning. I guess he didn't think it was the right thing to do, or maybe he was just trying to spare me embarrassment.

After the abortion, he prescribed some birth control pills. In general the pill is illegal. The Ministry of Health and Welfare says there are enormous side effects. Maybe Japanese pharmaceutical companies are not very advanced in this area. I don't know why it's still difficult to get. It's hard to tell. The doctor can prescribe it to those who have reasons coming under the Eugenic Protection

Law: women who might have a hereditary disease or some mental defect in the family. Even to those women healthy enough to have children who have already had enough kids. It's the doctor's decision really.

My doctor charged a prohibitive amount for the pills— 10,000 yen [$40] for a month's supply. The abortion was not cheap either—70,000 yen [$280]. That may not sound like a lot now, but that was fifteen years ago. And when you're twenty-one, that's a lot of money.

I continued taking the pill for three months. But I felt sick and dizzy and always tired. So I stopped. I know it was the easiest way of contraception, but . . .

Of course I didn't tell my parents about the abortion or that I was living with my boyfriend. Many of my friends were living with their boyfriends, too. There were a lot of popular songs then about living together. I don't think it was a fad. People still do it, and they're more open about it today. My boyfriend and I were economically independent. We shared the rent and food costs. It's hard to do if your parents live in Tokyo. But a lot of students come from other prefectures to study here or in Osaka. Their families don't know exactly what their son or daughter is doing, so those young people have an easier time of it. But some of the major companies don't employ women who aren't living with their families. And whether young people can afford to have an apartment together on their small salaries once they start working is another question, too. It's economically difficult.

I myself have never been to a temple to buy one of those *mizuko jizo*. I don't like the idea of *mizuko*. You admit that there should have been a child. Some people write the name of the child on a wooden tablet and the date he or she . . . well, passed away. If I had had a miscarriage and wanted the child, it would be different. Then I'd buy a *mizuko jizo*. But I've refused to admit its existence. Rather than feel sorry for the unborn, actually, I feel sorry for myself for having to make that decision. I decided not to ask forgiveness. It doesn't matter what religion you believe in, any woman who's had an abortion certainly feels guilty, whether it's to God, yourself, or Buddha.

I'd say more than half of my friends have had abortions. Some have had two. One friend of mine had five abortions before deciding to have children, and now she has three kids.

I had a second abortion myself. After the first one, I thought I might go to France to study European theatrical arts. But a friend told me about a job at the Japan Cultural Institute of Italy, so I went to Italy and taught Japanese for four years. Then I came back to Japan with the idea of importing Italian fashion. I started the business but it didn't go so well.

At the time, I was about twenty-nine and had a boyfriend, a businessman, and we used the same combination of condom and rhythm. But rhythm is not exactly very reliable. And since condoms may interrupt the feeling, at times we didn't use them at all. So I got pregnant again. We talked for a long time about whether to get married or not and decided against it. Then we went to the clinic together, a different clinic, and I stayed in the hospital for two days. It cost 100,000 yen [$400]. I never told my parents, of course, but this time I did talk with some friends. Of course, I felt guilty again. When I was under anaesthesia during the operation, I had a scary dream that I still see sometimes at night—a deserted earth from which all human beings have vanished. It makes me so afraid.

Anyway, we broke up and I went to New York for two years. First I studied English at New York University for two semesters. I got some pills from NYU's Women's Clinic. There was a feminist group conducting research on women's usage of the pill. I had a very thorough body check before they prescribed the kind and dosage of pill.

Then there were follow-up visits. My Japanese doctor never did anything like that. I was surprised at how irresponsible he'd been.

Next I got a good job preparing business reports for a Japanese research company. I talked with dealers and consumers of electronic appliances to check the level of acceptance of Japanese products in the United States. I did interviews over the phone.

Then I was transferred to the headquarters in Tokyo to work in a new division that published an industry magazine about the marketing of electronic appliances. It was a very good position, a responsible job, that I did for three years. But I wasn't involved in the decision-making. It being a Japanese company, I might never have been. So I decided it was time to move on, and I joined this advertising company three months after it started.

I've been living with my boyfriend for two years now. I don't know if we'll have a big ceremony or wedding reception, but we intend to register at the town office next month. I've finally met someone I'm sure I can live with the rest of my life. I never talk about my boyfriends to my mother, but I told her about him, and she approves. Actually it's not my first marriage. After returning from New York, I married when I was thirty-two. We only lived together for eight months. It was just a mistake. He was seventeen years older, and we decided to marry right after we met. He was president of an advertising agency and seemed like he knew everything. He seemed like someone I could rely on. As I look back on my own history, I'm surprised I had so many boyfriends.

I guess I'm unusual in that I've made all the decisions in my life myself. Most Japanese women consult with their parents. I have worked hard to have my own life. And I'm not ready to give it up for my child or husband. Of course I'll keep working after the baby. Otherwise I'd feel guilty. I have sacrificed so much to have my own world.

I think the high number of abortions in Japan is due to the lack of sex education here. I was a typical case. Even though I went to an all-girl high school, I learned nothing about sex. Oh, they may tell young women they are capable of bearing a child but nothing more. Yet high school is the time when you're most interested. At this age you can fall in love and so on. So it's a problem we all must face.

I believe there should be more sex education in the junior high and high schools. Maybe even in the elementary schools. Children seem to mature much younger now. I wish the government would do something. There are two kinds of women: those who want children and those who don't, but at this time, the government only supports those who want children.

Sex is not discussed in the family either. My parents never talked with me about it. Sex is something to be ashamed of. Older men seem to know what to do and how to be careful. But young men know as little as the young girls—sometimes less. In my case I had to lead my first boyfriend. We young girls learn from each other. We talk very frankly. It was a girl in high school who first told me what's what.

I think sex should be discussed more openly in the family. If I had a little sister, I'd . . . well, to be honest, I . . . I don't know if I could discuss it either.

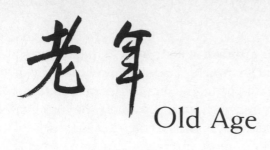

Old Age

  While the problems of sex and pornography, birth control, and abortion seem important to me, a female outsider, actually Japan and the Japanese are focusing very little attention on these topics right now. The nation as a whole is much more concerned with the graying of Japan and the aging of both sexes.

  In 1950, Japanese senior citizens aged sixty-five and older made up a small five percent of the population. Due to a lower birthrate and increased life expectancy, the percentage of senior citizens doubled to 10 percent in 1985 and will more than double again to 22 percent in 2020.[1] Many other advanced countries have a greater percentage of elderly than Japan: Sweden (16.6 percent), West Germany (15.5 percent), Great Britain (15.2 percent), France (13.5 percent), and the United States (11.4 percent). But Japan's rapidly aging society will bypass the United States in 1990, overtake Sweden in 2005, and by 2020 Japan will be number one.[2] More than one in five people will be elderly. Three workers instead of the present eight will split the cost of supporting one retired person. According to Nihon University projections, pensions (currently small by Western standards) will increase thirteenfold and social security nine times. Forty percent of GNP will be needed to support the aged, thus lowering Japan's growth rate to one percent per annum.

  Japan is understandably worried about this. Already the Japanese government offers subsidies to companies that raise their compulsory retirement age to sixty. The Ministry of Labor spends millions starting employment agencies known as Silver Talent Centers. The Health and Welfare Ministry subsidizes thousands of welfare centers for the elderly. Our neighborhood center offers classes in *go*, *shogi*, flower arranging, and traditional Japanese dance (Japanese have a saying that old age starts in the feet), as well as lectures and travel. One sixty-five-year-old widow in Sendai exuberantly described her center's overnight trips to hot springs. "Actually, we have to go somewhere educational first, like a factory, dairy, or water purification plant, if we want the government to pay for part of the trip. Then we check in early at the hot springs so we can soak for hours."

Since 65 percent of Japan's old people live with one of their children, it's good for them to have a place of their own to go to during the day, so they can stay out of the way of their daughters-in-law (some of whom boss them around the way their mothers-in-law used to) while keeping themselves mentally and physically active. Above all, no old person wants to be a burden. Many pray for a *pokkuri* (abrupt) death at special *pokkuri* temples.

In the old days, according to a legend-made-movie (the 1983 Cannes prizewinner *Narayama bushi-ko*), an elderly woman who reached the ripe old age of seventy would tell her son "It's time," and he would carry her piggyback to the top of a mountain where she would be left to freeze or starve.

Now many Japanese women routinely live beyond the age of seventy to eighty, the longest life expectancy in the world. (Japanese men, on average, live until seventy-four.) Women older than eighty outnumber men two to one.[3] A longevity list, published just before Respect-For-The-Aged Day (September 15), announced that those receiving silver cups for becoming 100 years old numbered 1,216 women compared to 347 men in 1984.

Any Japanese women aged sixty-five or more that I have met is an impressive person. When we had a serious midnight fire in our neighborhood, the seventy-two-year-old widow next door sprinkled water on her head and arms, and hosed down the land in front of her house before joining the crowds who stood mesmerized, as I did, watching one house burn to the ground and seeing flames sweep the second floor of another. Meanwhile, another widow across the street busied herself serving hot tea to all the neighbors. The two of them were so calm, I got the feeling they'd seen it all before, as well they may have. They are both old enough to have witnessed the chaos and fires of the Great Kanto Earthquake of 1923 and to have survived the bombings of World War II.

Japan's older women have known hunger, deprivation, and sacrifice. They saw the nation rise from the ashes of World War II. In their later years, they find the reward for their hard work in their childrens' college graduations, marriages, and children. Although these days fewer old women live with their families, more than half still do. The ideal, according to both young and old, is to live close enough so that soup carried from one house to another stays warm.

When an elderly man gets sick, if his wife is living, she takes care of him. Although some women regard their retired or ill husbands as nothing more than *sodai gomi* (bulky trash), I know one devoted couple who promised each other that, if the husband should die first (as he did), he would wait for his wife and they would meet "on the petal of the lotus blossom" (the sacred flower on which Buddha sits).

When elderly women get sick, the majority are cared for by their daughters-in-law. A daughter-in-law will probably see more of her husband's ailing mother (or father) than their own son does. Taking care of the aged is perceived as a "women's problem" and was the topic of the 1972 Japanese best seller *Kokotsu No Hito (The Twilight Years* by Sawako Ariyashi) in which Akiko, the wife of a salaryman, at first begrudgingly cares for her senile, incontinent father-in-law, who wears diapers, repeatedly runs away from home, and awakens in the middle of the night. Japan has few hospitals for the aged or special nursing homes. Ninety percent of the bedridden are cared for at home.[4]

Although the wives of *chonan* (first son) have the primary obligation for care of their husband's parents, young women these days increasingly worry about their own parents. One thirty-two-year-old Tokushima housewife, currently nursing her own mother, told me, "My parents are my first priority, but I will take care of my husband's parents someday, too. I have to admit I was happier teaching nursery school. I'd rather be around kids than sick people. But I'll do it anyway. It's my duty." Placing grandma in a nursing home still has a stigma attached, so this young mother decided against it. But as for herself, she says, "When I get older I hope they put me in a nursing home so I won't be a bother to anyone."

Sumie Seo Mishima, eighty-four, fully intends to avoid being a burden to anyone. "I am a Taisho woman," she says, proud of the progressive years (1912–1926) associated with democracy, labor unions, and the women's movement that influenced her as a student. "My mother was a Meiji woman who opposed feudal customs." Mishima-san's mother came from a wealthy family who, fortunately for her, had liberal ideas about women. So as a young woman, Mishima-san studied in America, graduating from Wellesley College in 1927. She also traveled extensively in Europe. Returning home four years later, overloaded with knowledge of the West, she eagerly sought to embrace Japanese and Chinese history and culture. So she married a professor of Chinese classics, a descendant of a noble samurai family.

"My husband was a great scholar," she says, tapping her temple with slightly arthritic fingers as if to jog her memory. "Books," she says. "Books everywhere. In the cabinet, on the desk, piled high on the floor. He ordered books without even paying for them. Samurai did not worry about money. I guess he thought I was responsible."

Not long after Mishima-san married, the war—the

central event in the lives of all Japanese over forty-five—broke out. She and her husband, his mother, and four stepchildren all survived the firebombing of Tokyo, which burned their two houses to the ground and killed 100,000 people.

After the war, Mishima-san worked as an interpreter at the War Crimes Tribunal. For forty years, off and on, she contributed to the monumental project of translating into English all the laws of feudal Japan.

But her primary job was always caring for her husband, until the day that he died thirteen years ago, a duty she dispatched with the dignity of a samurai woman. "True strength lies in patience and self-control," she was taught.

Mishima-san has a gentle and dignified face with small, intelligent eyes, beneath which a line has sunk diagonally across each cheek. Lines run across her forehead; combs pull back her gray and black hair, which is netted into a bun, and touches the silk collar of her slate gray kimono and *haori* (overcoat). She insists on wearing a kimono every day (only 5 percent of Japanese women still do). "It's economical," she pronounces.

SUMIE SEO MISHIMA:

I was born on July 15, 1900. My family lived in Kyoto where my father was a junior high school teacher. We had a nice big house near the Imperial Palace.

I was brought up in an old-fashioned Christian family. My father went to a Christian college in Hokkaido. His father had been a samurai, and samurai families were very poor after the Meiji Restoration [1868]. My father started his studies at Tokyo University, but it was so expensive that he moved to Hokkaido University, where there was no tuition and no textbooks. He had to copy his textbooks.

My mother had gone to Kobe Jogakuin, a Christian high school, which is now Kobe College. She was quite a bright girl, but she didn't enjoy or understand the Christian services. Yet all of the girls were very anxious to be Westernized. One of her teachers, Helen Serl, had graduated from Wellesley College, so she urged my mother to go to America. Since my grandfather owned a spinning factory and was a prosperous businessman, she could have. But he didn't want her to go. Instead, the family arranged her marriage to my father.

I was the third daughter. I had two older sisters, one older brother and two younger sisters. Since the boy needed a lot of care, and no one cares much about a girl baby, I was sent to my mother's parents' home in Kurashiki where my grandfather headed a textile company. They sent me to the family carpenter's home, and those people took good care of me until I was three years old. This was often the custom that a baby was sent to a nurse's home in the country for the good of the baby. I'm not comparing our family to that of Kyoto nobles, but they did this, too.

I was a self-assertive baby and a willful child. So when I returned to my family—my parents didn't want me to be away too long—I was scolded by my parents and teased by my sisters. I fought with my mother. She was hysterical, you know, with so many children. Anyway, no one cared for me. In a Japanese family, only boys are important. Girls don't mean anything. Only the outside people took good care of me.

My father died when I was ten years old. His sister who was married and living in Tokyo was kind enough to volunteer to raise one of the girls. My aunt had one son who had already graduated from Tokyo University. Since it's always the middle child who is sent out, I went to Tokyo to live with her and her husband, an engineer.

Later we moved to Osaka, where I attended a primary school near the gay quarters. (Many of those girls became geisha.) Each week I was sent to Sunday school, but I wasn't interested in the Bible stories. Oh, I suppose a few were interesting. But I went because each child's Christmas present was determined by her attendance. The Christmas present was usually a Western doll. That was all I was interested in.

I hadn't gone to church much in Tokyo because my uncle was an old samurai who hated all Western things. He had studied the Chinese classics like Confucius. He despised Japanese literature; he thought that was only for commoners. But he was good to me.

After four years in Osaka, we moved back to Tokyo. I began to go to church again, because I was interested in English, and my high school English teacher went there, too. And when I studied English at Miss Tsuda's School (a four-year post high school course), all the girls had to go to church.

I attended the Episcopalian Church. The service was so straightforward. And there was much more music and beautiful words like those of the Nicene Creed. They sounded easy and restful, so interesting to me even though I couldn't always understand.

One day the minister told me I was ready to be baptized. I wasn't so sure. But one of my friends wanted to do it, so the two of us went together and got baptized. That's how I became an Episcopalian.

At my school they asked me my religion and I always said, "I'm an Episcopalian." You had to be a Christian to go to these schools, you know.

When my father went to school in Hokkaido, he had to say "I'm a Presbyterian." He told me he became a Christian because he had to. Same with my mother. She was baptized so she could enjoy a nice school life.

I think I got too much Christianity, so now I'm interested in Buddhism.

Buddhism is ready to accept so much human weakness. But Christianity worries about sin and salvation and crucifixion. These concepts are so frightening to me. I believe both religions have a lot in common like 'Love thy neighbor,' but in Buddhism the same ideas are presented in a more roundabout, quiet way.

My Kurashiki grandfather made a lot of money with his textile business during World War I. When he died, he left much money and land to the eldest son [of three brothers and three sisters]. My mother and the others only got a little money and stock.

When my mother died, my eldest sister got all her money, because my brother had already died. So when the other children need money, she has the duty to help us.

At that time, there were no women's colleges and no women were allowed to enter boys' universities. So a young Japanese woman who wanted to go to college had to go outside Japan. Today of course, they can get educated here, so they only go to the U.S. for graduate school. There are very few Japanese students at Wellesley now.

Since the school agreed to pay my tuition and board, all I needed was traveling and pocket money, which my eldest sister and two rich uncles gave me.

Since I had always worn kimono, I had to buy some Western clothes for the first time. They were made in Yokohama, where so many foreigners lived.

There were six Japanese girls and one American lady on the boat from Yokohama to Seattle. We all traveled first class, which cost $300! The only other women were some Japanese brides for the immigrants to America.

At Wellesley I wore my funny-looking, Japanese-American-style clothes until a Miss Cook asked me if I wouldn't be more comfortable wearing kimono (except during gym). That made me feel much more at home.

I studied ancient history, math, economics, Greek, Latin, and English. I was so interested in history then, and I still am—history, history, history. Actually, world history was mostly Egyptian, Babylonian, Greek, and Roman. Nothing about Japan, China, or India.

I had the hardest time in economics. Miss Perkins

said that I, as a modern, educated woman, must study it, so I did.

I felt closer to the professors than the students really. The girls were too active for me. They talked so fast and so directly. They would say, "Well, is it 'yes' or 'no'?" And I couldn't answer. Saying "no" is impolite in Japan. So you say "yes" in a vague way when you are not sure what to say.

I came back to Tokyo in Showa 3 (1928). On the way home, I had traveled through London, Paris, Munich, Venice, Florence, Rome, Naples, and Cairo. So when I returned I thought I was a grand person. The problem was that no one else did. Already there was a military mood about the country and an economic depression.

Only a few yen remained in my purse, so I lived with my two younger sisters who had both studied in Tokyo.

During the Depression, there was hardly any work, so I was lucky to get a part-time job teaching English at Miss Tsuda's School and Daisan High School. I tutored and was paid in presents such as dried salmon or kimono.

About this time, my aunt and her relatives began to get interested in me as someone's potential marriage partner. They told people I would make a good daughter-in-law, because I got good marks at school and I was good at sewing.

But I didn't care for this kind of marriage talk. I wanted to study Japanese and Chinese history. I felt so ignorant after studying so much English history and literature.

At this time, *Nihon Daigaku* [Japan University] was the only men's university that allowed women as auditors. They had a history department that was very progressive, and that's where I met my husband. He was a specialist in the economics of the Tang and Sung dynasties. Ahh, the Sung dynasty—the most wonderful age in

Chinese history. They were the most prosperous people in the world.

The Mishimas had a family tradition of studying Chinese literature. My husband's grandfather had taught Chinese classics to the Emperor Taisho. It was the Emperor Taisho, through the Imperial Household Agency, who gave him the money to start his famous school of Chinese classics.

I met my husband in an extra session in his home. He was married then to a really beautiful woman, who always wore beautiful kimono. I understand she came from a good sake-brewing family in Kobe. Strange, but my husband's first wife worked as a hostess in a big cafe bar. They had married very young, and she had had a hard time with their four kids and the family debts left by my husband's father. So she had to work. Her brother had started a very famous Ginza cafe bar named Cafe Haru [Cafe Spring]. I remember passing by it. Well, as it turns out, she met a nice man there and divorced my husband to marry this man.

My husband's mother said that if I would marry her son she would take care of the four children and give us a separate house of our own. I was thirty-one then—I was twenty-eight when I returned to Tokyo—and he was only three years older, so I thought it was a nice proposal. I wanted to study Oriental history, so I decided to marry into the Mishima family. Thus, both she and my husband proposed to me, and I accepted. My aunt and uncle approved. My parents weren't living then, but they would have approved too, because the Mishimas were an important family in Okayama Prefecture where my mother grew up.

Houses were so expensive at that time that we all ended up living together. My mother-in-law was nice to me and fond of the children, but I had to work and we had to live together, so in a sense she got in the way.

I continued to teach English at Daisan, my old high school, and at Miss Tsuda's School, but when the military rose to power, I was asked to leave. I was considered too liberal, and besides my husband had openly denounced the military government. He was head of a group of scholars called the Democratic Historians Association. They were crushed by the special police, who took away some of his books. One day they took him away too, and I was so worried, but he was released that night.

Then the war came. It was early in the morning when we heard about Pearl Harbor. The radio said the Japanese Army was at war. But we didn't know anything about it beforehand. I thought the American planes and the American Army would come right away. I was so afraid. But nothing happened. It was a nice calm day. The war still seemed far off.

My oldest girl worked in a hospital during what would have been her last year in medical college. The hospital corridors and entrances were full of wounded people. The eldest boy had started Tokyo University, but there were no classes. He was assigned work in an airplane factory. The second girl was in high school, and the youngest boy was about junior high school age, so they couldn't do much. But I do remember the younger boy worked in a factory that printed money.

In the daytime, we'd watch the Bees or *B-ko,* as we called the B-29s [*B-ko* means boy bee or rascal bee], as they flew 10,000 meters over Tokyo. They looked like birds until they dropped the bombs. Do you know that when the plane is right overhead, you are perfectly safe? The bomb doesn't fall straight down but in the direction that the plane is headed.

Most of the time the Japanese guns couldn't reach the American planes. Only once did I see an American plane come down. I wondered what the man in the plane must be feeling. I felt sorry for him.

During the war, we had *tonari gumi* [neighborhood

societies]. We were ordered to group together several households, because when a bomb falls your neighborhood can help you more than your brother who lives a mile away. We had a captain, like my husband, who would report how fast ten housewives could pass the water buckets. Each day we practiced our fire drill, but when the bombs came, it didn't work at all.

The night of March ninth, 1945, was the worst in Tokyo. All of downtown was destroyed. People were burned and bandaged. I saw them. We were dazed. We had no feeling, except to pray that the war would stop.

Finally in May the bombing came that destroyed both of our houses. They burned to the ground, and we became one of the "burned-out people." We had no time for regret. We were just glad to be alive. The food question was most important. The next question was where to sleep. Since many people had gone to the country, there were lots of empty houses. We moved to one of the houses that remained. More than twenty burned-out people lived in the same six-room house.

My poor husband was so dazed. When we went back to see the house, all he said was, "Oh, my books are gone." He had some wonderful antique Chinese books—even from as far back as the Sung dynasty [A.D. 960–1279]. These were books my mother-in-law had sold many kimonos and rings to buy.

For days the books burned slowly, and the ruins of our house glowed red at night. There was no water to put out the embers. The old Chinese books became shining white ashes, and the modern books were gray ashes.

I used these ashes for toothpaste and soap.

A few months later, there was just a small story in the two-page government paper that a bomb—not an ordinary bomb—had been dropped on Hiroshima. It was not until a few days later that we learned the truth. We didn't think it was awful. We were too dazed. All we thought about was how to eat, how to live another day. I had no feeling toward the Americans. We had no strength to hate.

Before the emperor's announcement about the end of the war, I didn't know if he had a human voice. Actually, on the radio, he sounded like a child. I never thought he was divine. To me, he was a curiosity appearing in a medal-laden uniform of the highest rank or in the oldest of court robes. But the majority of Japanese did think he was divine. Today I think of him as just a nice man. He's so patient. He never loses his temper. He has wonderful self-control. He was trained that way.

After the war, I worked for the Occupation forces in the defense counsel section of the War Crimes Tribunal. I had to work to earn money, and this section paid much better than others. I earned 1800 yen [$7.20] for a forty-hour week. Two years later my pay was 18,000 yen [$72]. I was so happy. It was the nicest place to work.

After the war, we all said no more atomic bombs and no more war, not for any reason. I still feel that way. So do most Japanese.

The war helped women. The new national Constitution gave them equal rights, and because of the Civil Code, women were paid equal wages at GHQ. Young women today have more freedom. They don't have to ask their parents' or husband's permission when they go out. So many of them work outside. They have fewer children but they need more money for education.

But now I think some women are going too far. Throwing away everything, the way they do. And they are getting so mannish. Men and women look alike. Women are becoming superficial, wearing Western-style clothes. No kimono. Living in Western-style homes. All the TV and radio shows are saying, "Oh how Americanized we are." I don't think too much of it.

I've had such a busy time all my life. Yet now I am more happy and comfortable than ever. I get a widow's pension, and I have no economic worries. For the first time in my life, I am doing what I want to do. I'm not taking care of others.

My husband died at age seventy-three, about thirteen years ago, of cancer. We didn't know what it was at first. He had pains in his stomach, so he entered a hospital near us that was started by a distant cousin. But the doctors couldn't find out what was wrong. When he came home after a few months, he looked well. But then he couldn't eat and the pains in his stomach came back. He returned to the hospital for several months, and the doctor finally found that he had cancer of the liver. The doctor told his eldest daughter first, not me, that he wouldn't live more than ten months. (She's a pediatrician.) But he only lived a few months after that. I went to the hospital every day. I sat and talked with him. Although the hospital fed him, I had to bring three meals a day for the special nurse we hired for him. No one liked the job, so they kept changing. Sometimes my stepson's wife came to help me. My husband was a lot of care when he was at home, too, because he belonged to two historians' associations, and so many people came to see him and I was kept busy receiving them and making tea for them. Even now they still come, particularly on New Year's, and I have to return the call.

My husband depended so much on me, whether he was well or ill. And I spent almost all of my time taking care of him. He was often asked to write essays, and his publisher would send over their people to see him all the time. I had to entertain them and feed them, so finally I just said, "Let me write it." I gave all my time to my husband and not so much time to the children. That displeased my mother-in-law. She kept saying I spent too much time with my husband.

I think Japanese husbands require a lot of care. But it's changing. They're supposed to help in the kitchen, but they still don't clean, I've heard. But I lived in a samurai family. In my day the man kept out of the kitchen. It was beneath samurai dignity to cook or clean. At least in literature the common people had some appreciation of women but in the samurai tradition women were totally ignored.

I think Japanese women spoil the men when they are young. So when Japanese men get old, they don't know how to take care of themselves. They depend on their wives for everything. You know it's mostly men in the old age homes. They are the ones who become senile. Women are more useful when they get older. They can help take care of the grandchildren. They can work. They have more strength to take care of others. Old women are stronger that way. Old men are burdens and no use. Japanese men are spoiled boys. Women are the foundation of this country, like the foundation of a house, something you don't notice, but something you depend on.

This is the first time in my life that I've had time to do what I want to do. I don't want to remarry. I'm enjoying myself now. In Japan, marriage means marrying a house and family not just a man.

All my high school classmates are widows. Very few want to remarry. They feel both lonely and relieved when their husbands die, as I did, especially if it was a lingering illness. We like to have class reunions a few times a year, to get together to talk about our children, grandchildren, old teachers, or cooking.

There's one elderly people's association in my neighborhood, but I don't have time to go there. I only go to the New Year's party. They are very good to old people. But now there are so many old people in our neighborhood that it must be a big burden to the local government. The old people take trips to places that present them each with a whole big box of nice-smelling soap. I get invited every year, but I haven't been yet because I'm so busy. I think Japan is a good country to old people. We are very kindly taken care of. But I don't know how long the country can keep up this kindness.

I live alone in an old-style wooden house. It's a small house with four rooms—two tatami rooms for living, plus a kitchen and a bath. My husband and I had it built about fifteen years ago. Although his retirement money from teaching at Senshu University was enough to build a small house, it was not enough to buy land, so we thought of building on the family graveyard. The land used to cover a whole hilltop, then the city walled off the graveyard and made the rest into building lots.

The eldest son owns the house now, and he pays the taxes on it. I know the postwar law says all children shall inherit equally, but the house and graveyard are one thing. You can't split it up. He sends me money once in a while, but I have enough. I get $3,200 a year—tax-free—half my husband's pension. I don't need to buy any clothes these days, because I inherited more than enough kimonos from my sisters. Young people say a kimono is too much work to put on, but a kimono is very economical, you know. When part starts to wear out you can remake it into squares of futon or a *haori* coat or even underwear.

I have the small *butsudan* [family altar], which my mother-in-law had until she died. The big family *butsudan* burned down during the war. Every day I burn two or three incense sticks in front of the *thai* [tablets with the deceased's posthumous name on them]. Our *butsudan* has so many *ihai,* and I didn't know any of the people except my husband and his aunt. I put flowers in the *butsudan*—mostly artificial ones that my stepdaughter brings me. It's very simple. I'm afraid I don't pray there. I don't know how, since I was brought up in a Christian home. I make sure to put flowers on the seven graves, too, during anniversaries of the ancestor's death. That's where I'll be buried, too.

The Seo family graveyard is in Nagoya. We had to move it once because the city had plans for our burial ground. My father, brother, and sister who didn't marry are all buried there. They all had the Seo name, so they are allowed to rest there. Since my three younger sisters all married, they lost their name. But when my sister who didn't marry was dying, she whispered, "Nagoya," so I knew she wanted to be buried there.

Oh, Nagoya is such an awful place. Those car people who make so many Toyotas would like to swallow up our graveyard. Why, they would even take our gravestones down!

I think the family feeling is still strong in Japan. I stay in touch with my stepchildren. The eldest stepdaughter is a doctor—she's very nice—with her own clinic that her husband manages. They have two children, a girl and a boy, and the girl has her own little boy. My eldest stepson lives with his wife in a tiny but well-furnished condominium. They have no children. He's an adviser to the Chinese classics school founded by his grandfather. When he went to Tokyo University, he became good friends with the man who now heads Seibu Department Store. That man gave my youngest stepson a job, and he and his wife have four children, three boys and a girl. My youngest stepdaughter married a dashing kamikaze pilot but later divorced him to marry a nice American man named Bill Shannon. Mr. Bill Shannon had a big house and a high salary. He bought nice kimono for my stepdaughter and her little daughter Sumie, who was named after me. And he bought them both wedding dresses. He and my stepdaughter had a son together—Michael Shannon—before Bill Shannon died of cancer. My stepdaughter Yasuko is an art director, and she's so nice. When she was little, she insisted I was her real mother.

Her son, Michael Shannon, studies biology at the University of California. He's been to Japan several times. My stepson Akira took him to Okayama to see the family castle. Way, way back, one of our family was the *shugo* [head of the province, the highest local official] of Bitchu [now Okayama Prefecture].

1 1 0

I have so many children and grandchildren that I can't die yet. They need me. Michael wants me to write the history of the Mishima family in English. He's such a nice boy, I'm going to do it.

I'm glad I'm still strong and well, so I can work on this translation project. I have no right to depend on my children. Feeding them was all I could do during the war. And after the war I didn't have much time to take care of them. My only responsibility these days is to take care of the graveyard. I will take care of myself.

I had an aunt who never asked for a doctor. When I lived with her, she taught me the virtues of hard work and plain eating. And she died at nearly ninety. The doctor came just once. That's what I'm going to do, too.

教育

Part II

EDUCATION

The years 1871 and 1872 were momentous ones in the history of women's education in Japan. In 1871, the emperor proclaimed: "We still lack an established system of education for women in this country, and they [women] are generally deficient in the power of judging and understanding things. How children grow up depends on how their mothers bring them up, and this is a matter of supreme importance. It is recommended that those who go abroad from now onward should take with them their wives and daughters or their sisters. They would then see for themselves how women receive their education in the lands they visit and would also learn the way to bring up their children."

That year, five of the fifty-eight students sent to America on the Iwakura Mission were kimonoed little girls ages eight to fifteen. Their goal was to absorb American culture and to bring back the best to Japan. Educator Yukiko Maki, eighty-two, explains that Western women were considered superior at that time. The empress herself even told the girls they must become an example to Japanese womanhood. (Although two of the little ambassadors returned after a year due to illness, two others attended Vassar and one went to Bryn Mawr. One of the Vassar students (Princess Oyama) later became a famous nurse during the Russo-Japanese War; the Bryn Mawr graduate opened her own Girls English School, now called Tsuda College, an institution known for its excellence in English instruction even today.[1]

The next year, 1872, the newly established Ministry

115

of Education, taking its cue from the emperor, in a major advance, introduced a universal compulsory system of primary education, ensuring for the first time that girls received at least an elementary school education.

Japan's leaders in early Meiji days had recognized that rapid modernization and industrialization was needed to prevent Japan's becoming just another Asian colony or sphere of influence of the Western powers. They could no longer educate according to class. They needed talent at the top and below that, an educated citizenry of loyal, submissive workers willing to give their all for the state. The government began to reach out in many directions at once: educating women of the lower and middle classes; sending study missions to Europe and America; importing thousands of highly paid foreign teachers and technicians. Not that the educational level of the Japanese wasn't already high. Scholar Ronald Dore writes in his book *Education in Tokugawa, Japan* that 50 percent of the men and 10 percent of women were already reading and writing, a literacy rate as high as England's at the time.

As early as 701 the Taiho Code established a school to train government officials. Confucian scholars tutored the children of nobles. After the rise of the warrior class in the twelfth century, young samurai, in addition to learning the martial arts, attended schools supported by the local feudal lord. Buddhist priests taught reading, writing, and the abacus to not only samurai but commoners as well, in the widespread temple schools.

Centuries ago, education for women was restricted to enhancement of their feminine graces. Ladies at court in medieval days learned music, art, dance, tea ceremony, and flower-arranging. Poetry was considered a mark of refinement for both sexes. But the arduous task of learning the thousands of characters necessary to read the Chinese classics was restricted to men. Upper-class women learned comparatively simple Japanese (and often surreptitiously some Chinese characters), but from this group of women emerged the great Japanese writers of the ninth through the twelfth century, such as Ono no Komachi, revered for her love poems; Sei Shonagon, the talented writer of the *Pillow Book*; and best-known of all, Lady Murasaki, the author of the greatest work of Japanese literature, *The Tale of Genji*. Well aware of his daughter's talent, Murasaki's father could only lament, "If only you'd been a boy!"[2]

Many samurai women learned how to ride horseback and to handle a sword so that they could defend their homes, if need be. A few accompanied their husbands into combat and died beside them on the battlefield.

By the 1700s, the feudal woman was encouraged to learn by heart the Confucian guide to the duties of a Japanese woman, *Onna Daigaku (The Greater Learning for Women)*. This bible of behavior taught her that, "The five worst maladies that afflict the female mind are: indocility, discontent, slander, jealousy, and silliness. Without any doubt, these five maladies infest seven or eight out of every ten women, and it is from these that arises the inferiority of women to men . . . Such is the stupidity of her character that it is incumbent on her, in every particular, to distrust herself and to obey her husband." Over and over the book reinforces the idea that "the great lifelong duty of a woman is obedience."[3]

The first few decades of Meiji were heady days for women who wanted to learn more than obedience. Foreign missionaries opened more and more high schools for girls. (A high school was a five-year school entered after graduation from elementary school.) People eagerly embraced the "Western knowledge" half of the widespread slogan "Japanese spirit, Western knowledge" (*Wakon, yosai*). A few even discussed whether English should become the national language. In 1885, there were ten mission, one private, and two government high schools for girls. By 1900, the missionaries had started more than forty girls' schools around the country with names that are still well-known today—Seishin, Futaba, Shirayuri, Miyagi, Kobe, and many more. But the bubble of enthusiasm for the mission schools burst in mid-Meiji days, around the turn of the century, when the country's mood became reactionary and nationalistic, and the government forbade any kind of religious teaching. Having won the war with China (1894–1895) and about to do battle with Russia (1904–1905), Japan needed women less as scholars than as mothers of future soldiers.

The Imperial Rescript of Education in 1890 reemphasized Confucian and nationalistic values. The heavy hand of the Civil Code of 1898 perpetuated feudal ideas about the role of women by making clear, in no uncertain terms, that in these tumultuous times the woman's place was in the home as a good wife and wise mother (*ryosai kembo*), thus upholding the "Japanese spirit" part of the slogan. The Civil Code reinforced the idea that the head of the household made all decisions. So what use were geography, biology, or English to a woman confined to home and hearth, producing and raising children? Such academic subjects could only put wild ideas—such as religious thoughts or romantic notions—into her head, causing parents to fear for a daughter's marriage chances. Enrollments in mission schools dropped sharply.

At least one good result of these decades of experimentation was that the desirability of having a high school education had sunk into the nation's consciousness. Since nonmission high schools emphasized proper subjects like domestic science, sewing, and Confucian ethics, their numbers continued to grow. In 1899, each of the forty-seven prefectures were required to have at least one girls' high school. By 1905 Japan had 100 girls' schools, and by 1910 almost all boys and girls finished elementary school.

Although the government did set up a few higher normal schools to train female high school teachers, it did not establish a single university for women. A few progressive

Japanese educators, however, influenced by the West, started their own private universities: Tsuda College and Tokyo Women's Medical College were founded in 1900, and Japan Women's University opened its doors in 1901. A handful of women were admitted to one national school, Tohoku Imperial University, and two private schools, Waseda and Hosei.

The second biggest period of change, after the Meiji reforms, came after World War II, when the country adopted the American model of six years of elementary school, three years of junior high school, and three years of high school. Only after the war did schools beyond the elementary school level become coed (no more separation of the sexes from age seven on) and girls study the same curriculum as boys. Compulsory education for all was extended to nine years. The postwar Constitution (Article 26) ordered that "all people have the right to receive an equal education, according to their ability." So in 1947, university entrance exams were opened to women, thus giving them full equal opportunity in education.

Women benefited greatly from postwar educational reforms. Today, more women than men go on to high school. Almost as many women as men go on to higher education, but women account for nine out of ten students at the two-year junior colleges that more or less double as finishing schools. Only 23 percent of four-year university students are women.[4]

Education Mama
(KYOIKU MAMA)

Japan's education system has been a key driving force behind this country's economic success by providing a well-educated work force. In Japan's mass education system, 94 percent go beyond the compulsory nine years of study—a higher percentage of the population than in the United States, where only 72 percent graduate from high school. More Americans do advance to college (60 percent), but about half never graduate. The Japanese are fond of saying, "In the States, it's easy to get in and hard to graduate, but in Japan, it's hard to get in and easy to graduate." Almost all of the 36 percent of Japanese high school students who enter university get a diploma four years later.[1]

One hundred years ago, the first minister of education, Arinori Mori, insisted that education was the basis of national wealth. Today it is still the key to success, and the key to Japan's future. No one knows that better than the legions of education mothers (kyoiku mama) who still take to heart the words of the Emperor Meiji: "How children grow up depends on how their mothers bring them up."

A woman's most important job is the education of the children at home and at school. And the "wise mother" knows that the right schools determine the destiny of her child. In Japan the paths to success are clearly mapped out. Some children, who start work right after high school, never take an entrance exam, but everyone knows that higher education is the key to social mobility and status. Getting into the best possible high school increases the chances of

120

getting into the best possible university, which means getting the best possible job four years later, since, when applying for a job, the name of the university counts more than the student's grades. University names like Todai, Keio, Waseda, Kyoto, Hitotsubashi open doors in a world of *gakubatsu* where (although the practice is weakening) former graduates help new graduates. Everyone in Japan wants to become a Mitsubishi man (or woman) or a Mitsui, Sumitomo, Japan Air Lines, Suntory, Hitachi, or NEC man (or woman). When introducing themselves, people say their company name before their own names. Big business has an enviable reputation among workers in Japan, because large companies offer the best pay, the best hours, and the best fringe benefits.

That's why *kyoiku mama* start pushing early to ensure their children's future. That's why, in addition to the cooking, cleaning, and other chores any mother does, the *kyoiku mama* busy themselves finding supplementary textbooks and workbooks, researching schools (determining which cram school and which university is best for the child), helping with homework, rewarding (perhaps spoiling) the child with the promise of a trip to Kiddyland toy store, an ice cream, or, if older, a stereo or *pasokon* (personal computer), if he or she is diligent in his homework. As a 1984 University of Michigan study noted, the Japanese emphasize effort more than ability. The belief is that you can get ahead if you just work hard enough. The same study noted that Japanese youngsters are already ahead of their American counterparts in math and reading by first grade![2] Japanese mothers do a lot of informal teaching, and two-thirds of all four-year-olds already attend kindergarten, compared to one-third in the States.[3]

The race is on from a young age to pass through the narrow gates of hell—"examination hell," as the entrance exams are known. One out of three primary school students attend afterschool classes—either cultural lessons or cram school to prepare for the junior high school entrance exams. During the last year of junior high, three out of four students attend cram school—the infamous *juku* (pronounced "joo-koo")—in order to pass the exams to the best high schools. Summer vacations that their mothers and fathers spent chasing butterflies and catching big black beetles are now filled with homework and spent in *juku* by nearly two-thirds of those students.

Families devote a sizeable chunk, 20 percent, of the household budget to education, and many surrender a portion of their precious little living space so that their child may have what is becoming a standard piece of furniture in Japanese homes—the study desk.[4] So many mothers coddle their elementary school age children that only 28 percent of Japanese children help around the house compared to nine out of ten American children who are expected to do chores.[5] The Japanese themselves call these youngsters the bean-sprout generation, because they grow tall and fast but lack substance.

Winter for some is a sad time in Japan. Examination pressure peaks from January through March. The national and public universities give a first-round, five-subject exam over a two-day period in January. Private universities give their own exams in February. And the second-round public university exams are given in March. (The idea of the uniform first-round exam, started in 1979, was to alleviate exam pressure by acting as an SAT-like indicator to universities. Instead it's just another hurdle to leap, because the universities still give their own separate exams.)

Every winter, out-of-town students (and often their mothers) fill up the Tokyo hotels, receiving package deals that include meals, lounges to relax in, and college consultants. The media announce weather and transportation conditions nationwide on exam days. Every year, the newspapers run an inspirational story, too, such as the one in February 1982, about an eighteen-year-old girl involved in a plane crash in Tokyo Bay who, despite her fractured leg and third-degree burns, arrived on crutches at the examination site.[6] Sad to say, another perennial feature is the suicide story. One month earlier that same year, a teenager who had already failed the exams twice, rather than repeat them again, electrocuted himself, placing electrodes on his chest and hand and linking them to the alarm clock timer set for his usual wake-up time of 5:00 A.M.[7]

During these three months especially, Japanese buy amulets or charms for luck from the Buddhist temples. At Shinto shrines, the number of votive wooden tablets multiplies with messages such as "My name is Yoshi Watanabe. I want to go to Tokyo University. Please help me, God. Thank you."

At the climax of this annual hysteria, in mid-March when the identification numbers of successful entrants to Todai are posted on a notice board, TV cameras pan the crowds for shots of jubilant students being hoisted in the air on the shoulders of their friends. Their futures are assured. But a much greater number of students are rejected than accepted to Todai, and they look crushed. Some openly sob in the arms of friends. Out-of-towners wanting to enter big-name universities often pay students to send them the news by telegram, and on that day the anxious applicants pray that the message will be something good like "Buddha smiles" rather than "The cherry blossom has fallen."

Only a handful of people these days defends the entrance examination system, insisting that it is a natural *rite de passage*. One professor said the exams contribute to the "fighting spirit" of Japan and teach the young people "self-control." But most mothers, fathers, teachers, and students think of it only as a "necessary evil," at best.

Few mothers are openly proud of being a *kyoiku mama* (and certainly not all women are *kyoiku mama*), so the following three women all requested anonymity, and I accordingly have changed their names.

Yuki Sasaki, a forty-five-year-old Kagoshima housewife, is a typical "education mama" who wants to get her boy into Todai. She pushes, pressures, and cajoles him, knowing that his success would fulfill her dreams for him and reflect glory on her. Even though her family returned from living abroad five years ago, she still worries that he has some catching up to do.

Wearing matching beige skirt, pumps, and Hermes sweater, she ordered café au lait in the coffee shop where we talked. Sasaki-san grew up in Tokyo where she attended private high school. Along with most of her classmates, after graduation she studied the traditional arts and skills that would prepare her to become a good wife. A few of her other friends went to junior college or got jobs. None went to university.

Like most Japanese wives and mothers, she dutifully (and contentedly) devotes herself to her children's education, the housekeeping, and the handling of the family finances. Her husband is president of a small manufacturing company in Kagoshima, where they live with their fifteen-year-old daughter and seventeen-year-old son.

YUKI SASAKI:

After graduating from high school, I spent three years learning many things to be a good housewife: tea ceremony, flower-arranging, cooking, and sewing. This is called bridal training *(hanayome shugyo)*. It's very useful and necessary. Tea ceremony, for example, teaches manners. In every movement, you are always thinking of other people first, always putting other people ahead of you. Since the housewife often has visitors in her home and since you always greet the guest with tea, the tea ceremony is very important. Tea ceremony also teaches graceful body action. Each action has meaning, and there are no unnecessary movements.

I learned flower-arranging *(ikebana)* so that if I want to arrange the flowers of my garden—even if it's only one flower—I can do it with good technique. And that helps me make a room more beautiful, more comfortable. I enjoy flower-arranging for myself and for my family.

As for cooking, it's important for women to cook well. Cooking is supplying food for raising human beings, so it's a very important job.

But I have to admit that I don't sew much anymore since we can buy inexpensive but good-quality clothes at the department store. Now I just make my daughter's clothes, and maybe a dress or apron for myself. Only occasionally do I sew a *yukata* [cotton kimono for wearing around the house] but not visiting kimono.

Yes, bridal training was very popular when I was a girl. And as far as I know it's still popular. Some OLs (office ladies) take cooking or *ikebana* lessons after work, just as some learn English conversation. It's a hobby that increases their enjoyment of life. The daughters of people I know enjoy doing it. I want my own fifteen-year-old daughter to take these lessons, too, after high school. But she wants to go to California to study. I hope that someday she will learn to enjoy and appreciate wifely skills as both a hobby and a job.

My other child is a boy, seventeen, in the second year of Chuo High School. [Japanese high schools have three years.]

We lived in London when he was two, three, and four, and in New York from his ages nine to twelve. Every Saturday from 9:00 to 3:00, he and his sister attended a Japanese language class for six hours, even when we moved to the States. Their teachers at American schools were very kind to them, tutoring them in English for twenty minutes every day after school.

I didn't mind living abroad when the children were in the first through third grades, because then the children are just getting used to school and the other children. But for an elementary school boy like my son, the fourth to sixth grades are very important academically. If we had been transferred when the children were in junior or senior high school, they and I would not have gone. We would

125

have stayed in Japan with grandfather and grandmother.

Overall, living in a foreign country is very good experience for children, but once they return to Japan, the Japanese schools aren't very accommodating. The children have trouble adjusting back to the more strict educational system. In addition, they are behind their classmates in math and Japanese.

It's too bad that the Japanese schools don't value the experience of living abroad. But it will be helpful to my children when they finish their studies and join the workaday world. Speaking English is much more useful for girls, though, than for boys. It's enough to get them a good job. For boys, it's only a means for doing something else. Boys must have other abilities as well, such as negotiating ability and political sense.

We moved back to Japan when my son was in junior high. He had to have a tutor in Japanese before taking the entrance exam to high school, but he passed and was accepted at Chuo High School, which is difficult to enter. It's a very good school, one of the top three in Kagoshima, and all the students go on to university.

Now my son is studying for the university entrance exams. He'd like to major in math or physics. He's not so good in English anymore. No, he doesn't attend *juku*, because he's going to a first-rate school. They give the students a lot of homework and try to finish the required curriculum early so that they can spend time preparing for the entrance exams. So if he just does well at school, he'll get into a good university.

My daughter does go to *juku* though, and next March she'll take the entrance exam for high school.

Right now my boy wants to enter the medical department of a first-rate national university or private university. Does he want to go to Todai? Oh, I don't want to name names. As you know, any medical department is very difficult to enter, so perhaps he'll change his mind to avoid the disappointment of failing. I'm recommending that he apply to the engineering or science department of a private university and that the university should not be so high level.

In the meantime, I help my son prepare for his exams by arranging my schedule around his schedule. I take care of his meals, his bath, and anything else he requires, because he doesn't have much time. I try to cook his favorite foods like teriyaki steak (very thin) and fried vegetables. I buy him chocolate ice cream and kiwi, apples, oranges, and grapes.

No, my husband and daughter don't arrange their schedules around him. Oh, sometimes she gives him her turn in the bath. She lets him go first.

Do I help my daughter in the same way? I only help her by picking her up from *juku* and her violin lesson. That's all. But I will be able to help her all my life, because the relationship between mother and daughter is always very close. After she marries, I can help her when she's sick or when she's busy with babies.

But the son or boy should be independent someday, so the period a mother can give something or help him lasts only until he enters university. Of course I want to help him during and after his university days, but a son doesn't like to be helped then. Besides, I think it's no good for boys to have too close a relationship with their mothers.

Sometimes my son tells me *"Chotto urusai* [could you please lay off], you are taking care of me too much. Please leave me alone." But I explain to him that this is my last chance to take care of him.

Am I an education mama? Well, other people around me say that I am. I am very serious about education for the children. I believe a good mother is always thinking about her children. My husband's role is to work outside and earn money to support the family. So I don't need to worry about financially supporting the family. I take care of the family. If the family has a nice, good, bright environment, then the husband can work well and the children can study hard in school without worrying. I don't feel well if a room looks messy, so I'm always thinking of cleaning the house, cooking the meals, and washing the clothes for the family. I take care of the children's education more than their father does. I watch out for everyone's health, plus I manage the family finances and give my husband pocket money.

After I raise the children, I'd like to do things for myself. I'd like to do something for my husband and all our parents. Maybe I'll take my mother-in-law on a trip to Europe!

But for right now, I just want to do everything perfectly for the children so I'll have no regrets later. I think if my son gets into school in Tokyo, maybe I'll move there, too, so I can take care of him.

Less well publicized and less numerous is the second kind of education mama who puts enormous pressure on her kindergarten-level child to enter a private elementary school. Women who want to give their children a head start (and not all of them think it's worth the pressure at such a young age, nor can everyone afford it) try to enroll their children in private "escalator schools," which automatically advance the students from elementary school through college, without their taking another brutally competitive, fact-packed entrance exam ever again.

Michiko Tanaka, forty, an upper-middle-class, fast-speaking woman, is an unabashed *kyoiku mama*, even though she knows that other people may disapprove. Right now all her energies are focused on her four-year-old son, who takes afterschool lessons five days a week, to the point that she pays only minimal attention to her businessman husband and two-year-old son. The younger boy will someday follow in the pressured footsteps of his older brother. But these days it is the first son who is preparing for the entrance exam to an *esukareta* (escalator) school—in this case,

Keio. If her son Hiro enters this school at the primary level and gets decent marks, he'll be assured a place in Keio for the next sixteen years of his life, from first grade all the way through university. He will be on one of Japan's few automatic escalators through the educational system. (Other *esukareta* schools are Doshisha, which starts at the junior high level, in Kyoto; Konan from kindergarten, in Kobe; and Gakushuin from first grade, in Tokyo.) Since this is the only shortcut through the entrance-exam jungle, the mother reasons it's worth putting the pressure on her son now.

But Tanaka-san looks tired from chauffeuring her son around and quizzing him at home and as they sit in traffic; she often naps in the car while waiting for him to finish his lesson, that is, if she's not inside taking notes on what he's learning or conferring with his teacher. Little Hiro usually falls asleep in the car on the way home at night.

MICHIKO TANAKA:

I can't tell you about the mothers competing—oh, how they compete—to get their children into private elementary schools like Keio Yochisha [Keio Primary School]. Americans will think we are crazy. You see, men work late and the women have no hobby so they focus on the children. They become education mamas.

I work six days a week taking our four-year-old boy to school. The child must learn what to do for the test he will take at age five or six in order to enter private elementary school. A school like Keio elementary leads to Keio high school and eventually to Keio University, without the child's taking another exam. So if I can get him in, there's no more rat race. No examination hell at age twelve for junior high or at age fifteen for high school or at age eighteen for university. And when children are younger, they don't feel this pressure. The little ones just do what their mothers tell them.

But even at this age, the competition is stiff. At Keio elementary school, there are 1,200 applicants for only ninety-eight places for boys and thirty-six for girls, so after nursery school, I go to *juku* or *okeiko goto* [cultural or sports lessons] with my son from 2:00 until 6:30 or 7:00 P.M. I watch and watch and make notes about his weak points. But I cannot say what I really think in class. I have to smile and nod at everyone—even to the other mothers. I can't admit my son's weak points, because other people will write letters about him to the principal and say what a bad boy he is. They try to pull out the legs from under the other boys. For example, our oldest boy doesn't look much like either one of us, and I heard a rumor that he was not ours! Can you imagine?

My boy is one of forty-six children who attend—can I call it M-san's school?—a minimum of three days a week from 2:30 until 6:00 or 6:30 P.M. (Classes on the other days are optional.) Today is Wednesday, so the children will be doing active work. They'll be using wooden blocks to make animals. The blocks are square, long, flat, and other shapes, too—about fifty pieces in all, and the more pieces the children use the better. For instance, the child who uses all fifty pieces to make a crocodile does better than the narrow-minded child who uses just ten pieces to make a giraffe.

Then on Thursdays, the children are divided into groups of ten or less, so that the teachers can watch the children more closely and give the kids more individual attention. The teacher might ask each child how many insects he can name. Some can give the names of ten insects, and some can say twenty-six in one minute.

After a two-hour session like this, the mothers are gathered together and told: "Your boy should study more" or "Your boy shouldn't study so much because he's nervous." You know some boys are very active and smart, but maybe their eyes move too much, which means they are nervous. Well, you are told to take such a boy jogging in the morning so he'll relax. This man M-san is like a doctor. He's been teaching children for more than thirty years. He just meets a child, and he can tell what that child is like. He's really a genius. So whatever he says to do, I obey. I always know he has his reasons.

Many of the things he teaches are useful throughout the child's life, too, and not just for the entrance exam. For instance, while the mothers are talking with some of the teachers, other teachers are organizing relay races outside for the children. The young ones enjoy athletics, and it's good for them to get some idea about competition. As you know, just having good character or a good mind is not enough to make it in this world.

We must train our children at home, too. Before my son can go to the school's thirty-day-long summer camp program, I was told that he has to be able to brush his teeth, wash his face, and change his clothes—all in five to seven minutes. Now, if I just say, "Hurry up," my boy says, "I'm hurrying." But if I say, "Let's see how long it takes you" (and I look at my watch as I've been told), then he rushes. Children can't always be relaxed, you know. They must learn to hurry up and pay attention. So this training is not just for the entrance exam.

Besides Wednesdays and Thursdays, my boy has writing practice on Saturdays. The children listen to tapes so that they can practice giving answers. All exams are on tape now. (That's because a few years ago some people complained that their children couldn't hear the teachers in the examinations.)

We also send him to two other optional classes: Monday music lessons (the children sing songs) and Friday drawing lessons. A Sunday run in the park is recommended, too. Jogging for an hour is good for the legs. The child has a chance to jump and bump around. Tuesday is the only afternoon that he is free.

Lots of people say that M-san's fee is so expensive that only rich people can send their children to his school.

They say that in a sarcastic way. Well, I think it's just an excuse. All children get some tutoring somewhere anyway. At his school the three-day basic program is $150 a month, and not $400 as you have heard. (Sometimes Japanese people can be very envious. They like to gossip a lot, you know.) The other classes are optional: $40 for music and $50 for drawing.

You know M-san coaches the parents, too, because after the child's one-and-a-half hour written exam, the parents are interviewed. If the interviewer asks us what we think of our child, we are supposed to mention only his good points. We are not supposed to say things Japanese style, like "Oh my child is not so bright" or "My child is a little naughty," as I might to a friend. In this case, modesty is not so good.

M-san tells us that all the questions boil down to our philosophy of education. That's what the school wants to know. I am already so nervous about the interview next fall that I have fifty answers ready for fifty questions. My friends say that the fathers are usually asked if they have a chance to talk with the children and what they talk about. I wonder what my husband will say.

Before the war, public schools used to be good, and that's where Mitsubishi and MITI men went. But after the war, private schools became best. The principal says that the admission procedure depends all on merit, all on talent. That's the *tatemae*. The *honne* is that it's 80 percent connections. Since big companies like Mitsubishi and department stores like Isetan and government ministries like MITI hire a lot of Keio graduates, anyone who works for those businesses or the government tries to use their pull. After all, those places could cut back on the number of Keio graduates that they hire, you know. I know one woman who isn't even trying to train her son for the entrance exam. She says he'll get in because they are—oh, I shouldn't tell you—well, they come from a family that started a famous, large company. Oh, connections are so important, and so many people have them. The boy may be the son of a professional golfer, baseball player, or actor. They are not all the sons of intellectuals or businessmen. Doctors can have pull, too, if they are associated with Keio Hospital. My husband is an entrepreneur in business—a successful one—but that's not as well-respected and well-connected as being a company man. So my son and I must work very hard to make a good impression.

Oh, so many things to consider. I'm sorry, I'd like to talk more. But I really have to go now. It's almost May. We don't have a lot of time before the exam [in November].

Thirty-nine-year-old Kamakura housewife Hiroko Mori was educated at Japan's foremost music school, Geidai, and at the best of America's performing arts schools, Juilliard. A virtuoso pianist, she turned down the chance to give concerts because it would have meant separation from her family. Despite her barely concealed ambition and abundant energy, there's no doubt in her mind, as she says in her characteristically straightforward way, that "the family comes first." Mori-san doesn't resent this; to her, it's just a fact of life.

These days she focuses her energies on her children's education, particularly their *okeiko goto* classes. A strict interpretation of *okeiko goto* is "practicing things many times over," but to most people the two words together stand for cultural enrichment classes or sports activities—all of which are in addition to a Japanese child's five-and-a-half-day school week. Little wonder Japanese children have the least playtime of any children in the world.

HIROKO MORI:

Many Americans are wondering now why the Japanese children have higher IQ scores. It's very, very simple. They do *okeiko goto*. The children are used to studying hard and playing hard, i.e., training, from a very early age. That way their brains work very fast. Both of my children have *okeiko goto*. I take five-year-old Takeo to his hour-long swimming lessons twice a week. Ear-training and piano lessons are also twice a week too. My daughter, Yuki, thirteen, takes piano lessons and ear-training too, plus English lessons. I know that in America children play after school. But Japanese children have afterschool lessons. It's the custom.

Of course, some mothers don't do this. They are too busy, especially when they have jobs. But if you really want to educate your children, you have to stay home. The mother can't work. It happened to me. I wanted to give concerts, but if I did, I would have had to travel a lot. I had a difficult time deciding. But what if one of my children became sick? Then I'd have to cancel the concert. Besides, my husband wanted me to stay home, too.

Japanese spend a lot of money on education, so we'll never get rich. Our family spends almost one-quarter of our income on the children. My husband doesn't like to spend money on a house or cars, but he will lavish money on the children's education.

Yuki's piano lessons cost $120 a month, her ear-training $43, and English lessons $34. The English lessons aren't so expensive because a relative who lived in the States for ten years teaches her. Takeo's piano lessons cost $25, ear-training $17, and swimming $21.

It's a lot of work to take the children here and there four days a week. For example, I have to drive Takeo to his swimming lessons, change him, and then he wants me to watch him from the gallery. In his swim school, each child advances from level eleven down to level one. At the end of every month, the swim teachers give tests in diving and different swim strokes to determine if the children should change levels. Takeo is level ten now. He has failed to change levels four times now, so it's so discouraging for him. He hates it. Whenever he has to go to swim school, he always pretends to have a headache, stomachache, or cold. But swimming is good training for him. My husband feels the same way. It builds up a strong body. The lessons are not just for his health alone. Swimming builds up his determination and courage. (When I was a girl, I used to be afraid to dive and my father was so disappointed.) Anyway, once we get into the swimming pool building, he looks so happy. He gives up on his stomachache or whatever. He smiles. He seems to enjoy it.

Do you know I signed him up for swim lessons when he was three and a half years old? (The children can start when they are three years old.) I had to wait one and a half years to get him into this class. You have to sign up early. Now that it's in fashion to go to swim school, there is a waiting list of 200 children.

When everyone goes to *okeiko goto,* no one complains. If all Takeo's friends are busy with lessons, he gives up wanting to play and wants to take his lessons. But if his friends are playing, he doesn't want to go.

So a group of mothers made up an *okeiko goto* list. They know Takeo has lessons on Wednesdays, Thursdays, and Saturdays, and I know which days their boys have lessons. So if Takeo wants to play on one of his lesson days, I just call up a boy who also has lessons that day. Then Takeo gives up wanting to play. We avoid calling the children who are free.

Usually more girls than boys go to *okeiko goto,* especially for music training. Boys often give up music training in the higher grades of primary school because they have to concentrate on their schoolwork. I'd say most children start lessons like these at age three and stop around fifth grade to prepare for the junior high school exams.

Some people say it's vain to continue to take the lessons when other children stop. Some people feel it's vain to take lessons at all. They say, "Let the children play."

(I used to have the same opinion, because my parents pushed me too much. I gave up piano for five years.) But I feel that, once the child has the training, he or she can pick up an instrument or whatever again when that child is an adult.

When I was a girl, I took *okeiko goto.* I used to love ballet lessons. I wanted to be a ballerina, but my father said he didn't want his daughter raising her legs in front of other people. I studied Japanese dancing, too, but I didn't like it too much; the movements were so slow.

When I was five, I started piano once a week. I was still playing at age twenty-two after university when I met my husband. We were taking piano lessons from the same teacher. He loved music, so he wanted to marry a musician.

By this time, I felt my parents had pushed me too much. I wanted to get married so I could stop playing the piano. I was sick of it. I hated music and my piano. So I asked my husband to stop all the music in the house. I wanted to have a baby and become a common housewife. This caused a great misunderstanding between my husband and me. He married me because I was a musician. But whenever I asked him, "Did you marry me because I'm a pianist," he had to answer, "No, I married you because I love you." He was so unhappy. This was the most difficult time of our marriage.

So I became a common housewife doing this and that for four years. Then suddenly I got sick of it. I hated housework. And one day I heard a record as I walked down the street and thought I'd like to play like that.

So I started touching the piano again—at first for only five minutes a day. My hands were like pudding, so soft. It took me four years to recover my strength, my sense of rhythm and intonation. I had to start from the beginning.

Then we were transferred to New York. Six months later my husband very timidly handed me an application for Juilliard. "Are you interested?" he said. I answered,

"I have a child. I don't have time." But he pointed out, "There are babysitters here in America."

At the time, I was practicing only an hour a day while Yuki took her nap. On weekends my husband took her to the zoo so I could have time to practice. At the entrance exam for Juilliard, I played terribly, but I passed, and thus began five years of study. So I owe my husband a lot.

Of course, I had to find a babysitter, and I was lucky to find a very good Italian-American lady. In Japan, nobody wants to be a babysitter. Parents and children are afraid of babysitters, too. When we came back to Japan, that's what I missed most about America. For three years, I couldn't go to a concert.

Here everyone thinks the mother should stay home until the baby grows up—maybe until the third or fourth grade. Mothers have to give up concerts and parties. Wives are usually not invited to parties anyway, because it's so hard to get a babysitter. (Actually, if we were invited and didn't want to go, not being able to get a babysitter would provide a good excuse.) There is no system of babysitting.

In Japan, men make their own world and women make their own world. Women gather in town during the day to have lunch while the children are in school. You'll only see women in the nice French restaurants at noontime. The women never complain, because everyone else is doing the same thing.

But in New York, couples are always invited to parties. It's only after living in the U.S. where husbands and wives do things together that the Japanese women start to complain.

In America we lived in Yonkers, and as in Japan, my husband never came home until late. I thought the American husbands were so kind. If I had trouble with some machine or other, my neighbor's husband would rush over to repair it. He had all kinds of tools and could fix anything. I respected him.

And when it snowed, all the American husbands rushed out to shovel before the snow became ice. Only my husband didn't appear. He didn't cut the grass. He didn't rake the leaves either. He was the enemy of the neighborhood. In Japan, those are women's jobs, unless the husbands like to work outdoors. I did them for a while—until I learned I could pay the neighbor's boys to do those things. That's another thing I miss about America.

I tried to explain to my neighbor that, often when my husband wanted to go home, he'd get a telex from Tokyo (due to the time difference of fourteen hours) that he'd have to answer. She couldn't stand to see Yuki neglected, always left alone with her mother, so she was always saying, "Divorce your husband. Divorce your husband." Even today, she still hates him. Every Christmas she sends us lots of presents: about ten gifts for Yuki (she loves her), four for Takeo, and two for me. Nothing for my husband. He always says, "I guess she still hates me."

In Japan, you don't just divorce your husband. You have to think about the children. Do you realize how much power I have? I could really damage his career—particularly at a big company. They're so conservative. I wouldn't dare destroy a man's future. After a divorce, his chances for promotion would be much less good. The company reasons that if a man can't manage his own home, how can he manage business affairs?

Right now, my husband and I are discussing whether Takeo should go to public or private school after (private) kindergarten. I want him to go to public school so he'll get to know many different kinds of people: the sons of shop owners and fish market owners—all kinds of classes. My husband feels differently. He wants the children to be with children of the same class and the same intelligence level. This is something we discuss all the time.

In truth, we do have high expectations of Takeo, because his father went to Todai and his grandfather went to Todai. So I must protect him. Actually I'll do both: I'll pressure him and protect him. His father will want him to go to Todai. So I must protect him, especially if he doesn't get in. I want him to know that getting into Todai is not the only thing in life.

We had a big discussion about Yuki's education when we returned. My husband wanted her to go to the mission school, a private Catholic school, where only the rich people go. I had gone to this school, and I didn't like it. All the children were so snobby. The only thing the teachers do is train the students to be polite. I hated it. But it is good in that they teach English from first grade.

She ended up going to public school. Since her public middle school ends in two more years, she will have to choose soon which high school to aim for. Geidai is a well-known, national music school—very hard to get into. (Yes, I went there.) Toho is a well-known private music school and also very good.

Yuki had the biggest adjustment when we came back from the United States. In America everybody played after school, so I let her do the same thing. But here all the children go to *okeiko goto* after school, and in the beginning it was torture for her.

At first her level of piano was very low. I had to push her very hard. She had *okeiko goto* five times a week: lessons in piano, ear-training, English, singing, and swimming. We did too much. Maybe we overdid it. But we settled in after a few years. Really it was a new life for us, after eight years in America.

After living in America, I could see many things more clearly in Japan. When you live in a foreign country, you don't necessarily get to know that country, but you do get to know your own country. There's a saying that the frog in the well doesn't know the ocean. He can't see the world very clearly. He believes he's the only one in the world. When I talk to housewives here, I've found that they don't think about the rest of the world at all. They just think about their children. They should know that the world is bigger. Japan is only an island.

Schools and Teachers

The school year in Japan starts in April and ends in March and lasts 240 days—a full third longer than the 180 days in the United States. Every day, Monday through Friday and a half-day on Saturday, the little girls with red leather book bags and little boys with black leather book bags bouncing on their backs arrive at the neighborhood elementary school. They put their shoes (often sneakers) in their lockers and step into canvas-covered, rubber-soled shoes. Before the day's lessons start (or at the end of the school day), each group is responsible for cleaning its own classroom. First graders do simple chores like dusting, while sixth graders handle tasks beyond their own classroom, such as cleaning the library, music room, lavatories (in schools without janitors), and doing the gardening and weeding.

The class of Mizue Kuroda, a fourth-grade teacher in Osaka, consists of forty pupils. Very good, good, and poor students are all grouped together during the compulsory years of education. "That way," she explains, "those who are behind can learn from the better students." Kuroda-sensei ("sensei" is a term of respect for teachers and doctors) admits that having a class of all very good or all very poor students would be easier from the teacher's point of view, but wonders aloud how the not-so-good students would feel about grouping by ability. "They might get an inferiority complex," she says. "Besides, the parents would be embarrassed to have their son or daughter labeled as a poor student."

This is the Japanese version of democracy in education. To them, this is egalitarianism. They treat every student as equal regardless of ability. The positive outcome of such a policy is a high rate of literacy and a well-educated pool of labor. But in order to produce the well-rounded many, the interests of students at the top and the bottom are sacrificed. The few brilliant students become bored in class, and the slow learners become frustrated because they can't keep up. And this frustration is occasionally—and increasingly—manifesting itself as violence toward teachers and schools.

Nevertheless, the Japanese hold to their educational policy of the greatest good for the greatest number. They actively want to be all alike. For this reason, no student is held back a grade. "What's important is how many days the student shows up," says Mizue Kuroda. "As long as the student comes to school two-thirds of the required number of days each year, he can go on to the next grade." Thus, only a lengthy illness could prevent a child from being promoted.

Although it is an exaggeration to say that all children of Japan study the same page of the same book on the same day, there is a standardized national curriculum, and teachers must use Ministry of Education-approved textbooks. Such uniformity combined with the students' native ability and the efforts of all concerned (students, parents, and teachers) has produced the enviable national literacy rate of 99.7 percent. Japanese youngsters routinely run away with top honors in tests given in math and science to many nationalities. They scored an average of 111 on IQ tests compared to a test average of 100 by American children, according to a study by Dr. Richard Lynn, a psychologist from Northern Ireland.

All is not rosy, however. Students learn mostly by rote. They do have occasional give-and-take discussions with the teachers on the primary and junior high school level. But during the high school years, with the university entrance exams hanging over the students' heads like the sword of Damocles, the emphasis shifts to lecturing nearly 100 percent of the time. Teachers stuff as many dates, formulas, and grammar rules as possible into their students' minds. There's no time to develop creative problem-solving or critical reasoning skills, a failing many Japanese recognize today.

Mothers and teachers cooperate closely during the children's school years. At least once a year, teachers like Kuroda-sensei visit the home of each of their pupils to get to know the family members, family background, and the child's living environment. Membership for mothers in the PTA—another import from the United States during the Occupation—is, without anyone saying so, mandatory. Mothers are occasionally summoned to help clean up the grounds or wash the school windows. They attend the children's sports festivals and speech contests, the results of which are published in the PTA newspaper. The PTA also acts as a women's club, sponsoring lectures about child-rearing and nutrition and organizing sports for mothers such as softball, Ping-Pong, and jazz dancing.

A few mothers grumble about the necessity of participating in PTA activities. But, in general, since mothers have more education and fewer children these days, they do have more interest in their children's schooling—and more complaints. Only 39 percent of Japanese mothers thought the schools were doing a good or excellent job, compared to 91 percent of Americans who were satisfied, according to the University of Michigan study.[1]

Thus, Kuroda-sensei says, "Gone are the days when the teacher was a person next to God." In the Tokugawa era (1615–1868), students were taught, "The teacher is like the sun and the moon." Until recently, teachers selflessly devoted themselves to their students (their studies, their problems at home, their hopes and aspirations) twenty-four hours a day. Now parents complain that teachers act like salarymen to whom the school is just a company.

But *sensei*—at any level—still have more status and respect in Japan than in the United States. They are paid more than other public servants, and they get good pensions. Despite the increasing number of problems such as bullying, school violence, and examination pressure, the psychic rewards appear to still be there, too. Every week on TV, Kinpachi-sensei, the long-haired hero of junior high classroom 3B (on a dinnertime show called *San-nen B-gumi Kinpachi-Sensei*), successfully helps his students overcome all kinds of problems, from school phobia to potential suicide. Each program ends with Kinpachi-sensei, book bag slung over his shoulder, hair flying in the breeze, walking home with a satisfied look on his face.

It is not surprising that a man plays the junior high school teacher. Although one out of two elementary school teachers are female, only one out of three junior high teachers and one out of five high school teachers are women. Few rise to the position of principal. In public elementary schools, only one out of twenty principals are women; in junior highs, one out of 104! And not one woman is principal of a Tokyo public high school.[2]

At least the number of women teaching primary school is growing, but many people see this trend as a problem. An engineer explains that "Mothers prefer male teachers, because they are eager to help the children after school, whereas the female teachers want to get home to make dinner." This is not just a male perception. A female university senior says, "Mothers do think women teachers are irresponsible because those teachers don't prepare as much for classes, they take leave for pregnancy, and they stay home when their children are sick."

Few women are likely to become principals in the future, according to one especially capable sixth-grade teacher who has actively considered it, because principals must transfer from school to school and spend at least one-third of their thirty years in rural areas. "That means being separated from home and family," she says. "So women can't do it."

Students

Since 1950, the number of junior high school girls in navy blue British sailor uniforms and boys in black Prussian military uniforms advancing to high school has more than doubled, from 42 percent to 94 percent. At the university level, the figures are even more impressive, leaping from a mere 5 percent of the girls in 1960 continuing their education to 33 percent today. (The number of boys has risen from 15 percent to 40 percent.) Statistics can be misleading, though. The Japanese refer to both the two-year and four-year students as university students. In fact,

61 percent of the "university women" do not enter four-year colleges. They opt instead for the less challenging, more home-oriented two-year junior colleges, which actually outnumber the universities.[1]

The junior colleges started as a stop-gap measure during the Occupation, when teachers and facilities were in short supply, and were made permanent in 1964.[2] They continue to perpetuate the myth that women are less capable. Although girls today have exactly the same educational opportunities as boys—including the sex-blind, rigorous university entrance exams—parents' expectations of boys and girls do still differ: 76 percent of parents want their son to go on to a four-year university, while only 16 percent have the same ambition for their daughters. The majority say that a high school or junior college diploma is sufficient for girls.[3] Unfortunately, for the two-year graduates, these schools do not act as a stepping-stone to a four-year university. Junior college leads only to a nursery school or nursing home job or to life as an OL (office lady), sales clerk, or, most importantly, wife.

It is often said that higher education will free the Japanese woman and raise her consciousness. Certainly postwar coeducation has led many young women to be increasingly ambitious. However, most girls, whether two-year or four-year students, still pick societally acceptable majors. In junior colleges, the most popular majors are home economics and preschool education; in four-year colleges, humanities and education.[4] Why do the young women shy away from math, science, law, and engineering (a phenomenon not uncommon in many countries)? The director of the Women and Youth Bureau of the Ministry of Labor, Ryoko Akamatsu (herself a graduate of the law faculty of Todai), says, "Girls feel those subjects are not useful for married life." Many young girls feel that a "tough" major or four years of education would frighten off potential suitors.[5]

They may be right. I have a late-twentyish Japanese

male friend whose work brings him into daily contact with foreign journalists. He reads *The New York Times* every day, he has visited the United States several times—in brief, he's very Americanized. A few years ago as a student at Sophia University, he dated bright, articulate girls who could talk about Nietzsche and politics with him. But when it came time to marry, he returned to his hometown near Nagoya and married a sweet, young junior college grad. Why? "When I come home at night," he says, "I want to put my feet up, read the newspaper, and smell the miso soup cooking in the kitchen."

Most Japanese girls want to be known as *kawaii* (cute). That's the highest compliment a young women can be paid. All of the next three girls in this section—the junior college girl, the university student, and the high school graduate who failed the university entrance exam—would qualify as *kawaii*. In addition to cuteness, *kawaii* connotes an innocence and naiveté—almost a childishness—that is considered very attractive in girls. Although female American university students prefer to be called "women," Japanese still act like, and think of themselves as, girls.

Those young girls who take *kawaii*-ness to an extreme are a comparatively new phenomena known as *burikko*. (The word is a combination of *buru*, meaning to put on airs, and *ko*, meaning child.) According to high school teacher Makiko Fujita, *burikko* have always existed. But the word and concept first gained popularity four or five years ago with the original *burikko*, cutesy-wutesy singer Seiko Matsuda, (now twenty-three), one of a long line of innocent, virginal *talent-o* dressed in frilly, petticoated party dresses and adored by Japanese boys and girls alike. In a female variation of the Peter Pan complex, *burikko* try to act young and purposely vacuous. (So unlike the average American or European teenager, who desperately wants to appear older and more sophisticated than her years!) They wear cute bows, cute shoes, cute ribbons, and cute, girlish party dresses. Like other young girls, they carry Snoopy book bags, "Hello Kitty" notepads, and wear Mickey Mouse sweatshirts. But the real tip-off is the giggling. All Japanese girls tend to giggle a bit, but the *burikko* have raised the art to new heights.

Although Japanese boys find *burikko* attractive, foreign men have just the opposite reaction. "One day after summer vacation, at the beginning of the new school term," remembers an English friend, "I heard a girl screaming 'Ahhhhhhhhhh!' But when I rounded the corner to save the young women from a fate worse than death, I found it was just Machiko-chan's way of greeting her friend Akiko-chan, whom she hadn't seen for six weeks. Now, these young women are the same age as Princess Diana! Yet they are conditioned to act like overage high school girls."

"Act" is the key word. A Yokohama acupuncturist once told me, "The Japanese woman is trained to be an actress." Adds a female university student, "If she acts strong, the boy will say 'Bye, bye, you can live by yourself.' Maybe these *burikko* are actually very clever. They unconsciously know how to survive."

In Japan it is who you are attached to (whether it's a company, for men, or a husband, for women) that counts. The popular American song, "I Want to Be Bobby's Girl," which often plays at the crowded Shakey's Pizza Parlor in Shinjuku, could easily be, "I want to be Yutaro's girl. And when I am Yutaro's girl, such a simple, thankful girl I'll be."

These three young unmarried girls, ages nineteen to twenty-three, describe their lives growing up and their lives today, the days that are considered late adolescence in Japan rather than early adulthood. They will in all probability act like teenagers and be treated like teenagers until the day they become wives. Only once a girl marries does she become *shakaijin*, a grown-up and responsible member of society.

1 4 7

JUNIOR COLLEGE STUDENT

Not unlike other young girls, Mutsumi Hioki, nineteen, a second-year junior college student in Kagoshima, on the southern island of Kyushu, has two goals: to marry by age twenty-five and to have a single-family house. She favors the American preppy look currently popular among her age group—a powder-blue Brooks Brothers button-down shirt over a Scottish tartan skirt, and brand new Topsiders.

Her answers were occasionally rather vague (she had to struggle to remember what she took in school last year), but she became visibly more interested (although still somewhat shy) when the topic shifted to boys. Unfortunately for journalists in Japan, her society considers fuzzy thinking more of a virtue than a flaw among young ladies.

She giggles when I ask whether boys go to junior college. "Oh, no," she says, "To get a good job, boys have to go to university."

Hioki-san's parents, both of whom work in the savings department of the post office, are divorced. She lives with her mother.

MUTSUMI HIOKI:

I attended Yamashita Elementary School. I had to take an entrance exam for Junshin Junior High [a private school], another one for Junshin High School, and a final one for Junshin Junior College. At some schools with the same name, you are automatically promoted, but at Junshin you have to take the entrance exam each time, the way outsiders do.

I didn't go to *juku* to study for the junior high school entrance exam. My grandmother tutored me in math. That's all. Of all the exams, I felt the most pressure when I was studying for the junior college entrance exam, which covers English, math, and Japanese. I couldn't concentrate on studying because of the pressure.

Actually at first I didn't even plan to go to junior college. I was going to get a job, but then I realized it's easier to find a job after getting more education. Nowadays girls usually go to school at least through junior college. I thought this was a good way to get to know people from universities too.

My junior college has a total of more than 360 students. Of the four majors offered, English is the most popular. Home economics is the second largest department, followed by art and nursing.

Since I majored in art, I've taken it both years. My first semester, first year, I studied art, English, social studies, home economics, and psychology. Art included painting, pottery, embroidery, and weaving. And since it's a Christian school, I also took *ningengaku,* a kind of religious study.

Now I'm in my first semester of second year, and I'm studying art, home economics, French, and data processing. Art this term includes oil painting, watercolors, pottery, and poster drawing. Since we don't have four years to study, we have to cover a lot in just two years.

If I had gone to a four-year college, I'd have more education, more experiences, and more interaction with people. But companies prefer to hire junior college girls because they stay longer on the job before they marry and quit. Besides, people say companies think that four-year college students are usually *namaiki.* That means they are too intelligent, and they have too much self-confidence. Those girls act without thinking of others. They don't want to pour tea either. They refuse. But a junior college graduate doesn't mind. She does whatever the company asks her to do.

I've applied to one company to be an OL next year. Companies looking for OLs want someone who has a bright character, someone who is obedient, lovely, and healthy.

149

Kone [connections] are very important, especially this year when the job market is so tight. In my case, my sister—she's also an OL—got her boss to introduce me to the director of the company that I'm applying to. This leasing company specializes in computers and agricultural implements.

At school, I belong to a tennis club, which has about forty members. We meet Kagoshima University boys through this club. Sometimes we meet boys during the college festivals at their school and at our school. Another way is through *kompa* [from "companionship"] which are get-togethers between junior college and university students. We meet in a local coffee shop or restaurant to talk over tea, coffee, or a meal, then we go out to dance at a disco or drink beer at a beer garden. The group is no larger than ten boys and ten girls and is arranged through clubs or friends, usually during the summer vacation and the Christmas holidays.

If possible, I'd like to have a love marriage someday. I don't have a boyfriend right now—well, I do know one boy, but he's just a friend. I don't want to have any particular boyfriend. I don't want to have a close relationship. I don't want to get calls at home. That would be troublesome for everyone. It's not that I'm shy. It's just that, at this point, I'd rather have many friends. I've never kissed a boy. It just doesn't interest me.

About 60 percent of my friends do have boyfriends, though. I think that half of all girls have some sexual experience before they marry and half don't. But almost all of the boys don't want their wife to be their first lover. As for me, I'd like my husband to be the first man I sleep with. It's O.K. to sleep with him once we're engaged, of course.

Since I don't want to be poor, I'd like to marry someone who can support me. That's the role of the father— to support the family and make the final decisions on everything. The role of the mother is the children's education.

I'd like to marry about age twenty-five, and I want to continue my work. What I mean is that, once I have a baby, I'll leave my job, but when the children enter junior high school, I want to work again.

Mutsumi Hioki is not alone in never having kissed a boy. The two sophomore boys at Kagoshima University I talked with had never kissed a girl either, and as one of them, a twenty-one-year-old electronics major blustered, "And I don't want to!"

Understandably taken aback by the directness of my next question ("Do you want your wife to be a virgin?"), once this boy recovered his composure, he said, "The most important thing is her heart, not her physical condition."

A good answer, but some young men out there must care about the virginal state of their brides-to-be. Why else would vaginal repair clinics exist? (They are admittedly not widespread. I've only heard of two in Tokyo, but I imagine any gynecologist who wanted to could provide the necessary stitch or two.)

Although statistics on sex are always suspect, one survey certainly confirmed my sense that Japanese young people indulge in less premarital sex than Americans. In 1981, a survey done by the prime minister's office of 5,000 high school and college students indicated that 9.8 percent of seventeen-year-old boys had some experience with sex, as did 7.6 percent of seventeen-year-old girls. The figures rose to 26 percent and 17.1 percent of Japanese nineteen-year-old boys and girls, respectively. Comparable statistics from the Guttmacher Institute revealed that among American boys and girls ages fifteen to seventeen, the numbers are 44 percent and 34 percent. Among the nineteen-year-olds, 80 percent of the boys and 70 percent of the girls are sexually experienced. [1]

The percentage of Japanese with sexual experience has no doubt risen somewhat since then. But what concerned the Japanese in a 1982 survey of more than 20,000 young people, ages fifteen to twenty-three, in seven cities was that more girls (8.8 percent) than boys (7.9 percent) had had sexual experience. Those statistics produced dismayed headlines like "Feminization of Boys?"[2]

UNIVERSITY STUDENT

Twenty-three-year-old senior Yumiko Kusama is a charming, well-mannered, rather conservative young women majoring in mass communications at Tokyo's Seijo Gakuen—a school she herself calls "not the highest rank." To her father, a Tokyo Gas engineer, and her mother, a housewife, this escalator school has been the perfect place for their little Yumiko, an only child, because once she entered Seijo in junior high, her college future was guaranteed. With no more entrance exams to take, she could afford to spend her junior year in high school in the States.

Kusama-san lives in a three-generation family, she and her parents in one house and her ailing grandfather in an adjacent house. Her mother takes care of her husband's father, cleaning his house, serving tea to his visitors, and at mealtimes cutting up his food into bite-size pieces. "It's a lot of work," says Kusama-san, "but my mother doesn't complain." Young Kusama-san and her mother alternate going out during the day so that one of them is always home to take care of *ojiisan* (grandpa).

YUMIKO KUSAMA:

I went to a public elementary school in Tokyo, and from junior high through university I've attended Seijo Gakuen, a coed escalator school that goes from kindergarten through graduate school.

Most of the Seijo college students enter in junior high.

I started preparing for the exam by going to *juku* in the sixth grade. Most students start in the fifth grade, and some even start in the fourth grade. One evening a week I had a private tutor in math for an hour and a half. And on Sundays I went to a big *juku* called Yoyogi Seminar from 10:00 to 12:30 in the morning. Each time we were given a mock test similar to the entrance exam. The teacher would correct our papers and tell us our grade, so we could try to do better next time. These tests also helped us get accustomed to the tense exam atmosphere.

In order to go to *juku,* I gave up English conversation and ballet lessons—all my afterschool lessons—except piano, which I studied for ten years, and Girl Scouts. I didn't really like Yoyogi Seminar. I wasn't accustomed to such huge classes. We had more than a hundred students in one room, whereas in elementary school, we had forty students per class. But Yoyogi Seminar is very popular for both national and private schools.

When you are age twelve, a student in elementary school, you have three choices. You can take the entrance exam for national junior high school or private junior high school (as I did) or continue on in the public junior high school without taking any exam.

More than two-thirds of the students go on to public junior high school because that's the easiest way. Many of them want to stay in their own neighborhood with their elementary school classmates.

In order to enter Seijo, we only had to take tests in two subjects, math and Japanese language. But other private and national junior high schools also test social studies and science.

If I had failed the entrance exam for Seijo Gakuen, I could have gone to the local public school. Actually, some parents would rather have their boys go to public school so they'll have to take the college entrance exam which means a lot of hard work. I'm not against feminism, but it's a very competitive society for boys. If a boy wants to get a good job, he has to go to a good college. And in order to get into a good college, he needs more exam experience. He has to be tough.

But for girls it's the opposite way of thinking. Some parents feel that it's too hard for girls to take an exam every three years. My parents chose this way for me, so I wouldn't have to suffer through so many exams. I didn't really participate in the decision. I didn't realize how the decision would affect my life. I was just thinking about my friends and my school life.

Many parents think that private girls' schools like Shirayuri, Seishin (Sacred Heart), and Futaba will teach the girls manners. The girls learn to walk very quietly and use very good language—*keigo,* the honorific language that's used with elders and superiors and on formal occasions.

Parents worry that the atmosphere is very tense and competitive at a public school. The students have to wear uniforms, often dark blue and white, and some parents fear that the children will lose their individuality. You see, private schools can make their own educational policy, so the thought is that maybe they make more active children. They use the same Education Ministry–approved text books as public schools, but can use other texts as well.

Since education is compulsory through junior high school, schools are free, except for lunches. But a private junior high school costs 300,000 yen [$1,277] a year plus an entrance fee.

We go on to high school by choice. But most of the *esukareta* schools expect us to continue our education and to do it in their schools. It's nice not to have to take a high school or university entrance exam. Then we don't have to study so hard every day at school. Without really thinking, I can go through the system. In order to be promoted from Seijo High School to Seijo University, you must have a two-point-five (out of five) average, which is not hard to get.

Our school is not the highest rank, maybe upper middle. It's hard to say. It's very, very competitive to get in—I'd say three out of ten students are admitted to Seijo High School, but once you get in, it's not hard to stay there. So most of us stay until we graduate. But students who go to an *esukareta* school may not take advantage of their potential since they are not as challenged.

It takes a lot of effort to leave an *esukareta* school for another college. You have to study harder since you're going to take an entrance exam, but you can't ask the school to help. You have to arrange your own tutor and *juku*. You have to have a strong will. Actually, I did secretly take a university entrance exam, but I failed. (I could only do this because I also had a U.S. high school diploma.) If I had told Seijo that I applied to another school, I would have lost my seat at the school.

Many girls prefer to go to two-year rather than four-year colleges anyway. It may sound like a contradiction, but it's easier for a two-year school graduate to get a good job. Since the employers expect all women to quit once they marry or have children, they figure a junior college graduate will work longer. The girls are only needed for very simple jobs anyway—copying, rewriting, or answering the phone. But some companies are changing their policy, particularly those that need computer programmers, word processing experts, and translators. They recognize that women's motivation has changed a lot. Young women want to continue working after marriage. So some companies are beginning to trust four-year graduates. But the change is slow, *really* slow.

Sometimes girls feel that unless we go to a very good four-year college, it's a waste of time. I mean, it's good to go to a four-year school and major in English literature if you want to be an English professor or a translator, but that major is useless when applying for any other job. I had a choice between majoring in English literature and mass communications, and I chose mass communications because it sounded very new and it's part of social studies. English literature was just reading Shakespeare; you don't read the newspaper or practice daily conversation.

Girls who go to junior college want to get a good job and get married in a few years. Many people say that the best way to find a husband is not at university but at work. That way the girls know they'll have economic stability. So they work to find a future husband. That concept may be changing a bit, but it's still largely true.

I'd say there are two kinds of girls who go to four-year schools. The first group are those who want to study special subjects, and they study very hard. The second group—and that's most of us—want four years of free time. (Actually, these groups apply to boys or girls.) We have to work so hard from elementary school up through high school that the only time in our lives that we're free is university. It's our paradise.

We are supposed to attend classes, but we skip them if we want. If the professor gives the same old lecture every year, we take turns going to class and make one big notebook or we get the notes from our club *sempai*. (Anyone in your club who's older than you is *sempai*.) *Sempai* give or lend *kohai* [their juniors] their notes or used textbooks. They tell us which teachers or subjects to take because they're easier and where to eat and drink—you know, how to have fun.

I don't study all the time, but I got all *yu*'s in my required subjects, and *yu*'s and *ryo*'s in my electives. Our system is *yu* (excellent), *ryo* (good), *ka* (fair), and *fuka* (fail). University subjects aren't so difficult, so it's easy to get *yu*'s. I cut some of my classes when the professor isn't interesting. But if a lecturer is good, I'm happy to go.

Professors cut classes, too. I was really surprised

when I started university, but sometimes we show up, and there's a sign on the door canceling the class. The professor has some business appointment like appearing on TV. He doesn't tell us why, but that's the real reason. Nobody complains though. We go play. That's what all Japanese students are like. We don't have much homework. Lots of people just study the night before an exam. They spend the day before an exam reading the one textbook.

We have a lot of vacation too. School starts in April, and we have exams in July, then we have the rest of July plus August and September off. The next semester goes from September 25 to December 22. After two or three weeks of exams in January, we have another break until April. National schools have less vacation, but all in all we have about six months of study and six months of vacation.

During vacation we take a club trip. We use this time to practice whatever our club does (sports, art, English) and as a chance to get together and make friends. One summer our English newspaper group went on a four-day trip to the mountains, where we spent our time climbing and cycling. We also talked about what kind of articles we'd like to publish.

And each year our club takes one overnight a year to welcome the new freshmen members. Usually we go on a Saturday after morning classes to a vacation place that the school owns near Karuizawa. We arrive about three or four in the afternoon, play cards, and after dinner, we have a *kompa*—you know, drinking. We introduce ourselves and say what our major is and hobby is. I don't know why, but Japanese like to use alcohol to make friends. Maybe it's because the Japanese are shy, and liquor loosens them up. It makes them feel free to talk. We like to go to drinking after an exam, too.

Many people take a lot of credits their freshman and sophomore years, so they'll have lots of free time their senior year. Like most of my friends, I have enough time to do *arubeit-o* [part-time work, from the German word "to work"]. I'm working for the Japan Center for International Exchange three days a week from nine-thirty to six. And I'll work for them full time after I graduate in March. We arrange exchanges around the world for politicians and top management.

Most Japanese students do have a part-time job. We can earn a lot of money in a short time. The best way to earn money is tutoring. You can tutor once a week for two hours and earn 4000 yen [$17]. And that's just for doing follow-up work right out of the student's textbook. If you're tutoring a student who's going to take the entrance exam, you have to teach a lot more, but you get paid more too. Usually you're paid according to the school you attend. A Todai student can charge a lot more, because all parents think Todai is the best. The second most popular way to make money is being a waitress at a fast-food place like McDonald's. But the pay is very low—only 500 yen [$2.13] or 550 yen [$2.34] an hour. I've never done it because I didn't think I could be sociable to people I didn't know. Other *arubeit-o* include teaching tennis, working at an inn in the summer or a ski lodge in the winter, or office work. Being a companion girl is interesting work, too. A companion girl is one who demonstrates or explains the product at a food fair or a car show. Only girls can get this job. Basically we just stand around and smile. And for this we earn 7,000 yen [$29.79] a day and a free lunch ticket.

Most of our *arubeit-o* money goes for travel overseas. Students like to go to Hawaii, Guam, Europe, and the West Coast of the United States. My parents paid for my month in the States, so I spend my money mostly for coffee and subways. I'm saving a little, too. Other students use the money for clothes, stereos and cars. Since most of the things we really need are paid for by our parents, our money is spent for what we want. We earn money for fun. It's different from the States.

In my third year of high school (1978–1979), I spent one school year in a public high school in San Diego. I stayed with my mother's former English teacher, an American, then with a family of a friend of mine. The family had five children.

American high school was very different from Japanese high school. It seemed more like Japanese university. The American high school had many elective subjects, and for each subject we went to a different classroom. So it was hard to make friends at first. In Japan we have homeroom, and the same students are together for the same subjects all day. Only the teachers change classrooms.

The teaching method was quite different, too. In Japanese schools, we copy down what the teacher says or writes on the blackboard. We don't speak out or say what we think. We are supposed to be quiet. We only answer when the teacher calls on us by name. In an American school though, they raise their hands to answer a question. They have a discussion with the teacher. American students have much more homework, too, although I may say that because I was at a private school in Japan. And sometimes at the American high school, I was asked to write an essay. We had to think by ourselves! And write our opinion! The Japanese educational method is passive, and the American way is the opposite, so it was very hard for me to adjust. I'd been trained to be passive, and I was.

I thought American teachers were very informal. Not only students chewed gum during classes, but so did the teachers! I was really shocked. And the way the teachers dressed—if it was really hot, they'd wear shorts! And they sat on their desks. It's really extreme. In Japan, the teachers always stand. They only sit down when they are giving an exam.

Class seating is arranged differently, too. Everyone in Japan sits in rows facing the teacher and the blackboard.

But in the States sometimes the students sit in a circle. And in the U.S., the school buildings are always flat; here they are taller. Usually the first year students are on the first floor; second year students are on the second floor; and third year on the third floor.

At my high school in California, I took a course in Contemporary Living, which included lectures on sex education, family life, and how to get a job. The first week we had to get our parents' written permission to take the course. If the parents didn't want their children learning about birth control, the students couldn't take the class. That made sense to me. We saw a film showing how a baby is born, and the teacher brought in birth control samples: diagrams [sic] and condoms. You know, that kind of class would never happen in Japan. This society is really closed about sex education. The teacher would be really embarrassed, and well, to tell the truth, so would the students. We tend to learn about sex through magazines for boys, and for girls, the weekly magazines, and our friends. All we learn in school is about menstruation. For one day during fifth grade, the boys are sent home and the girls are all gathered in one room to see a film about menstruating. That's it for sex education. One day.

I had a lot of trouble adjusting back to Japan, especially the first month. Japanese students are so quiet. American students are much more noisy. And when I wanted to speak up or say something—even if the teacher was wrong—I couldn't. In Japanese schools, only the teacher speaks and we listen. It was hard for me to be quiet.

Since I could speak English better than the other students, the English teacher was always asking me to read aloud. I didn't like that at all, but I had to do it. Then the other students felt I was different, and in Japan you don't want to stand out. In America it's O.K. to be different. After doing things individually in the United States, I didn't mind going home by myself or shopping by myself, but

Japanese girls are always doing things together, like buying snacks and taking the train home. So they expected me to join them.

Another problem when I returned was that I found myself behind in school. I was surprised that I'd forgotten so many *kanji* [Chinese characters].

In junior high school in Japan, very few young people date. Oh, maybe you talk with a boy or study with him, but that's all. And in senior high school, we have no prom as in the States. In Japanese society, adults think dating in high school is not a good idea. So the most you can do is meet in school or after school. Maybe you meet at the station and take the train to school or back home. But the situation is really different in the U.S., since those teenagers can drive a car. The parents trust the children (at least the family I stayed with did) and let them stay out really late. The curfew was midnight. In Japan the curfew would be 10:00 or 10:30 at the latest, and the young people don't drive. Parents would worry about girls getting home as late as they do in the States.

But in our university days, we have more freedom. We have more opportunity to get together through club activities and classes. In general, we tend to do things as a couple or with a group. Both groups and couples like to go to movies, plays or concerts together or play tennis or go driving. On a date, usually the boys pay, but some girls feel that since we are all students and equal, the girls should pay too.

Drinking is quite popular. People in clubs like to go out drinking together. And a small group from a boys' school and a small group from a girls' school may have a *kompa* to get together and go out drinking. University students drink a lot. In the summertime, everyone drinks beer. In the winter, it's whiskey, wine, or sake. They go to a Japanese or Western-style bar, sit at long tables and order drinks and food like fried chicken, fried potatoes, potato chips, peanuts, and dried squid. Personally, I don't go to these places.

Most people meet each other through their clubs. University students spend more time on club activities than they do on their studies. Everyone joins a club to make friends. We have many clubs at Seijo—sports clubs like soccer, basketball, tennis, baseball, and volleyball; music clubs like guitar; art clubs like painting and drawing; and of course an English Speaking Society.

Most students belong to a club that meets two days a week. The English Speaking Society is the most popular one. It has eighty members. So does the chorus for classical music. Golf is very, very popular, too, maybe cause my school very strong in golf.

I used to belong to the English Newspaper Group. I wrote articles about such topics as what foreigners living in Japan think of Japanese university students. Then I joined the Japan-America Student Conference (JASC), a student exchange program in which the students plan everything. The Americans come to Japan for a month in the summer, and we discuss social issues and our cultural traditions. The next summer, when I went to America, we stayed in university dormitories and American homes. We visited Los Angeles, Washington, D.C., Duke University, Baltimore, New York, and Boston.

I met my what you call "boyfriend" through JASC. (In Japan, it's possible for a girl to have three boyfriends, because we don't mean a steady. A boyfriend is just a friend. We call a steady *kare* [he] or *kanojo* [she], although the terms boyfriend and girlfriend, the way Americans mean them, are becoming more popular.) Maybe half my friends have a boyfriend or girlfriend, the way you mean it. It's difficult to say how many of those are lovers. I'd say maybe half, but they don't really talk about it. It's very different here from my American high school: the way they showed emotions was too much. In between classes or at lunchtime, I could see them kissing in the garden. Or maybe it's just that the weather in San Diego makes people crazy. Japanese would never kiss in public. We'd be embarrassed. Here, a young couple might hold hands in public. I've seen some young couples do this on the train, but my boyfriend and I never would.

However, what we do in private is not so different from what Americans do. Do we hug and kiss? Ahh, well . . . yes, I'd have to say that we do.

Whether the girl remains a virgin or not depends on the school she attends. Some schools are very liberal, you know. And we are influenced by our friends. We don't want to be different. But at my school, the kids are really conservative.

It's not that the boy feels the girl has to be a virgin when they marry, but . . . I think a girl is kind of careful in this matter. If she can't trust the love of her boyfriend, she can't do . . . uhhh . . . that thing. It's a personal matter though, so I don't really know what people think. Since we worry about what other people think, I guess you could do it as long as you don't talk about it, as long as other people don't know. I do know that some of my male friends say they don't care if their wives are virgins or not, they just want a good partner in life.

I think some people will do it when they are engaged or when they think that they will become engaged. I know one of the girls where I work was pregnant before she was married. But I want to wait until I get married.

When I go out with my boyfriend, we go to the movies or we drive to the mountains. (We don't stay overnight, of course.) Sometimes we go sightseeing in Kamakura or Yokohama. Sometimes we just go out for coffee and cake. We often do things with our friends as a group. Once in a while we meet at someone's house, and sometimes we all go overnight to a seminar house, a university-owned house, where we stay up all night and talk. It's very inexpensive, really—only about 2,000 yen [$8.50] each. When you get really tired, you can go into one of the small

1 6 3

rooms to sleep. There are four beds to a room. Nobody sleeps together. We all know each other so well that if someone did something like that, we'd feel uncomfortable. Our group is self-disciplined, I think.

It's possible that I'll marry my boyfriend, because I'm approaching *tekireiki,* the appropriate age for marriage. Age is very important for girls in Japan. I don't think boys feel it as strongly as girls. Boys marry at about age twenty-seven or -eight, three to four years after they start working. When a girl graduates from college at age twenty-two and has no boyfriend, the parents and relatives may begin to worry. They say, "Would you like to do *omiai?*" But I don't think I want to do *omiai.* How can you understand someone's personality in such a short time? I think it's important to have some common interests and shared experiences with your future husband. You can get to know each other better with your friends around. You can ask them, "Well, what's he really like?" My boyfriend is trustworthy, has his own beliefs—he's quite independent for a Japanese boy—smart, and hardworking. He's majoring in economics. For many girls, their first priority is the boy's appearance, but when *tekireiki* approaches, then they start to care more about the boy's occupation. Their tastes change.

When I get married, I don't want to stay home and do housework. I'd like to work outside. Volunteer work is O.K. I don't have to earn money. But I want to have social contacts.

Among my friends, most of them want to work—at least until they have children. But if their husbands get transferred—as often happens early in a man's career—they have to quit their jobs. And once you quit, it's hard to get a good job. The job market is so small. And companies are prejudiced against women. They all think that once a woman gets married and is busy with household work, she won't pay the same amount of attention to her work at the office as she used to. Besides, some people think it's more important to stay home and take care of the children. But if you have a special skill like English, you can work. Fortunately, I'll always be able to tutor English.

Our parents' generation thinks that men are superior to women. They say women are too emotional, they're not logical, they don't know what's going on in the world with politics and economics. It's changing now, though. There are some very smart women. And studies show that girls are more hardworking and get better grades in college than men. Yet still in a company we girls are always the assistants and the boys are the future managers. Companies still believe it's a waste of time to train women, because they will quit when they marry or get pregnant. And they do. But some people say women should have more choice. I think so, too.

Japanese women, regardless of education level, have a hard time being taken seriously. (This is the number-one complaint of foreign women working in Japan, too.) Once, when I asked an early thirtyish Japanese male friend which universities (coed or single sex) were the best for women, he laughingly answered, "Which do you mean—the ones that make the best housewives or the ones that make the best academics?" I didn't think it was funny. His wife forced a laugh.

Of course Todai is at the top of the wish list for both sexes. Then for young women come the girls' schools—the Smith and Wellesley of Japan—Ochanomizu and Tokyo Women's College, followed by Seishin, Gakushuin, and Japan Women's College (the last three being particularly good for housewives, my friend noted). Favorite coed schools are the national public schools like Kyoto and Hitosubashi, and private universities like Keio, Waseda, Sophia, and International Christian University.

In order to pass through the hallowed gates of Japan's major universities, the advice given to entrance exam test-takers is, "Sleep four hours, pass. Sleep five hours, fail."

Obviously, not every one is a winner. In fact, less than half of Todai's 3,000 coveted seats are won on the first try. Overall figures are that about one-third of all college freshman have attended *yobiko*, the year-long prep schools, which cost about 400,000 yen [$1,667]. One *yobiko* teacher told me that his job is half-instruction, half-encouragement for these disappointed young people. The teachers work the same full day as a public school teacher but often make two to three times as much money. Fewer girls than boys attend the more than 200 *yobiko*. ("All a girl needs is a husband," explains one sixty-eight-year-old retired teacher turned *yobiko* prof). The students call themselves *ronin* (masterless samurai), because like the warriors of old, the students wander around, in some cases for more than a year.

RONIN

Earnest young Toshiko Maeda, twenty, works as a clerk in her father's steel supply company. She lives in the traditional town of Kanazawa, located on the "other" side of Japan. She tells the story of the "other" side of Japan's notorious entrance examination system—those who fail. When she failed the entrance exam to public high school, she took the test for a private high school and was admitted. However, after failing the tests for her favorite universities, there was no time to apply elsewhere. She became one of Japan's annual 77,000 *ronin*.[1] She gave up after six months of study.

TOSHIKO MAEDA:

I was born in Showa 36 [1961]. I think Showa 36 is a year of the cow. I'm like a cow; a cow is slow and doesn't like to move.

Twelve people including my brother work for my

father's steel supply company. People come to him to buy steel cut to a proper size. My sister, mother, and I work part-time for him. We don't count, but my father needs my brother.

My father was born in Showa 11 [1936] and lived in Osaka. He only went to high school one and a half years, because he had to quit to support his family. When he was a boy, food was so scarce sometimes he'd walk five or six hours to find rice. When my parents married, they just lived from day to day. They didn't even have enough money for one day's rice. Now they aren't rich, but they have enough money for food. When I was a child, my parents said if you leave even one grain of rice in your bowl, you will be blind. I was so young I believed them. Nowadays, I know it's not true, but if I leave any rice I feel guilty. They don't want me to waste. I understand.

I started nursery school at age five. Then I went to elementary school and junior high school. I failed the exam for public high school, but later I passed the exam for private high school.

My brother and younger sister went to public school, where the tuition was about 3500 yen [$14.58] a month. But at private school, I paid double that amount. I spent a lot. Although it's hard to get into private schools in Tokyo, it's much easier here.

I think I aimed too high for the public school. Kanazawa has about ten public high schools and about five private schools. Each one has a rank. Since the exam for all public schools is held the same day, you have to pick just one. Maybe if I'd aimed lower, I would have gotten in.

The public school exams have five subjects: English, Japanese, math, social studies, and science. After students take the tests, teachers correct them. Then a few days later you learn if you succeed or not. Your number, junior high school name, and your name are printed on a bulletin board at the high school and in the local newspaper. In Kanazawa, we also have a television show about the results, which runs for four hours.

When I failed to get into a public high school, I wasn't embarrassed because only the names of those who succeed are shown and not the names of those who fail. If you are successful, your relatives and friends call to say congratulations. And you get a postcard in the mail. Since it's boring to spend four hours looking for your name on the television, most of the students go to the high school to look at the bulletin board. I didn't. I watched TV, and I cried at home. I didn't want to cry in front of people.

The private school I did enter was a Christian school where all the teachers were Japanese. (Only about one-third were real Christians who go to church.) Out of the five private schools in Kanazawa, three are for girls only, like mine.

Since Japan has a six-three-three system (six years of elementary school, three years of junior high, and three years of high school), it was only two years later when I began to study for an entrance exam again. I worked hard for one year before the university entrance exams. I studied at home like most of my friends. I had a tutor in English twice a week for three hours. He'd start at 7:00 P.M. and sometimes stay as late as midnight teaching me, my brother, and my sister. *Juku* do exist here, but the teachers aren't so good, so those schools aren't as popular as in Tokyo.

During that year before the exam, I slept just four hours a day, sometimes three hours. I hate to tell you this, but I slept during my classes. My school was not high quality, so I slept during the day and studied at home at night. To enter a private Japanese university, you only have to pass three subjects—English, Japanese, and social studies—not science or math. So each day at school I woke up for my English and Japanese classes. It was no good. Some other students tried to do the same thing, too.

You see, at higher ranked high schools, they help their

students study for the exams, but not at my high school. Only about twenty or thirty students out of my class of 240 studied hard. Since my school belongs to a college, it's easy to get in. All you have to do is pass an easy test and have good marks in high school. So most of my classmates went to college there or in Kanazawa or they started working. Only about two or three went to university in Tokyo. It's unusual to go to Tokyo or Osaka. But I really wanted to go to Tokyo, specifically to Dokkyo in Saitama, which has a good English conversation and literature program. Only a few universities emphasize spoken English at all. Sophia University is the best of all the schools teaching English, but I knew it was impossible for me to get in there.

In January, one month before the exams, I was so tired that I didn't study as hard as before. I guess I got lazy. I started to sleep standing up on the bus. It's possible. You can do it while holding the strap. You just rest your head on your arm like this . . .

The entrance exams for private schools are always in February. You hear your results after about a week, and if you are admitted you have to pay an entrance fee within two to three days.

My best friend and I had studied together. We were trying for the same private university. One week after the exam, she phoned to say she had received her success notice. She got a postcard, and I didn't. The university officials had told me, "If you fail, we won't mail you a notice." But I thought maybe it would come in the next day's mail. Although I realized that there was maybe a 50 percent chance that I had failed, I still had hope. I waited in bed all the next day. I couldn't move. I was so depressed. I didn't want to face the fact that I'd failed. I couldn't look at my parents. My mother had really supported me, because she hadn't gone to college and she wanted me to go so much. But my father didn't want me to go away to school in Tokyo. Since we have no relatives in Tokyo whom I could have lived with, he was really worried. So he was relieved when I failed.

I felt I had done my best, and I vowed to take the exam again next year. I didn't cry. I endured. When I talked to my teacher, she encouraged me by saying, "Don't worry. You did your best." Only then did I cry.

So for the next six months I was *ronin*. My high school had four *ronin*. Everyone else went to college or to work. (Not many went to work, only about ten out of forty in my classroom). I heard that in Tokyo a first-year *ronin* is not unusual. But in Kanazawa, it's no good. People said, "Oh she must be lonely." I felt real pressure because everyone kept asking me. "Which university do you want to go to?"

My father had said that it was a waste of money to study English at a Japanese university. It is true that students who major in English can't speak well. So he said that if I wanted to learn English, I should to to America or Canada. So instead of taking the exam again, I went to Canada for a year. That was the end of my being a *ronin*.

Now I work from 8:30 to 5:30 as a clerk. I don't like my job. All I do is make tea, answer a lot of phone calls, take a lot of orders, and do the bookkeeping.

What I'd really like to do is teach little kids. Or teach English to high school students. But to do that you have to finish university. Now I don't want to go to university. It's a waste of time and money.

Anyway, I have to work. I want to continue my English studies though, so two days a week I listen to the English-language programs on NHK-TV from 7:00 to 7:30 in the morning. I also listen to the radio lessons every day, Monday through Saturday, from 6:45 to 7:00 A.M. I really like being with and talking to people, so maybe I'll be an interpreter or tour guide. That kind of job would suit me. But first I need certification. I take English correspondence courses for 42,000 yen [$175] a month. If I went to school, the cost would be 50,000 yen [$208], so it's better to do it at home. That way I can work during the day and study at night. But it is difficult to study after work.

The Challenge Ahead

In the early 1980s, one frustrated *ronin*, a two-time failure, came out swinging with a baseball bat. Having been scolded by his father for taking money out of the bank without permission and chided once again by his mother for his laziness, he stewed in his room for several hours and started drinking before bludgeoning both parents to death as they slept. His behavior shocked the nation but was symptomatic of one of Japan's biggest social problems today: school violence. (Although called school violence, it extends to the home as well, where mothers, of all family members, are the biggest target.)[1] Increasingly, teachers have been beaten, struck, or knifed. The law prohibits corporal punishment of students by teachers. Thus, a quiet, shy junior high school teacher, Yoshito Yagi, thirty-eight, often harassed by school bullies for being an A-bomb victim, made headlines when, after a student threw a metal doormat at him, he stabbed the pupil with a fruit

171

knife. A few weeks later, the local suburban Tokyo school board accepted his resignation. Two months later, he paid a $400 fine, a lenient penalty since so many people sympathized with him.

What has led to this volcanic explosion of violence? Junior high school teacher Shugi Uchiyama, forty-five, of Sapporo explains the buildup of stress built into the system that may lead to such violent release. He says Japanese students are pressured "every day from elementary school until college." Although he approves of the use of discussion, as in U.S. classrooms, he admits frankly that, "In Japan, we don't have time." As an English teacher, he regrets that the number of weekly foreign language classes has been cut back from four to three and that only ten minutes out of the fifty-minute lesson can be spared for conversation, because "The entrance exam tests vocabulary and grammar, not how well the students can speak." Everything is geared to the entrance exams—even in the summer. This year, forty out of forty-four of his students put their noses to the grindstone at *juku* during the sunny days of July and August. Year-round, they have very little time to play. "When I went to the United States and saw the students playing football or soccer in the afternoons, I envied them," he says. "They are very happy young people. Here in Japan they are always preparing for some exam."

More than 90 percent of incidents of school violence take place in junior high schools, according to National Police Agency data. In 1983, the schools reported about 2,000 incidents of violence between students (up 60 percent from five years ago) and more than a thousand attacks on teachers (almost five times the figure five years ago). Nearly one out of ten junior highs has some episode of violence each year. And elementary school pupils feel the stress as well, so much so that fourth-grade Osaka teacher Mizue Kuroda says that the number of children refusing to come to school is rising, even in her school, which is located in an upper-middle-class neighborhood.

172

Everyone has a pet theory for what or who is to blame. And everyone's pointing the finger at someone else. Prime Minister Nakasone blames families first and foremost, for their overindulgence of the children, but also schools and communities. The Sapporo junior high school teacher cites a lack of discipline at home. Meanwhile, parents blame teachers for the children's lack of manners. Education Minister Mitsuo Setoyama even blamed the U.S. Occupation!

But students are blaming the teachers, too. One survey cited teacher favoritism as a major reason behind the violence. One fourteen-year-old girl charged that, "Teachers neglect those who do poorly and love only those who get high marks." The poor students have trouble keeping up with the fact-filled curriculum. What is usually a difficult time for adolescents anyway is made doubly difficult by the psychological pressures of the junior high and high school exams. If they fail to pass the exam to the right high schools that prepare them better for the exam to the right universities, they can see the door to opportunity shutting already at the age of only fourteen or fifteen.

Although the total number of acts of violence nationwide has peaked and is less than the yearly amount of school violence in New York City alone,[2] such actions are shocking to a people accustomed to respecting authority and to having a relatively crime-free society where the group takes responsibility for the individual. (Indeed, one prinicpal committed suicide to take responsibility for the violence that occurred in his school.) There is a real feeling that the Japanese—not a few Japanese, but all Japanese—have failed, that something is wrong. The public is ready for and actively wants major change in the educational system.

This would be only the third time a change has been made in the educational system (early Meiji days, post-World War II, and now). In 1984, Prime Minister Nakasone appointed a twenty-five-member ad hoc reform council that will report to the prime minister in three years, after hearing the opinions of parents, teachers, administrators, and other experts. He has encouraged the council to make emergency recommendations along the way. What he wants in the long run is a system that turns out "a kindhearted, patriotic, yet internationally minded people who will serve the country well."

Just how can the country eliminate school violence, reduce exam pressure, and deemphasize memorization? What will some of the reform council's recommendations be?

There are no easy answers, no quick fixes, but several ideas are gaining support, some mentioned in recent studies by the Japan Teachers Union and the Ministry of Education. Since most young Japanese advance to high school anyway, why not combine the junior high and high schools and thus eliminate at least one exam? Another idea: stress extracurricular activities more in the admission process. Do away with the uniform first-round exam, a widely acknowledged failure; reduce the number of subjects tested for public university from five to three; have private schools give their exams on different days so that students can apply to many schools; start the school year in September rather than April to help young people returning from abroad and to facilitate international exchange. Students should be allowed to transfer from one university to another, and to enter four-year schools if they have good records in the two-year colleges or technical schools. A more flexible grading system is needed, too. The current system is a bell-shaped curve that gives as many As as Fs (in Japan, 5s and 1s). Under this system competition is so stiff that, when a boy who customarily gets one of the few 5s moves out of town, says the Sapporo teacher, all the children who usually get 4s are delighted because there will be one more 5 available. The *hensachi* score is another bell curve monster. Students take a mock high school entrance exam and use the score as an indicator of which high school's exam they will most likely pass. Since the exams are given on the same date, the students can apply to only one high school per prefecture.

Most of the proposals have to do with reforming the examination system, making it easier or less important. But Prime Minister Nakasone wants to reemphasize something more basic to the children's character—moral education, a once-a-week, hour-long lesson in how to behave, already a required subject during the nine compulsory years of elementary and junior high school. Many teachers lecture about inspirational leaders or heroes in Japanese history. Sapporo teacher Uchiyama recently gave an example to his homeroom class of a school trip made by a group of students. The night before climbing the mountain together, a few rowdy pupils stayed up all night talking and partying, even though their teachers had warned them not to. The next day they made it to the top and back down to the bottom, but the teachers and other students remained angry with them anyway. Why? Well, what if the weather had turned bad all of sudden, Uchiyama asked. What if the tired students hadn't made it to the top? But more importantly, these students had disobeyed the rules of the group. That was the point of the story.

Called *shushin* before the war, Occupation authorities prohibited the teaching of morals, thinking (rightly) that the subject had been used to stir up nationalistic feelings. But it crept back into the curriculum in 1958 and is known as *dotoku* now. These days, however, some teachers, fearing a resurgence of nationalism, would rather not teach it at all; others use that hour as a time for entrance exam preparation.

If the Japanese people really want change, though, it will not be enough to change the educational system alone. The long-term goal of the most able students has always been to enter a large company. The one major change needed in the business community to complement the various changes in education is the widening of the employment pool and the criteria for selection. At this point, large companies only hire graduates of a handful of elite universities and give just a passing glance to their college grades and extracurricular activities. These employers should heed the words of the hardworking sixth-grade Tokushima teacher who reminds her students. "The best student doesn't always make the best man." One reason that TV star Tetsuko Kuroyanagi's book *Totto-chan, the Little Girl at the Window* was the biggest best seller since the war was that it showed that there is more than one way to educate children. Asked to leave her first-grade class in public school because she was so noisy, Totto-chan attended an alternative school (unfortunately burned down during the war) that combined joy with learning and valued her exuberance. Once companies emphasize the need for well-rounded people and not impressive test-takers, only then will the rest of the educational system follow suit.

The biggest single change within the educational system itself must come in Japan's encyclopedic method of learning and teaching. "With all the information surrounding us today," says teacher Shugi Uchiyama, "We need creative ability, not the ability to memorize."

Japan's *kyoiku mama*, concerned fathers, devoted teachers, and administrators have a mighty challenge ahead of them—a worthy goal that could be reached by the twenty-first century, if everyone makes it a priority—to put the joy back into learning.

仕事

Part III

WORK

Ask any Japanese what the secret to the country's success is, what Japan's greatest strength is, and without hesitation, men and women alike, from all parts of Japan, will give the same answer: *kinben*—diligence. Not lifetime employment, the seniority system, nor quality control circles, not one specific management technique nor one specific sex, but diligence, the virtue that pervades the entire Japanese economic sytem. Foreigners may call them "workaholics" but Japanese prefer the appellation "worker bees." And like busy bees, everyone moves quickly. The postman runs from his bicycle to our mailbox, the waitress runs from the table to the kitchen and back.

In 1983, one petite, hardworking Japanese woman, who could be called *kinben* incarnate, held the country in the palm of her hand. Her name was Oshin, a self-sacrificing, ever-diligent woman of great character and strength. Indeed, her name derives from the word *shinbo*, meaning perseverance.

Phenomenally popular, Oshin was only a TV character, a composite of the lives of 300 actual Japanese women, but all of Japan sat glued to their television sets, watching her life unfold. Ninety-eight percent of the Japanese saw the show at least once. O-syndrome gripped the nation like a fever, because Oshin's life paralleled the life of Japanese women, indeed of Japan, in the twentieth century.

Born in 1901 to an impoverished family of tenant farmers, little Oshin watched wide-eyed one day as her mother tried to induce an abortion of an unwanted pregnancy by standing in an icy river. On the same river, at

179

the tender age of seven and about to be sent off to work as a maid for a well-to-do family, Oshin tearfully stood on a raft, clutching her wooden *kokeshi* doll, and waving good-bye to her beloved mother. The nation wept as she cried *"Okasan!"* (Mother!).

Oshin carried the baby of the merchant's house on her back while she did chores, just as she carried her own children on her back years later when she and her husband lived on his parents' farm with her tyrannical mother-in-law. During her life many misfortunes befell her—a tragic stillbirth, a son needlessly lost in World War II, and a husband who committed suicide. Despite all, she perse-vered. During her eighty-odd years, she had many jobs—maid, farmhand, hairdresser, fish shop owner, and fi-nally co-owner of a chain of supermarkets in partnership with her penurious first son.

I watched the show most mornings at breakfast time because I considered it good drama. Just a story, I thought to myself, until I met a fifty-eight-year-old cleaning lady who told me she, too, had been sent away at age thirteen as a maid. Prewar, with high taxes to pay and poor crops, many farmers (and in those days 70 percent of the nation were farmers) feared rather than welcomed another mouth to feed. Young girls were sent away to work as baby nurses and housemaids, just to put rice in their bowls and a roof over their heads. "This was not unusual," a friend assures me. Older girls could earn wages in textile factories or be indentured to geisha houses.

In those days, as throughout Japanese history prior to World War II, the Japanese woman's work never seemed to end. She drew water from the well or stream; she hewed wood; she planted rice; she cooked, cleaned, washed, spun, wove, and sewed from dawn until dusk. Survival was her goal, not comfort. And that was Oshin—the Japanese ideal of womanhood—what Americans today call a superwoman capable of juggling work and home. Never complaining, always diligent, unstintingly devoted to her children, Oshin progressed from being just an extra mouth to feed to being a successful businesswoman. That was perhaps the one element of Oshin's life that did not ring true—her enormous success as an owner and manager. Only a handful of Japanese women own their own business (and many of these are inherited from their husbands) or hold managerial positions.

However, it is true that since the end of World War II, as in Oshin's life, Japanese women stepped through a time warp from feudalistic days to the modern era. For women accustomed to obeying the head of the household (usually the father-in-law), always shuffling three steps behind the husband, and generally having no rights at all, the changes—urbanization, democratization, and increased industrialization—could be called no less than a revolution. Urbanization spawned the nuclear family, which released young wives from the meddling of a live-in mother-in-law and the authority of the patriarchal three-generation family house. Democracy, as embodied in the Constitution and subsequent laws, ordered equal pay for equal work and equal access to higher education. Increased industrialization meant more jobs for all.

These plus other changes—a longer life expectancy, fewer children, fewer family workers, and more paid employees—have resulted in more married working women, more women working for a longer number of years, more mothers returning to work, more women working in tertiary industry (banks, supermarkets, travel) than secondary (manufacturing) or primary (farming) industry, more university graduates, and more part-timers. Quite an encouraging list of "mores," and the bottom-line good news is that the number of female employees has more than doubled to 15 million in the last twenty-five years.

Certainly Japanese women have come a long, long way, but they still have far to go, according to some of today's young working women—the new generation of Oshin. Consideration of other people and hard work still

1 8 1

come naturally to the female white-collar workers in their twenties and thirties, but the new Oshin are different from their mothers: the young women have never known the hardship of war or hunger; they have more education and skills; and they want more out of life. As a group, they have made successes out of magazines with names like *Arubaito* and *Torabayu* (from the German and French words *arbeit* and *travail* meaning "work"). And unlike the soft-spoken, ever-subservient, and willingly subordinate Oshin, they do complain—although certainly not at work and generally not in public.

But even though a vague disquiet and frustration permeates the thoughts of many young women, in the long run more of them will spend their energies trying to accept less. Less opportunity, less pay, less interesting work, less prestigious work—what they consider their lot in life—rather than demonstrating in the streets and demanding more.

The first four working women describe the life and work of four kinds of today's white-collar women in their twenties and thirties: the dedicated career woman; the job-hunting college senior; one of the increasingly numerous part-timers; and what to most Japanese is the quintessential Japanese working woman—the office lady.

Career Woman

Dressed in a white ruffled silk blouse, black linen suit, and matching pumps, Kiyomi Saito, thirty-four, projects a cool, confident image. Saito-san is a *kyaria wuman* (career woman) in a nation where women in prestige professions are few. They represent a small proportion of scientists (6.4 percent), engineers (2.4 percent), and lawyers (9.3 percent).[1] Only 6.2 percent in business are managers.[2] Saito-san works as a management trainee at Bank of America (Tokyo office) because she thought her chances for recognition and promotion would be better in an American company. After all, more Japanese women executives work on Wall Street than in all of Kabuto-cho, Tokyo's financial district.

Saito-san grew up in Tokyo, where her parents work together in a small hotel that they own. Like her older brother, whom she much admires, she majored in economics. After graduation from prestigious Keio University, she passed a rigorous, competitive entrance exam for the *Nihon Keizai Shimbun* (Japan's *Wall Street Journal*), where she was allowed to be a computer programmer but not a reporter, a male-only domain. Saito-san met her husband in a tennis club, a popular site for love matches ever since the crown prince met his wife on a tennis court. She and her husband married, moved to the States, and subsequently divorced.

Saito-san returned to Tokyo to begin work as secretary for Sony Chairman Akio Morita, one of the best-known businessmen in Japan. Seeing that her job, though challenging, led nowhere, she decided to go back to university. In 1982, Saito-san became the second Japanese woman ever to graduate from Harvard Business School.

Most of the time, she sounds like the forward-looking, freshly minted Harvard MBA that she is. Occasionally, however, the Japanese shadow of womanly self-doubt creeps in and her *shikata ga nai* (it can't be helped) fatalistic training from childhood eclipses her ambition to become a director of a Japanese company.

KIYOMI SAITO:

I had a hard time finding a job after college, because I had majored in economics. When companies come to the campus, they are looking for English or French majors. That's all. Nobody wants a female economics major. But for a man, it's an advantage to have majored in economics or law.

My brother majored in economics at Waseda, and he influenced me. I wanted to be a literature major, but he said, "You can read novels as a hobby the rest of your life, but if you don't major in economics, you'll never learn about it." I loved reading books, but he said that's why women become so foolish.

My brother married the typical Japanese woman. She went to university but didn't study a lot. She did the usual lessons in bridal training: cooking, flower-arranging, and tea ceremony. (As did I.) After graduation, she worked for about two years. She saved all her money for her wedding. Actually, it was mostly her money that paid for the condo they bought when they married.

After I graduated from Keio, I took the examination for *Nihon Keizai Shimbun* or *Nikkei*, as we say [Japan Economic Journal]. I was so glad to be accepted at this newspaper. I ranked at the top of the exam, and I thought that was wonderful, but I was mistaken. *Nikkei* only wanted to hire me as a computer programmer. They have an ironclad rule against hiring women as reporters.

To tell the truth, I think women are not so conscious of the business world when they are twenty-two or twenty-three and just out of school. I was the same way. I just wanted to have a family when I was that age. So I married at twenty-three. I met my husband at a tennis club. I had had many boyfriends when I was growing up. My parents thought I would find a boy for myself, so they didn't try to do *omiai*. No one brought me any photos. They didn't push me a lot to get married. I did feel strong pressure from my friends, though. I didn't want to be left behind.

More and more young men would like to have a partner, not a housewife. They are still the minority though. These young men would rather have their wives work outside so that they can have something to talk about together. But even those young men often encourage their wives to quit once they have a baby.

Japanese companies have no written rules about leaving once you marry or have a baby, because it's illegal. But it's a fact that many women are forced to quit. I had a friend at Nomura Research Institute, which is quite a good place to work. She made it known that she'd like to stay on after marriage. So several of the managers took her to lunch about a week before her wedding in order to persuade her to leave. But she told them she didn't want to quit. So when she distributed her wedding invitations, they all made up excuses, and none of them came to her wedding. There was no one from her company to make a speech for her at the wedding reception. She managed to stay on at that company for two more years, but eventually she was made so uncomfortable that she quit. These stories are not uncommon. Women aren't upset by them. It's just part of the way we are brought up.

Do you know how Japan keeps its unemployment figures at only 2 percent? The full-time, lifetime employees are all men. The second tier of workers are full-time women who are forced to quit after two to three years when they get married or have babies. The third tier of workers are the part-timers who are housewives. They receive no social security benefits or bonuses. (Most Japanese companies give twice yearly bonuses.) The worst thing (or the best thing from the employers' point of view) is that women are not calculated in the unemployment figures. (You have to earn a certain amount to be included.) In this way, women are not considered people. People who are born women have already lost the business game. This gets me mad. Then I hear people always talking about the prosperity and economic success of Japan. To me, the key success factor is the sacrifice of the Japanese women.

In Japan, most men are at the office by 8:30 A.M. But the girls have to be there by 8:00 A.M. in order to wipe off the desks, clean the ashtrays, prepare the tea, and get the day's papers ready. When there's a ten-minute break at 3:00 P.M., the women have to run to the coffee machine or coffee cart to get a drink for the men. The women never stop working. Yet they don't complain. They just accept this situation. Most Japanese women are content. Why? They can't imagine any other world. We were brought up to be a woman or a girl. We learn that men start dinner first and women should follow men when out on the street. (When I was in the U.S., I felt so uncomfortable at first walking with men. It took me a year before I could go through the door ahead of a man.)

My husband and I got divorced when we were in the States. He was studying at MIT. Here in Japan he works as a rocket designer for NASDA [Japan's NASA]. The main reason I didn't trust him or respect him or like him was that he became a typical husband after I married him. He bossed me around and said, "I earn money for both of us, and you don't do anything." Yes, I'd quit my *Nikkei* job after a year and a half to go to America, but I did have a part-time job at that point, so these words hurt me.

After we were married, no one called me by my name. I was always Tadakawa-san's wife. I wanted to be called my own first name. I lost all my personality. Even my own friends only asked about my husband—how he was, what he was doing. No one asked about me or what I was doing. They just asked questions about cooking or shopping. I didn't have a baby yet, so there were no questions about children. Maybe I wasn't mature at that time. I wanted to keep my independence.

Divorce is a very bad thing in Japan. You do it only as a last resort. Only when women have more financial power will more and more of them divorce. When I was divorced seven years ago, I had no real skills, so I couldn't get a job easily. I was too old. I was twenty-four. Most job advertisements in the paper were for women under twenty-three or even under twenty (the high school and junior college graduates). The best most divorced women can do is a part-time job at a factory or work at a supermarket as salesgirls or secretaries. Most end up working for small companies.

Very fortunately for me, I was hired as an administrative assistant and secretary for Mr. Morita, the cofounder of Sony. He's quite a dynamic guy. I thought that as an "old" woman I was lucky to be hired by Sony.

Traditionally, a woman has this job because the managers are afraid that a man might accumulate too much power. After all, this person controls who sees Mr. Morita and who doesn't. The managers know that a woman can't be promoted. Besides, they thought I would be there for a long, long time since they knew that, as a divorcée, I wouldn't get married again. (A woman usually stays home with her parents if she wants to remarry. Once a woman goes out to get a job, she's kind of committed to not remarrying. At that time, I didn't want to remarry. But now that I have a boyfriend, I might reconsider. I don't know.)

I worked very hard at Sony. Sometimes I'd be there until 2:00 A.M., but I never received any bonuses or recognition. I began to realize that the job was a dead end.

Women weren't promoted at Sony. The company may have an international image, but after all, it's still a Japanese company.

I wanted to do something with my life. I decided to invest in myself, so I applied to Harvard Business School. I was the second Japanese woman to attend this school. (The first one graduated seven years ago, so I didn't get a chance to talk to her.) The first year was particularly tough because I couldn't speak English well. But I survived.

Like most Japanese, I can read and write English, so I could read the cases and everything on the blackboard and I'd read my classmates' notes after the class. Since classroom participation counts for half the grade, I'd raise my hand during the first part of the class before the discussion got heated and complicated. I didn't have time to go to parties. I just studied.

After business school, I thought at first that I wanted to stay in the U.S. where the discrimination against women is not so severe. But then I thought I should do something for women back here. I knew I'd receive a lot of recognition here. I guess you could say I'm kind of a rare commodity.

Since Japanese companies hire their employees right after graduation from college, I knew I'd have to work for a foreign company in Japan. I think Bank of America was very courageous to hire me as a management trainee. Even women who graduate from Tokyo University are usually hired as clerks, not as officer material. The women have no chance. After Bank of America hired me, they accepted two women straight out of college as management trainees. I'm glad that maybe I helped create the momentum to change the Bank of America.

I've heard that the foreign manager of a small consulting firm decided to staff his company with the brightest Japanese women from the best schools. His strategy paid off. The women were grateful to be given a chance and the company has been very successful. On the other hand, the First National Bank of Chicago once hired all women as lending officers, but the customers didn't like dealing with them, so the bank put them all in the back office. I think the bank should have been more patient.

When I came back to Tokyo six months ago, I wondered myself how I would be treated. I thought I might very well have to return to the States in two or three months. However, once I am introduced to customers as a management trainee and a Harvard MBA, I have no problem. I can talk their language. It surprised me, but in fact sometimes it's an advantage to be a woman. The men are curious and they talk to me a lot, so I can pick up a great deal of information for my company. Also, at a big party they can remember me, even if I don't always remember them.

My friends say that when I talk English I am very aggressive, but when I'm using my own language, my strategy is to be a woman. If I talk like a man, I know the men will feel resistance; they will tighten up and feel uncomfortable. But the disadvantage of speaking women's Japanese is that I have to humble myself constantly. So I'm better off speaking English. Then I can talk at the same level.

Only once did someone think I was an interpreter and that man was a foreigner, not a Japanese! My frustrations are more inside the company, where men try to isolate me. It's a very subtle form of discrimination. They try to cut off the flow of information, and in my situation information is key. I'm still a trainee. I work for two Japanese bosses. One is a high school or junior high school graduate who's worked for the bank for thirty years. He's still an assistant manager, which is one of the lowest levels for a manager. As his assistant, I have to know what he is doing so I can give answers to the customers' questions. But he doesn't give me any information at all. That decreases my effectiveness and reliability because the customers think I don't know anything about the business and they don't want to come to me anymore. Also, the clerks and operational people at the bank think I don't know anything either. They don't trust me anymore. They just think I'm not effective. The good thing is that the American managers do trust me. They give me lots of different jobs. My other Japanese boss is very good, too. He delegates a lot of responsibility to me. So I've proved myself to them. These people know I am efficient.

I find that people high up in Japanese companies can treat me as an equal. They don't discriminate against me as a girl. They are not scared. They are not threatened by me. They know they have their own expertise.

I'm in charge of foreign companies in Japan. The problem here for foreign companies is that they can't hire good Japanese. Most of the Japanese men working for American companies are dropouts from the mainstream of society, second-class citizens. They aren't secure, so I don't get good treatment from them.

Why is there a stigma attached to working for a foreign company? Well, all the good students are supposed to go work for the government and large companies. Once these students pass the company entrance exam and interview, they are accepted by a large company or the government, and that means they are good. The other graduates must go to work for smaller companies. In a foreign bank, Japanese men don't mind if the women work in the trading section. It's O.K. That's hidden in the back office. But there is resistance in the credit section which has traditionally been a man's domain. That's the heart of the bank.

In a way, I hope I'm transferred. In Japan, people aren't promoted fast enough. Seniority in the company—even an American company in Japan—is still the most important factor. Even if I do outstanding work, I will still have to wait. Meanwhile, I'm frustrated with the number of slow-thinking and slow-acting people. Maybe I should go back to New York to make my mark while I'm still young and healthy.

Did I ever think of going back to Sony? No, Mr. Morita wrote me a very good recommendation to business school, but he advised me not to return because there were no opportunities for women at Sony. Anyway, it wouldn't be a good idea to go back where I first worked as a girl.

After twenty years, who knows? I may be near the top of a foreign company. There's still a racial problem though. Minorities don't get good opportunities. I think I can be an executive vice-president, but that's all. I can't fully understand the American mentality, so it's not fair to elect me president or chairman of the board. But I can function quite effectively as an executive vice-president. I don't blame the company. It's natural. If I were a minority from the U.S., then that would be discrimination. But I'm from a different country.

My real dream is to be hired at a high rank, as an outside director of a large Japanese company. If I can prove myself competent, it's possible. They do make women directors, and some of the women are outside directors. For example, Ichiko Ishihara, who heads the public relations section of Takashimaya Department Store, was promoted to that company's board of directors. But she worked her way up from inside. There's another store, a chain of supermarkets called Daiei which hired a woman named Teiko Baba. She came from outside.

I think Japanese are learning a little from the example of the American companies. Those men who go to the U.S. to do business see women working, and they also see foreign women visiting their companies and working here in Japan. Besides, nowadays it's not so easy to train the young men. They are not as enthusiastic as the traditional Japanese man who has worked all his life from eight in the morning until eight at night. The younger generation don't want to do overtime. If they have a date at 6:00 P.M., they leave the office immediately. They don't care if their superiors think that they are not working hard. They just don't care about that kind of evaluation from their boss. The younger generation want to have their own individual lives. More importantly, they know how to play—something the older people do not. A member of the older generation usually has just one hobby like golf, mah-jongg, or pachinko. But the younger generation knows how to ski, play tennis, play musical instruments. Lots of things. It's good for them, but it's not so good for the economy of Japan.

I'm not totally pessimistic on the outlook for Japanese working women. I think the situation is changing, albeit slowly. As the Japanese companies need more and more labor, and as women show more and more capability, management will no longer be able to ignore them. Then as women gain confidence, they too will want more.

Now if a Japanese woman is a mother and working, she feels guilty. You see, if a wife works, it's often considered shameful for the husband. It implies that he doesn't earn enough. So some working mothers don't tell anyone that they work. We have some cleaning maids at our hotel who pretend that they have gone out shopping or to classes. It's O.K. for them to work only as long as the neighbors and relatives don't know. Some children don't even know that their mothers work. So when my parents or I see one of these maids after work, sometimes we don't say hello. It's not that we look down on maids. We don't have rigid classes here. Usually a man doesn't mind if his wife is a maid. What he tries to conceal is that she works. I can understand why a housewife would want to be a maid. Many women want to get out of the house even if only for a short while, and it's hard for them to get jobs.

You American working women should really appreciate General Electric. Many Japanese don't have room for a big freezer or a huge refrigerator. They only have room for a small one, so they have to go out shopping every day. Most homes don't have dryers yet either. So the housewives must hang out their clothes to dry.

Women do dominate the home in Japan. That's where their power lies. Usually a Japanese husband hands over his paycheck to his wife, who manages the family's finances. Then the wife gives her husband an allowance. (I know a man who writes articles and appears on television after work. He puts this extra money in his pocket and never tells his wife about it. That's pretty typical, I think.) So women feel equal in the home and can talk about anything at all. But outside the home, we are taught to be quiet. We learn early to keep our mouths shut.

My old college friends who are married are all housewives. I don't keep up with them now. We don't talk any more. We have nothing in common. They look down on me. I'm not a complete woman to them. Since I don't have a family, I'm defective.

Job-Hunter

Yoko Suzuki, the daughter of a Tokyo salaryman and a housewife, attends prestigious Sophia University. Like most young college girls, she still lives with her parents and will until the day she marries.

As a senior, in the fall before her springtime graduation, she was caught up in the whirlwind of *recruit-o* season. In Japan, under the classic lifetime employment system, students go job-hunting only once in their lives and join a single company until the day they retire. Job-hopping is taboo (although increasingly done). Large companies hire only recent college graduates—mostly male—to mold them in the company's image according to the company's needs, making raw recruits into seasoned veterans who will lead the company to success a quarter century from now. Young women, management assumes, work only to fill the time before they marry. Personnel managers have lots of clout in Japan due to the competition for talented human resources—Japan's only abundant natural resource—in a process known, appropriately enough during harvest time for a formerly agricultural nation, as *aotagari*, harvesting yet green rice.

Quiet, poised Suzuki-san sighs as she talks about the getting-a-job war (*shushoku senso*), the "other big battle," second only to the college entrance examination war (*juken senso*). Everyone scrambles to find a slot in a large company, but for girls the competition is doubly fierce. More than 70 percent of the large companies do not even accept applications from female university graduates. Of those who do, 60 percent give the girls different training from men or no training at all.[1]

Little wonder the young women look nervous as they pound the pavement in Otemachi and Marunouchi in Tokyo, location of many company headquarters. Suzuki-san can easily spot the harried fellow job-hunters. "Their facial expressions are stiff; they have *rikkuruto-cut-o* [recruit-cut] hair styles; and they wear *rikkuruto-style-u* clothes: a dark blue suit with a white blouse and a bow." Some girls go so far as to have cosmetic surgery (nose, lip, or eyelid fixes) to enhance their attractiveness and thus increase their chances of being hired.

Although offered a job by Sumitomo, which her parents encouraged her to take, Suzuki-san opted instead to become one of the 150,000 young women who work with foreign firms, where they tend to be treated with more respect and have a better chance at receiving promotions and more responsible work. So popular is this domestic brain drain among top-notch young women that each year foreign banks receive hundreds of applications for a handful of entry-level positions.

YOKO SUZUKI:

For graduating seniors, the two most important dates are October 1 and November 1. On October 1, a senior is allowed to visit any company. Before that date, it's not "legal" to start job-hunting activities. But lots of people do. First they look around for contacts—either alumni, relatives, or friends. The higher up the personal connection, the better the chance of getting a job. Of course, you have to have good marks, but that's not really so important.

Many companies make recruiting phone calls to boys from good schools like Todai before October. The recruiters say, "We want you so badly that you don't have to come on October 1 or take our test on November 1. You're on the list if you just say yes."

It's much easier for men to find a job since so many more companies are open to them. After visiting three or four trading companies over a seven- to ten-day period, they can usually find some company that will accept them. So most male seniors know by the middle of October what they are going to do next April after they graduate. The written test they take on November 1 is nothing, because they know they've already been accepted.

But for women, it's not that easy. They are usually still struggling to find a job in November. Since so few companies hire female college graduates, the November 1 exam is critical. In the next step, the interview, recruiters look for obedience more than anything else. In men, they look for energetic, cheerful, and cooperative types. But if

195

the company hires an energetic, strong-willed woman, she will want a promotion, and then the employers will be in trouble. Employers expect girls to do what they are told.

Since the more qualifications a woman has, the better her chances of winning a job, it is mostly women who take qualifying tests in skills such as English. They think they will be able to use their language training in their work, once a bank or trading company has hired them. But the reality of the situation is that companies don't allow women to do any important work. They make them do secretarial and supplementary chores: copying papers, running errands, and in general doing things under men.

When men and women first graduate from school, they stand on the same line in terms of education and ability. But from then on, women are forced into a different path. Women aren't given a chance at promotions since people expect them to work only about three to five years. Actually, women do quit their jobs after a few years.

In general, junior college graduates stand a better chance of getting a job than university students because companies figure they will work a few years longer than the four-year college graduates before they marry and quit the company. A junior college graduate usually works five years compared to three for the university graduate. Also, university graduates are considered more *namaiki*—that is, smart, so smart that they speak up and talk back if they are treated unequally in the company. It may not be so, but that's what companies think.

Eight or ten years ago, when I was little, the number of women who tried to get a job was smaller. Most women graduates spent their time in *hanayome shugyo* [bridal training] learning tea ceremony and flower-arranging. But many women college students like me no longer want to spend so much time or energy on the ritual ceremonies. More women want jobs instead, and more women have higher education than ever before.

Meanwhile, corporate attitudes toward women have

been changing, but very, very slowly. The number of companies that open their doors to women is increasing, but their expectations remain the same. They have a fixed concept of sex roles and don't evaluate each woman's ability or willingness to work. I think their attitude toward women who'd like to continue to work after marriage and children is changing too, but again very, very gradually.

This year Japan Air Lines [JAL] was the most popular company, the first choice among female seniors surveyed by the Nippon Recruit Center. At JAL, they use your ability. The door is open for hiring (although not really for promoting) women. Secondly, JAL looks fancy. It's very fashionable to work for an airline. It's just a feeling you get when you see an ad for the company. That's really important to female seniors.

The best thing about JAL is that they let women come back to work after they've had children. Again, that doesn't mean they'll be promoted or anything. You know when we say that "the door is open" at a company, we mean that they hire more women than other companies. It sounds good, but actually it's not.

The second most popular company was Suntory, the distillery company. It is popular because it takes an interest in cultural things, and it holds symposia on international affairs at Japanese universities.

This year the third most popular place was Sumitomo Shoji, the trading company. It looks attractive to both males and females, because it is said that you can get in without any *kone* [connections]. At Mitsubishi Shoji [Mitsubishi Trading Company], only those who are children of someone working in the Mitsubishi group of companies or those who know someone working in management or someone who does a lot of business with Mitsubishi can get in. And even if you do have *kone*, there is a ranking of *kone*. We say if you know someone who's a vice-president of Mitsubishi Shoji, you have a good chance. But if you know a person who's only worked there for seven or eight years, it's no good. It doesn't really help. In that case, it's better to know someone who does a lot of business with Mitsubishi. The *kone* is stronger.

Let's take another example. Let's say I'm a senior and I want to work for the Bank of Tokyo, and so does another girl. My uncle is an executive in a good position, but she knows someone at the Bank of Japan. She will probably get the job because Bank of Japan is higher than Bank of Tokyo and has a big influence on them. So, strictly speaking, you should have *kone*. You'll have absolutely no chance if you don't know anyone.

Kone counts more for women than for men. This fact tells a lot. Men have to have ability because they must make money for the company. But most companies don't expect much from women. They would rather have the security of hiring a woman they know, say someone's child or niece.

We students know which companies are recruiting because they post an information sheet at the school. It tells how many people are wanted, what they will be paid, and when the explanatory sessions, interviews and written exams will take place. In addition, there is a space where the company can write any other specifications, such as wanting people who have been born after a certain date. You can't be *ronin* or have repeated a year in college—that shows laziness—or spent an extra year in the United States as an exchange student. You're supposed to go to school for the right period of time.

The information sheet might also specify that the company wants girls who commute from home. This is an important factor, so it's harder for my classmates who come from outside Tokyo to get a job. Some of them don't bother to apply at all here in Tokyo because they know most companies have this preference. They give up and go back where they came from to find work. This is called "U-turn phenomenon."

198

Those out-of-towners who realize all along that there is less opportunity for them often decide to go into teaching. Here the competition is fair. Everyone takes the same written exam. But even if you pass, you must find a place that's offering a job. Since there are many more teachers than are needed in Tokyo, you do have to have *kone* to teach here. There's really more opportunity in local towns. That's why these young women go back. Graduates of big universities are much in demand locally. The more rural the better. Thus, education is a good profession if you like teaching. But it's miserable if you don't. Another way to be treated equally is to work for the government, but again you have to take several tests, and it's incredibly competitive.

I had no interest in becoming a teacher or working for the government. When I applied to private companies, I decided not to expect too much. This trend of treating women unequally is not going to change overnight.

So I chose to work for a foreign bank. There are more chances for women to be hired since Japanese young men would rather work for a Japanese company. You see, the most a young man can become in a foreign company is the local branch manager. So girls have a better chance to be hired and to be promoted, whereas there's hardly any chance for promotion for them in a Japanese trading company or bank.

I'd like to teach you one more word: *koshikake*. *Koshikake* means chair, but it also has another meaning. It's the kind of chair you sit on for just a little while. After graduation, lots of girls are just waiting for the time when they will get married. So they're just working for a while. They have no real desire to self-actualize or make the most of their abilities. They work without any future ambition. Here's a typical conversation. One girl says, "Why do you want to work? Are you going to be a career woman and continue in your job?" The other girl says "No, my work is just *koshikake*. I'm just working for a while, until I'm

199

twenty-four or twenty-five and must get married."

After I graduate I'd like to get married, but first I'd like to work for a while. I wouldn't call it *koshikake* because that implies a kind of superficial person with little ambition. I want to work until I get married and have babies. After that I'd like a certain kind of job: not full time, because most husbands—even young husbands—still don't want their wives to work outside all day long. I'd say more men are less conservative these days and they understand the wife's desire to do something besides cleaning house. Still, they don't want their wives to be away from home Monday through Friday, nine to five.

I'd like to make the most of my abilities and what I learned at Sophia. I think it's important to stay in touch with the world, to know what's going on. Besides, I don't think I'm home-oriented—the good-wife-and-wise-mother type. I don't think I would be satisfied just doing housework, cooking, and cleaning. My boyfriend thinks it's reasonable to work for a company now, and after we have children for me to find something part time to fulfill myself.

One last thing I'd like to add. Lots of women complain that they are not treated equally, that they are discriminated against. Do you know the word *amae*? It means being dependent in the way that a baby is dependent on its mother. I feel women are more dependent on men. (Men have *amae* on women but in different ways and not in the working world.) Women don't really feel they have to work to support the family or themselves. They feel they have husbands who will take care of them. Those who do work don't want to be sent to developing countries or somewhere very far away from Japan, and not very many women want to work full-time after they have children. So women in Japan are still dependent. *Amae* is the reason that women in Japan are not independent—not just economically but mentally. They know they definitely have someone who will take care of them.

Because few women have been continuous members of the work force, we are in the position of a baby to its mother, always in a position of dependency. Until that changes, the role of women will never change. We will always be dependent on men, like a baby to its mother.

A long time ago, I read a Chinese proverb that said: "When you see something wrong, turn your gaze inward." Along with medicine, architecture, religion, and Confucianism from China, the Japanese seem to have adopted this philosophy as well. In the end, Suzuki-san blames only herself and other women for their situation. Although she describes a clearly discriminatory employment system, she neither harangues men nor blames society. "What is, is" pervades her voice, and she clearly intends to live her life within the limits of the system—as it is.

Yet what Suzuki-san accepts as fact in the workaday world, such as the standard argument of management that women-quit-so-why-train-them, no longer reflects reality. The great majority of working women who give birth continue to work after birth. In 1965, 49 percent of working women who gave birth did "retire" (an offensive euphemism for being forced out by the company's and society's expectations.) But by 1981, the figure had dropped dramatically to only 22 percent.[2] Yet management's long-standing perception of women's commitment to the company did not change.

Another favorite management shibboleth holds that junior college graduates make better long-term employees. Yes, junior college girls do tend to work a few years longer before they marry, but twice as many university graduates want to work ten years or longer than junior college students do. One in three university graduates wants to work until retirement, compared with one in ten from junior colleges. And if they do interrupt their jobs to raise their children, more than half fully intend to return to work.[3]

Some companies recognize that in women they have

an underutilized source of labor. "Some women are willing to take the same attitude toward life and their jobs as men," admits Hiroshi Takeuchi, chief economist of the Long-Term Credit Bank of Japan. "But," he adds, "the companies cannot distinguish these girls." So, he concludes, "It is more profitable to make them serve tea . . . than to take the trouble to train them."[4]

What really makes junior college and high school grads more attractive to employers is that they are paid less than college graduates, willingly do menial jobs, and, best of all, they leave. (Japan's seniority-driven wage system makes older employees more expensive than raw recruits.) Instead of proudly pointing to four-year female college graduates as an educated resource and a symbol of an advanced economy, the personnel heads of many companies dismiss them with a wave of the hand as "overqualified." Thus, a vast, rich amount of energetic talent in this resource-strapped country is ignored.

非常勤者

Part-Timer

Part-time working women of all educational levels now make up fully 22 percent of the female labor force and that number is expected to increase. Indeed, today the three million part-timers are quadruple the number of twenty years ago.[1] More women spend their free time fattening the family budget than frugally stretching each thousand-yen note. Although many college students do temporary work, the majority of part-timers are housewives working to meet rising educational costs or the monthly housing loan payment during hours that don't interfere with the family. That qualification is key. When unemployed women scan the want ads for jobs in the newspapers, the flexible hours of part-time work look very attractive.

Companies have eagerly welcomed female part-timers in good times (the days of double-digit growth that expanded demand for laborers) and bad times (particularly since the oil shock of 1973) rather than acquire the costly overhead of regular employees. Recognizing a bargain when they see one, department stores, fast-food shops, supermarkets, and offices increasingly count on the low-paid, easily hired-and-fired part-timer as an economic buffer. According to one survey of 485 businesses, 40 percent reported that they use part-timers as their main source of labor. More than half of the part-timers work in small companies (fewer than thirty employees) and another third for medium-size companies (fewer than 500 employees).[2] These employers have discovered a savings gold mine in part-timers who, although defined as those who work less than thirty-five hours a week, often work full-time hours (more than a quarter do). Best of all, part-timers require none of the standard fringe benefits of "full time" employees—paid vacations, social security, housing loans, and family allowances.

Shy but energetic Keiko Ambiru, twenty-nine, works as a part-time clerk at Japan Productivity Center in Tokyo. She realizes that as a woman she is being taken advantage of by being hired as an ill-paid, benefitless part-timer when, indeed, she does full-time work. And she resents being expected to retire and have a baby.

Ambiru-san is a good example of the Japanese women caught in the middle between modern and traditional expectations of women. Like so much of Japan that appears Westernized on the surface (from hamburgers to jeans to skyscrapers), she looks like the average American working woman in her tailored brown tweed suit. And she can spout American slogans about equal pay for equal work, knowing the average Japanese woman is paid only 53 percent the wages made by men.[3] (In the U.S., the comparable figure is 68 percent.)[4]

But scratch the surface of this young woman, and beneath the Western-style business suit beats the heart of a traditional Japanese woman who, as contradictory as it may seem, also sincerely believes women are inferior to men. For many Japanese women, modernization is only skin-deep.

Before marrying and moving to Tokyo, Ambiru-san worked as a secretary near Nagoya in central Japan, where she was born and raised. Due to family financial problems she and her older brother were unable to go to college, even though they both very much wanted to. She began working right after high school.

KEIKO AMBIRU:

At age eighteen, I started work as a secretary at an electric power company. I spent my first three years in the head office in Nagoya and the next three at a branch in my hometown of Ichinomiya, about an hour by train from Nagoya. Since I was a secretary, I sat and waited. I watched the boss. Whenever anyone asked me for a xerox, I made a copy. Our company didn't employ any female college graduates, because we had no positions to utilize their abilities. There was only clerical work. So we used to say, "An electric power company is a man's office." The women are secretaries and tea servers. They copy, type, and occasionally run errands or do accounting.

204

Most companies want to hire young girls as clerks because their wages are low. When a company has employed a girl for a long time, her wages tend to be higher, so the employer would rather hire a girl fresh from school. And he'd prefer to hire a high school instead of a college graduate, because the girls are paid according to age, education, and number of years they've worked.

For the first two years, both male and female high school graduates are paid the same wages. But after three years, men get paid more money. More is expected of them. Women will get married someday, and the employers assume they will leave the company. But men keep on working until they are sixty. Do you know that the wages of a woman in her fifties who hasn't married and has stayed on are the same as the wages of a man in his thirties? I know these things because I worked in the labor department of my electric power company.

I do regret not having gone to college. Last April I started taking a labor law correspondence course from Keio University. The fastest I can complete my major is in four years, and the longest time allowed is ten to twelve years. Every three or four months I get two or three new books. I am tired when I come home from work, but I study anyway. I am also studying for the English language ability qualification exam. Many people take this exam for certification, which helps them get a job or better pay. There are also qualification exams for accounting, auditing, typing, real estate, driving, and even household consulting. I'd like to take the insurance specialist test someday, then I could have small and medium-size companies as clients. I'd teach them how to cope with insurance problems. My husband says I am too interested in too many things. He always tells me to concentrate, to narrow my interests.

I've always liked to try many things. I've taken lessons in making hats, sewing Japanese kimono, flower-arranging, tea ceremony, French conversation, violin playing, and porcelain-making. I wanted to go to college so much that I tried studying many subjects via the radio and TV, such as history, science, English, French, German, Chinese, Spanish—everything. My father used to say, "You do too many things. That's why you can't get married." He'd turn off the TV lesson, and I'd get so angry.

Before I turned twenty-five, my parents had been very anxious about when I was going to get married, because of the importance of *tekireiki*. But after age twenty-five, they didn't care so much, because they wanted me to live with them. I wanted to please them, of course, whatever they wanted. But when I met my future husband at age twenty-seven, I changed my mind; I wanted to marry and live with him.

I stayed home for the first year that I was married, but I didn't like it. I almost got neurotic. I was weeping all the time. I was alone every day, and I wanted to do something. Usually I'd go shopping in department stores or wandering around galleries and museums. Sometimes I'd go to meetings or lectures. There is something to be learned from meetings and lectures, but you have to pay for them. So money is going out of the house rather than coming in.

I wanted to have a goal. When I had worked, the money was always coming in, and I could aim at a certain goal. And when I had reached it, I always felt some spiritual satisfaction. For me, that's the most important reason to work.

I also just wanted to get out of the house. Although we are building a house across the street, right now we live with my husband's mother, and, to tell the truth, my relationship with my mother-in-law is not so good. It's quite different from the true parent-child relationship. Our minds do not communicate so easily. I try to do something nice for her and I irritate her. Let's say I empty the water out and clean the bath. Then she says, "I was going to use that bath water to wash clothes. I needed it for today's laundry." Or let's say I want to buy beer and sushi from my favorite shops. She says, "You should buy beer at this place and sushi at that place"—so I can't even pick out where I want to shop.

When we started planning our new house, she got angry with me. She said, "Mother has been kind enough to rent a part of this house to you. Thinking about building a new house and moving out is rude." His sisters told me the same thing. She did eventually accept the idea, but then she started telling us what to do: the entrance should face this direction for good luck; the roof should have that shape; and we should change the position of the car park. You see, to his mother, my husband is still a child. [He is forty-three.] My mother-in-law thinks she was robbed of her son by me. She told me, "You are a latecomer, so you should walk one step behind me. We are parent and child, and you are not." You see, I am at the bottom of the Ambiru family because I am the newcomer.

When I decided I wanted to work again, my own mother encouraged me and said, "It's a good idea." However, my mother back in Nagoya is not so important now. My mother-in-law has much more to do with me. When I asked her about working, she said, "Be patient and stay home, at least for a year." I didn't want to worry my husband because he has his own job, and when he comes home, he's tired. I was a good wife at the beginning, and I didn't complain. Finally, though, I told him, "I can't endure staying home anymore. I want to work." At first he didn't give me a good answer. Nor did my mother-in-law give me a good answer. Neither person gave me a straight "no" but they weren't so sympathetic either. So I asked them if I could work for just two months. My husband said, "O.K.," and my mother-in-law said, "All right."

But after two months I didn't stop. I kept on working, and I still work at the Japan Productivity Center in the international communications exchange department. I type, proofread, xerox, and I prepare seminars. I work from 9:30 to 5:30 and earn 80,000 yen [$355] a month, i.e., an hourly wage of 650 yen [$2.89], plus a half-price ticket for lunch and a subway pass to and from home.

I am a temporary employee, so my wages are about half that of a full-timer who works the same hours. And I have no paid vacation days and no sick leave. It's terrible, but many Japanese companies have a lot of temporary employees. It's better for them to keep people as part-time workers. That keeps wages down. Many companies employ women for a long time this way.

Since I am a married woman, the company thinks I might quit the company any time to have a baby. It's not fair, really. I can't help that I'm married.

Would I quit if I had a baby? Oh, yes, when I have a child, I'll stop work. And when the child is four or five years old, I'll go back to work, although I know it's not easy for a girl to reenter a company after quitting.

My husband says that a man is more likely to encourage someone else's wife to work. That's because in their heart of hearts, most Japanese men hope their own wives will stay at home.

When my husband's friends ask me, "Why do you work? Why don't you stay home?" I tell them that I want to work. Then they say, "You're a young girl. It can't be helped because you are still young. But if you have a baby, you'd better stay home." And whenever I have to work late, some man always says, "Why don't you go home soon? Girls are not supposed to work so much."

In Japan we have a few special labor laws for women. For instance, women have menstrual leave. I think it lasts about three days a month, but most girls don't take it. One friend of mine does, though. The other girls say that she is brave or that she has a nerve, but she told me that she's only exercising her rights. I never took that kind of a day off, but I have to admit I think it's a good idea. Now a few people say that men need menstrual leave, too. No, I'm not joking. Men have times when they feel uneasy or sick also.

As for hours, women work about the same number as men—about seven. Women can work overtime, as I have, but there is a limit of two hours a day and six hours a week. This is specified in the labor law. When I worked for the labor department, I was always checking to see whether anyone was infringing on the law.

Why are the hours limited? Oh, because of women's physical inferiority. I believe it's a good law. You know, I feel sorry for those women who think they are not inferior. And I am also sorry for able women, but an able woman is the exception. They are just a minority group of women's liberation. Those women's lib people say that they are superior to men. They say women can work like men. I am not a women's libber. We are less strong. We are weaker than men.

A woman who has the same ability as a man may think she can do the same work, but she can't. There are exceptions, but on the whole, women are both physically and mentally inferior to men.

Another woman whose own self-limiting expectations (principally, her belief in women's inferiority) hold her back, Ambiru-san brings up the Labor Standards Laws of 1947 (a hornet's nest of controversy within the recent Equal Employment Opportunity Law debate), which "protect" the delicate sex from long hours, night shifts, and dangerous work. It is believed by many that these laws "overprotect" women right out of advancement to responsible positions, all of which require overtime work, and confirm men's perceptions of them as the weaker sex by requiring the company to offer two to three days of menstrual leave—which, incidentally, most women do not take.

The few women who have become managers get around the overtime and late-night restrictions by simply ignoring them, yet employers still use these provisions as their excuse for not giving women responsible work. Curiously enough, a long list of exceptions has been made to the

209

10:00 P.M. curfew: hostesses, radio and TV announcers, telephone operators, nurses, airline stewardesses, and even sardine and crab canners!

The only two provisions in the Labor Standards Law that all women agree should remain in effect are maternity leave—allowed for six weeks before and six weeks after childbirth—and nursing leave, which provides for two thirty-minute breaks per day for mothers to nurse babies under one year of age. Practically speaking, however, few companies have childcare facilities, and few workers live close enough to exercise this right.

In 1984, the government finally took some action to improve the lot of part-timers by issuing guidelines (which in typical Japanese fashion only urge but do not order) that would not allow part-timers to work longer hours than full-timers and that would give them written contracts, paid vacation for those who worked five-day weeks, and thirty-day notices of dismissal for those who worked more than a year.

The unfortunate part-timers working at home (a separate category of workers called *naishoku*) received no government attention at all. These invisible part-timers, more than a million of them (and 90 percent are housewives), labor under the most blatantly discriminatory conditions of all, doing manual work—embroidering sweaters, assembling radios, addressing envelopes—for which they receive 322 yen ($1.43) an hour or less than two-thirds of what the already underpaid office part-timer receives, according to a Labor Ministry survey. Small and medium-size companies, as with part-timers, account for the lion's share (97 percent) of this piecemeal work.

婦人事務員

OL (Office Lady)

When Japanese think of a working woman, the first image that springs to mind is a young, single, pretty, and uniformed OL, or office lady, the term coined in the early 60s for a member of the legion of female office workers who answer the phone, greet customers, and pour tea for companies both large and small. One major corporation's best-selling *Anthology of Office Lady Common Sense* offers detailed advice on how the model office lady should behave, including seven pages on apologizing and thanking, nine pages on serving green tea, and a whole chapter on bowing.[1] Not exactly the kind of job that most American women would jump at, but in Japan fully one out of three working women—more women than in any other profession—hold this much-sought-after position.

According to one newspaper columnist, "Perhaps nowhere in the world will you find such fortunate and enviable girls."[2] Why is so much attention paid to these much-surveyed, much-written-about, over-glorified assistants? It certainly isn't because of the work they perform, which is by any standard menial. The reason is freedom. Freedom in a land of obligations. The image of the OL's life as carefree has made her the object of envy in the press. On the job, she is free from responsibility and overtime work. After hours, she is free from family responsibilities (until she marries), free to spend her money on herself (for clothes, records, movies, and eating out), free from financial cares (she usually lives with her family), and free to travel (to Hawaii, Guam, America, and Europe)—all freedoms that will be sharply curtailed once she marries.

2 1 1

Even four-year university students want to be OLs, because if a young graduate "makes it" into a large company, she acquires the prestige of that company, no matter what her job. In Japan, status is by association—you are who your company or husband is. Any new OL proudly wears the company uniform that Western women would find offensive to their individuality. That is her badge of belonging. (Men do not wear uniforms, only company pins in their lapels.) The parents are pleased too, because their daughter has landed in the perfect place to find a good husband. She herself likes the good atmosphere (a secure company with a good image) and good pay (starting salaries for both sexes of the same educational level are not so different at first; the gap widens as the years pass). Her average annual income is a respectable 1,950,000 yen ($8,125).[3]

Nevertheless, one farsighted manager in a large company warns: "They are happy now just to be allowed into the big companies, but wait until a few years from now, they'll be frustrated in these boring jobs." The future seems to be arriving already. One survey of OLs revealed that 42 percent wanted to change jobs.[4] An August 1984 survey of 500 young women working at Dai-Ichi Kangyo Bank, Japan's largest bank, revealed that 17 percent were not satisfied with their jobs for the following reasons: no changes in work, too simple work, and incompatibility with the job. (Nevertheless, 49 percent were satisfied with their jobs; and 34 percent were neutral.)

Women are far from shouting "No more tea" in the streets but on the other hand fewer OLs are content to be "office flowers" (*shokuba no hana*), discarded from the company as they age and marry; more of them want to continue working. One survey showed that about 40 percent wanted to work until they retire.[5] These OLs have benefited from a 1966 court ruling (Suzuki v. Sumitomo Cement Co.) against forced early retirement for marriage. Companies cannot legally fire a woman employee for marrying; however, they can (and do) exert a lot of pressure.

The force of financial need prompts some married OLs like Etsuko Takahashi, thirty, to overcome societal pressures and remain on the job. Hardly a women's libber, Takahashi-san, the wife of a sake company clerk and mother of a three-year-old boy, works because she must. Her family needs the second income. Four months pregnant with her next child, softspoken and sweet, but clearly capable, Takahashi-san continues to work at a small miso and soy sauce manufacturing plant in northern Japan.

Each day, Takahashi-san proudly dons her crisp, bright blue uniform (vest, skirt, and jacket over a clean white blouse). "It makes me feel like one of the group," she says, as she heads for the same job she has performed for ten years. She, like 70 percent of female Japanese college graduates, has no hopes for promotion.[6] In Takahashi-san's mind, managing is men's work.

ETSUKO TAKAHASHI:

I was born in Sendai in Showa 29 [1954] on January 30. My father worked for the employment office of the municipal government. Now he's retired. My mother worked on a factory assembly line before she married. After marrying, she got a part-time job to help the family. She worked eight hours a day, just like a regular employee, but received lower pay and fewer benefits. I wanted my mother to quit and stay home to take care of us, but I never told her that because I knew she was just trying to help the family. We were four children: my twin sister and I, a younger brother, and a younger sister. (My twin sister is married and has one boy. She worked as a telephone operator before the baby.) My twin and I always got up as early as my mother and helped with the morning meal before going to school. Then we washed the dishes and cleaned up.

When I was eighteen, I graduated from an all-girl

Catholic high school in Sendai. In my high school we were divided into two groups: those who wanted more education and those who wanted occupational training. I decided to join the second group, because I wanted to help my family financially. Right after graduation, I got a job at this miso and soy sauce factory. Most of my classmates went to work, too. [Out of fifty girls, only ten went on to junior college.] Although some of my classmates married right away, most waited until *tekireiki* at age twenty-five. I lived at home, as did most of my friends. If you stay with your family, you can save money. Having an apartment is costly.

My marriage was a company marriage [*shokuba kekkon*], that is, my husband was also employed by the same company, but he later switched jobs, and now he works as a clerk for a wholesale sake company.

Before we married, my boss had tried to do an *omiai* for me with his brother-in-law. Since my boss's wife knew and liked me, she thought I'd make a good wife for her brother. I already knew another man (who later became my husband), but at that time he had said nothing definite about marriage, so I did the *omiai*.

Once my mother met my boss's brother-in-law, she liked him very much and insisted on my marrying him. I cried a lot, because I wanted to have a love marriage. My parents and grandmother had always said I could marry whomever I wanted. But my mother liked this man, and besides she didn't want to say no to my boss. But I liked the other man at my company better. Finally, my family let me do what I wanted. Most of my friends have love marriages, too. There are very few *omiai*.

The advantage of love marriage is that I knew my husband-to-be for three years before we married. So I already knew his personality, habits, everything, and ever since we married, we've had no problems.

From the time I joined this company at age eighteen until now (I'm thirty) my duties have been the same. I do general office work such as typing, copying, social security, pensions, health insurance. I feed data about monthly salaries into the computer. Since I've been doing the same job for more than ten years now, I know how to do everything. It's automatic.

We had our first child when I was twenty-seven. At that time, I got forty-two days off before the baby was born and forty-two days after the baby was born. Our company regulations are based on the Labor Standards Law, so we have a monthly menstrual leave too. But I don't take it. I don't do heavy work and I don't feel so badly on those days.

Once the baby was born, I could have taken off time to feed the baby, but I didn't take advantage of that rule, because my mother was taking care of him, and our house was a little far away from work by bus. A friend of mine who lives close to the company did take advantage of this time though. She left work during her lunch hour and then she went home one hour early, at four o'clock instead of five o'clock.

I felt no pressure to quit once I married or had children. Today most OLs want to continue working until they have a baby. Then they quit, because they want to take care of the baby by themselves rather than having their parents do so. But I wanted to continue working for economic reasons among others. I like working in this company. My coworkers are good people. (And if I didn't like them, I would quit.) But I have to admit that, if I were rich, I'd stay home.

Fortunately, my mother lives across the street from us. If she didn't, I'd have to leave the company, but if I'd done that, once the baby had grown up and gone to kindergarten, I'd go back to work. I couldn't leave the baby with someone I didn't know well, though. I'd feel unsafe. But if a relative takes care of your baby, that's all right. Those female workers who don't have any relatives nearby and who must work don't have any choice but to leave their children at a daycare center.

My pay is 130,000 yen [$575] a month plus a twice-a-year bonus. When I started this job, I had no vacation. After the first year, I'd earned six days, and every other year I get one additional day up to a maximum of forty days, including those left over from previous years. Now I get ten days off a year, but I have fifteen vacation days coming to me, including those I didn't use last year. After I had my baby I wanted more days off, but now it seems like enough. Before I was married, I took many holidays because I like to travel. I went to Izumo, Kyoto, Hokkaido, and around Yamagata with my girl friends. But now I seldom go on a trip. Only when my three-year-old son is sick or needs a checkup do I take a day off. Last year I took about six out of ten days off. Everyone gets off New Year's [December 31–January 3] and *Obon* [August 15–16], because the company is closed on those days.

A good OL must be loyal to the company. She must be well-rounded so she can handle anything. She should be obedient, energetic, hardworking, cheerful, and last but not least, she should have her own opinion so she can insist on what she thinks. I must express my own idea even if it's not accepted.

Since, like everyone else, I work on Saturdays, I don't have enough time to play with my son. I believe it's very important to have good communication with him. What I really want is to do two jobs well: at home and at the office. I'm trying to do both perfectly. It's hard to say which is more important, my family or the company. My own family is as important as the company. Actually, I guess the family comes first. But, you see, I've been working so long that this company is like a second family to me.

On an average day, I get up at 6:30 A.M. and prepare breakfast and our lunch boxes. Sometimes I make a Western-style breakfast of ham, eggs, toast, and salad. Sometimes I make a Japanese-style breakfast of rice, miso soup, salad, and *natto* [fermented soybeans] or salted fish. We eat at 7:00 A.M., then I clean up and get dressed. My husband reads the newspaper and drinks tea. I'd like him to help with the housework, but he doesn't. That's natural with husbands, isn't it? Next, I take my son across the street to my mother's house, then at 8:05 on the dot, my husband and I get in the car. He drops me off at work ten minutes later, and it takes him five more minutes to get to his company.

The first thing I do when I arrive at 8:15 is to change into my uniform. I like being in the same uniform as the other girls. That way I feel we belong to the same company, the same group.

A few men are already working or reading the newspaper, even though work for them doesn't start until 9:00 A.M. We have seven girls and eighteen men in my section. The OLs are supposed to start cleaning the room from 8:30, but I get there a little early, so I start dusting and wiping off desks as soon as I've changed into my uniform. And I serve tea. My hours are 8:30 to 5:00.

Although my position hasn't changed over the years, my pay gets higher, and I get more responsibility. I could never be a manager, though. And I wouldn't want to. In this company a father and son manage the business.

From 12:00 P.M. to 1:00 P.M. everyone has lunch. Miso soup (one of our products) is served free in the corner of the company gymnasium. Like most employees, I bring a lunch box [obento] with things like rice, a Japanese-style omelet (with egg, salt, and sugar), or fried ground meat and mashed potato and ground fish and vegetable mixed-and-fried. Every day at 12:45, I watch TV before going back to work.

After lunch, it's the same routine until the end of the day. Since my husband finishes work at five, he has to wait outside in the car until I finish around 5:20. We get home at 5:50. (It takes longer than going to work because there's more traffic at that time of day.) Then I pick up the baby. I make dinner, although if I need something, I rush out to the nearby convenience store. (Usually I do all the food shopping for the week on Sunday. Most wives in Japan shop every day.)

We eat at 6:30 P.M. Last night, I made sole meuniere with lemon, fried cabbage with green pepper covered with egg and Japanese mushrooms, plus pickles, a lettuce-tomato-cucumber salad, miso soup, rice, and Japanese tea. For dessert, we like to have an apple or tangerine. (We can't afford cake.) Since it's important for a wife to be able to cook well, I went to cooking school at night before I married. But I'm still not so good at cooking.

After dinner I do the dishes while my husband watches TV. He likes samurai drama, quiz programs, and Western movies. But about this time my son often wants me to read him a book. Since I have to clean up first, my husband sometimes reads to him, even though he'd rather be watching TV.

Around 8:00 P.M. my husband and the baby take their bath together. I get their pajamas ready and prepare the futon for the baby and my husband. When I'm pregnant, my husband helps me make the bed because the futon is heavy. But when I'm not pregnant, he doesn't do anything.

The baby goes to bed around 9:00 P.M. And at 9:30 or 10:00 I take my bath. Then my husband and I have a cup of coffee and talk about our boy. He's our main topic of conversation. Since I do the laundry at this time, usually I talk while I'm hanging out the wash on the balcony or doing the ironing. I go to bed around 11:00 or 12:00 P.M.

On Sundays I like to sleep in until 8:00 A.M. because I'm so tired. After I get up, I clean the house and do laundry before we eat brunch about 10:00 A.M. I do our week's food shopping about 1:00, then we go to my parent's home across the street. My boy is so attached to his grandmother. She has a big house that he loves running around in. While they play, I just rest and drink tea around the *kotatsu* [a foot-warmer with a quilt over it]. My husband—when he has the chance—likes to go out to play pachinko [a pinball game] before we eat dinner with my parents. Since our feelings about family are still strong, we always get together on Sundays—about thirteen of us— my fifty-six-year-old mother, my father, my sister and her husband and her boy, plus my aunt and her husband and their children. My brother (he'll inherit the house some-day) can't come because he lives in Yamagata Prefecture, and my younger sister lives far away, too. All the girls who are there—the sisters and daughters—do the kitchen work so that my mother can rest. Then we go home around seven o'clock.

Although the young, single OL continues to be the stereotype of the Japanese working woman, the married working woman (whether she be an OL, doctor, or super-market cashier) is the reality. Ever since 1977, more mar-ried than single women have worked. Proportions flip-flopped in two decades: in 1960, 55.2 percent of working women were single and 32.7 percent of working women were married; in 1982, 31.5 percent were single and 58.8 percent were married.[7]

Like Etsuko Takahashi, most of them work a double day, first at the office, then at home. Their husbands con-tribute a mere seven minutes of housework (in all fairness, many of the men work overtime), while women do house-work an average of two hours and thirty-six minutes a day.[8]

The bigger obstacle, though, and the number one problem for working mothers, is childcare. Takahashi-san is lucky her mother lives close by. As she readily acknowl-edges, she couldn't work without Grandma taking care of her little boy. Ironically, the traditional, three-generation family system which used to oppress young brides can free the modern working woman from childcare duties.

Not everyone has the "Grandma" option, however. One top newspaper editor had to leave her newborn baby girl at the hospital for a year and visit her for an hour or two each morning before work. She says, "I knew if I quit my job, I could never go back." Japanese have only one shot at the coveted lifetime employment system of a large company. In general, once you get off the treadmill—male or female—you're out. Companies expect a twenty-four-hour commitment, which doesn't leave much room for childbirth or childcare.

In 1950, the Child Welfare Act established the first daycare centers to care for young children when the parents could not, due to work or other reasons. (Parents pay on a sliding scale according to income.) Since then the number of daycare centers has mushroomed from 1,476 to 22,684, to meet the urgent need of the increasing numbers of working mothers. [9]

As noted in a Tokyo government report, working parents still need public nurseries for babies under one year of age, longer daycare hours, and nighttime care. [10] In response to these needs, thousands of unlicensed nurseries, more popularly known as baby hotels, have sprung up to cater to the offspring of female clerks, teachers, nightclub and bar hostesses. Many suffer from insufficient space and unqualified staff. Three infant deaths, primarily from neglect, in a one-month period finally prompted government promises of future regulation. [11]

Japan does have a law that urges all employers to give their pregnant employees a one-year childcare leave (the Working Women's Welfare Law, 1972). The Ministry of Labor offers incentive pay of around $1,500 per mother to the employer, but only a paltry number of companies (14.3 percent) have taken advantage of this law. [12] Hoping to set an example, the government passed the Childcare Leave Act of 1975, which provides one year of leave to new mothers who are teachers, nurses, or other workers in public institutions.

As for the older children of Japanese working mothers, they are called *kagikko* [key children] because, like the latch-key children in the States, they wear a key around their necks to let themselves in their apartment or house after school. A female columnist laments, "Are women going to make their homes into *waribashi* [disposable chopsticks that come with delivered meals] homes?" She sighs, "To me, this would be a very sad loss of balance."[13] The mass media often speculates about the link between working mothers and juvenile delinquency. Curiously, no one ever asks if the high number of absentee fathers might contribute to the children's antisocial behavior.

The government often urges the public to help women "harmonize their work and family lives," yet precious few new daycare centers are being built. Both the public and private sectors would do well to address the working mothers' needs, or else a few more women may elect the alternative taken by an ambitious married chemist in a large electronics company and a talented married editor at a large newspaper. They have decided to have no children.

Blue-Collar Workers

Blue-collar workers in Japan work hard. Their work week is best described by the Japanese song "*Getsu, getsu, ka, sui, moku, kin, kin*" (Monday, Monday, Tuesday,

Wednesday, Thursday, Friday, Friday.) If farmers or fishermen, their lives are governed by the vagaries of nature and the market. They work every day they can, except Saturday, since the market where they sell their produce is closed on Sunday. If factory workers, they do overtime on demand. If they own a mom-and-pop restaurant, they work even on holidays when everyone else is off, because those on vacation like to eat out.

I don't think I knew what hard work was until I heard a fisherman's wife in Tokushima describe her day. She gets up to meet her husband at 2:00 A.M. six mornings a week. Together they sort his catch of prawns, crabs, turbot, sea eel, and such, which takes about an hour. Then he goes home to bed while she drives the fish truck to market. By 10:00 A.M., having squeezed in a breakfast of toast and coffee, all the catch is sold, so she heads home to do the laundry. Around 2:00 P.M., she makes her husband's meals, which he takes on the boat at 3:00. (He gets up at 10:00 or 11:00 A.M.) She and grandma take turns making lunch and dinner. (Grandma, fortunately, does most of the housework.) Although grandma and grandpa eat around 6:30, the fisherman's wife usually eats a late supper around 9:00 P.M. with her two children after they get home from work. (Both high school graduates, her daughter, twenty-one, works as a clerk in a department store; her nineteen-year-old son paints signboards.) After cleaning up, she goes to bed around 10:00 P.M. How can she work a nearly twenty-hour day? "I try to take a nap whenever I can." She shrugs and protests that she's not anything special. "Getting up early is not so tough," she insists. "Many housewives do it."

Although this woman works as hard, if not harder than most women did prewar, since World War II the face of industry has changed rapidly away from primary industry (farming and fishing) to secondary industry (manufacturing). Hot on the heels of this change was the shift to tertiary industry (service) prevalent today.

222

As in many countries, blue-collar workers are the backbone of all three kinds of industry, and in Japan women are the nearly invisible, seldom-recognized part of this backbone. In this section, three female blue-collar workers describe their day-to-day lives and work.

First, from the primary sector, a farmer. To understand the Japanese, one must understand the farmer, many Japanese say. Less than 100 years ago, most of the population still worked the land as they had done for centuries and centuries. Either everyone worked together when planting and harvesting rice and other crops, or everyone starved. Thus, many claim, the importance of the group took hold in Japanese society.

The second blue-collar worker is from the secondary sector—a factory girl. These girls who labored under Dickensian conditons in the silk and cotton sweat shops were key contributors to Japan's rapid prewar industrialization. Factory workers are still numerous today, making up the second largest group of working women.

The third blue-collar worker, at the bottom end of the tertiary sector, is the mom of the mom-and-pop noodle shop. Small restaurants, the size of two American dining rooms (or less) put together, dot the neighborhoods of Japan. They feed the busy workers (both white- and blue-collar) at lunch and dinner time (or anytime); they deliver their food by bicycle to elderly shut-ins and mothers too busy to cook.

FARMER

Beneath the white protective head covering, it's hard to tell whose body is hunched over in the rice paddies, but with increased urbanization and more men working in factories, the Japanese farmer has increasingly become a female farmer. In 1980, more than 60 percent of farmers were women.[1]

Historically, both men and women rose early enough,

223

as the Japanese say, "to step on morning frost" and "return home under the stars." More than any other women in Japan, the farmer's and fisherman's wives come closest to being their husband's true partners. As a sixty-year-old Tokushima mother and farmer told me, "Men and women in the farmhouse are all equal because we work together."

Today the name farmer is synonymous with wealth. Ever since the Occupation forces after World War II gave back the land to the people and ended the deprivations of the tenant farmers, farmers have wealth through ownership of the scarcest, dearest resource in Japan—land. Farmers have three times as much net worth as the average white-collar salaryman.[2] And farmers earn an average of 12.5 percent more than salarymen.[3] Picture a country that has factories, shops, schools, homes, apartment houses, and restaurants standing side by side, a country where rights to sunshine are fiercely contested, then picture a single, free-standing house surrounded by countryside (not a lot, mind you: the average farm is only three acres) but some flat, empty space nonetheless, and then you can understand why people envy the farmers.

Then why do farmers want their daughters to marry salarymen? Why do the sons of farmers have trouble finding wives? The Tokushima farm wife mentioned above married a farmboy soon after the war because she knew that in a farmhouse she'd always have food. But everyone has food these days. Young women avoid marrying farmers because even with increased mechanization and high-yielding seeds and fertilizers, few women want to wear muddy rubber boots, and acquire wrinkled hands and bent-over backs from the long days filled with hard work in the fields. In 1984, some young dairy farmers in Kyushu in the South were so desperate for wives that they took out full-page ads in the northern prefecture of Yamagata—home of the industrious Oshin—inviting young, single women on a get-acquainted tour of their area.

Although Japan would like to increase its self-sufficiency in food, the factories and cities continue to lure farmers away from the land. In the future, it is expected that more and more women will trade in their farm clothes for factory uniforms.

For wizened, toothless Haruko Muramatsu, seventy-six, it was neither the lure of the big city nor cash income but rather an unfortunate stroke that got her out of the fields at age sixty-two, after thirty-eight years of hard work on the family's rice farm in northern Japan. I was introduced to her by her grandson's employer. During the hour-long drive from Sendai, he and I passed rice field after rice field and step-terraces among pine-tree-covered hills. The leveled brown rice shoots were blanketed with snow. Not too far from the main road, we turned into a dirt driveway. There sat an enormous storehouse, higher-than-life-size stone lanterns, and a sprawling, tatami-matted family farmhouse. Although built only a few years ago, it does not have a flush toilet. In an upper corner of the living room sits a Shinto god shelf; in the opposite corner of the room, on the tatami, a TV runs all day.

Before *obaachan* ("Gramma," as she is affectionately called) came into the living room, my businessman friend left and I sat down. There was a lengthy and embarrassed silence. Finally, the eldest of Gramma's two daughters-in-law drew up all her courage to inform me in the sweetest way possible that I was in Gramma's seat at the head of the table.

A few minutes later, carrying a wooden cane and wearing a green sweater and green-white-and-black silk scarf over a dark blue kimono, Gramma entered the room and sat in her seat at the head of the table. With red-chapped cheeks and pepper-colored hair, Gramma is clearly the much-respected and much-loved matriarch in a four-gen-eration family. When her exuberant, pink-cheeked, seven-year-old great-granddaughter came home from school, the little girl paid her respects first to granny, who quietly an-swered "Welcome home" (*O-kaeri-nasai*).

225

Weakened by her stroke and perhaps prematurely aged by her years of back-breaking labor in the fields, Gramma speaks slowly. All the wrinkled lines of her face seem to lead to her lips.

While we talk, her two daughters-in-law take turns bringing food to the *kotatsu* (foot-warmer with a quilt and table over it) around which we all huddle. Big juicy sections of peeled apples, chunks of pineapple, sweet bean-paste cakes, green tea, hot coffee, more cakes, delicious tangerines—the food just kept coming and coming. ("That's the way they show their hospitality on the farm," my businessman friend told me later.)

Gramma remembers the war days when, as opposed to now, food was scarce, and they had to hand over most of the farm's rice to the government. ("We only had enough rice to eat because we hid some," she says.) She talks about women who came to the farm and pleaded with them to trade rice for their kimonos and jewelry. ("It hurt me so because I know how much women love their kimonos.")

Years after the war, daughter-in-law Chieko, now fifty-six, married Gramma's first son. "When I came here as a wife," she says, "Gramma was only forty-seven, yet already bent over from all her hard work in the fields." Indeed, Gramma may be more than the four feet ten inches or so that she looks. It's hard to tell because her back is bent at a forty-five degree angle. "But I didn't mind working hard," pipes up Gramma. "I just hated the way I was treated by my mother-in-law." Like the TV heroine Oshin and like many prewar brides, Gramma found that suffering continual slights and criticism at the hands of her mother-in-law was harder than working in the fields. Gramma had to be prodded to talk about it in detail. "Basically, I'm trying to forget it all," she says.

HARUKO MURAMATSU:

I was born in Meiji 41 [1908] on April sixth in Ko-
gota, about twenty minutes by car from here. I was the
fourth oldest of a family of three boys and four girls. We
had a rice farm, but not as large as this one. My parents
raised silkworms, too. Since silkworms require a moder-
ate temperature, we had to get up twice in the middle of
the night to stoke the fire and feed them.

I went to elementary and junior high school. Then I
went to sewing school, which was very rare. Only two out
of our whole class went on for two years of additional
study. I was twenty-four when I did *omiai*. Well, I don't
know if you can call it *omiai*. After all, *mi* means to see,
and I never did see him. But then again, if it had been a
real look-see, no one would have married me. I saw his
face for the first time on our wedding day. In those days,
a daughter obeyed whatever her father told her to do.

I was this man's fourth bride. The first three had run
away because his mother was so hard on them. The first
ran away after a year, the second after a month, and the
third after six months. My husband's mother didn't like
me, either.

But my husband's father was very kind to me. He
had lived outside Japan for seventeen years in both South
and North America before returning to Japan, so he was
very modernized. We still have the wash basin and agricultural machines he brought back from America. Yes, he
was very kind.

My husband was very good to me, too—a kind and
considerate man. He tried to protect me from his mother.
When I complained, he'd listen and say, "I understand."
And in the morning, he even washed the children's diapers. There was no dividing line in our roles as husband
and wife—even though my mother-in-law said men
shouldn't wash diapers.

Like all the women in those days, I worked in the

227

fields, came home, made dinner, washed, and cleaned. There were many things to do in raising the children. When I was pregnant, I worked in the fields until the day the baby was born. (I gave birth at home to all five of them with the help of a midwife.) Sometimes I brought the baby to the fields in a straw basket.

My husband and I always went to the fields together in the dark around 4:00 or 5:00 A.M. We worked for a while before breakfast in the one and a half hectares [four acres] of vegetable fields and eight hectares [twenty acres] of rice fields with the other employees (three peasants and ten daily workers). We took a break for breakfast, then we went back to work. It was hard work. But I was happy to be outside, working with my husband.

The hardest part of each day came when I returned home around 5:00 P.M. to help my mother-in-law in the kitchen. (It was our custom to feed breakfast, lunch, and dinner to our employees.) I would say, "I'm home," but she never answered. She just looked away.

Of course, every night there was always more work to be done in the house. We made our own miso and soy sauce, and we cleaned. Oh, how we cleaned. I can still remember my mother-in-law waving her duster in the air. We had to wipe and wipe and wipe. Everything had to shine for her. My husband's brother's wife lived in the same house, but since she was the daughter of a relative, my mother-in-law was kind to her.

We ate dinner around six, cleaned up the kitchen, and did all the cutting and chopping necessary for tomorrow's breakfast. We usually spent about an hour cleaning the rooms and the walls. Then there was the washing, mending, and sewing to be done for my own family of five children (three boys and two girls). I used ashes to wash the clothes. She let us have no light, no candles to work by. Being the lowliest member of the family, I was always the last to take my bath. And I had to clean the bathtub afterward. By this time, it was 10:30 or 11:00, and we had to be up again at 3:00 or 3:30 in the morning, so I washed in the dark and got up in the dark. I was so tired that sometimes I fell asleep while weeding in the fields.

Even on snowy days, my mother-in-law opened the sliding wooden door with a bang at 3:00 A.M. so that if the noise didn't wake us up, the snow, which flew in, did. I couldn't sleep, I had to get up—even though it was dark outside. Oh, how she nagged and nagged. But that's past, and I don't want to talk about it anymore.

My daughters-in-law are wonderful people, so I'm happy now. And I'm very well taken care of. We've never had any trouble. [Gramma points to Chieko; the younger daughter-in-law has a two-month-old baby girl in her arms] She does most of the farm work. She's very healthy and works very hard. During the busiest season of planting and harvesting, the men help with machines. Sometimes her husband works at night or during his vacation.

I can't thank my older daughter-in-law enough. I haven't been able to help her for the past fifteen years, but she doesn't complain. So I try not to be hard on her. When my mother-in-law was mean to me, I can remember vowing that I would never ever do the same thing to my daughter-in-law. I would do my best to get along with her. And let her be happy.

Now is the happiest time in my life. I know a very old lady—three years older than I am. She lives alone, and her daughter or son comes to visit her each Sunday. How lucky I am to have all my family. I've always lived with lots of family, so I can't imagine being alone.

Nine of us live here now: my daughter-in-law and my son, their son and his wife and their three children, plus my youngest daughter and me. But the Japanese family has changed. It's very rare to have three generations living together anymore. Many families live separately now— just the husband, wife, and children—because the man has to live near his workplace. We're lucky to be able to afford this big house. And we're lucky to be happy to-

229

gether. I couldn't bear to live without my family.

I'd say I have a very happy life. Eight years ago we built this new house, and since then I've tried to forget the old days and the experiences with my mother-in-law.

Women have changed a lot since I was a girl. Now women are very free. They can do anything they want. For example, they can go to their parents' home anytime they want. And they are more free in their minds. It's become a better world.

Every morning and night I pray to Buddha in front of the family shrine. I am both Buddhist and Shinto.

I get up around 7:00 A.M., and every morning before breakfast I pray to the ancestors, including my husband. (He died thirteen years ago.) That's the beginning of my day. And that's my only work.

Then we eat breakfast and watch the TV program Oshin around 8:00. I have a snack around 10:00 or 10:30. We eat lunch at midday, then I watch more home drama [soap operas]. Around 3:30 to 4:00, I have another snack of tea and rice crackers or homemade cake. (My daughter is very good at making cakes.)

Around 6:30 we eat dinner, then I watch TV. I like the soap operas and the samurai shows. I take my bath around 8:30. I'm the last in the bath because I like the water not-so-hot. (The baby and her grandmother go first.) Then I go to bed at 9:00.

To be together with my family and to eat are my greatest pleasures these days. I like a cup of coffee every day—the American kind. And I like things very sweet. You know, different generations like different foods. I don't like meat much, but the children do. They just love hamburgers. I prefer fish myself. We still eat twice as much fish as meat.

I'm old-fashioned. My son always tells me, "You have nothing to worry about. Just think how to live longer—even for a day or an hour."

230

FACTORY WORKER

Ever since Japan opened its doors to the West in the nineteenth century, Japanese factory women have been the backbone of the country's effort to catch up to the West and overtake it. Between 1894 and 1912, women represented 60 percent of the Japanese industrial labor force.[1] Until 1930, more women than men were wage earners.[2] Working twelve-hour-plus shifts in dark, unheated, dust-filled factories, women reeled the silk and spun the cotton that became Japan's top two sources of foreign exchange. Women powered the industrialization miracle of prewar Japan.[3]

But what a price the Japanese women paid. At first factory work was promoted as patriotic; daughters of former samurai trooped off to the mills, and the government built a model plant in Tomioka in 1873, to which government officials (to set a good example) sent their own girls. But word soon spread about the harsh life there and even worse conditions elsewhere. So factories hired labor recruiters to crisscross the famine-ridden countryside looking for impoverished farmers willing to sell their daughters into service for one to five years. For many families who desperately needed yen to pay their overdue rent and see them through until the next harvest, the choices narrowed to sending their daughters (some as young as eleven or twelve) to the factory or sending them to a brothel. When the girls left the farm, they at least could eat, and some factory promoters even promised bridal training lessons in tea ceremony and flower-arranging. Many gave enticing and much-needed advance payments to the parents. So the girls were sacrificed for their families. They lived in overcrowded, locked dormitories and worked to exhaustion, constantly harangued (and occasionally abused) by their supervisors. Some ran away; others committed suicide. If they got tuberculosis (as one in four did), they were sent home to die.[4]

"We were like galley slaves," remembers an eighty-five-year-old dressmaker who started work in a Tokyo silk mill at age twelve. "When we were pushed too hard, we had to strike, or we'd collapse and die."[5] Although trained to be docile and submissive, as these girls were, they did strike. Japan's first strike occurred on June 12, 1886, at the Amamiya silk mill in Yamanashi Prefecture. Driven to the edge of survival and human dignity, 100 factory girls walked out to protest increased hours and reduced wages. They returned to work four days later when the company agreed not to extend the already fourteen-and-a-half-hour workday by thirty minutes. The company made no concessions about wages. Other strikes occurred, but not much changed. Women still worked long hours for pitifully low pay.[6]

The government finally passed a factory law in 1911 that cut back work time to a maximum of twelve hours a day, prohibited night work between 10:00 P.M. and 4:00 A.M., and required one hour of rest a day and two days off a month. However, the actual impact of this law is questionable: not only was it unimplemented until 1916, but also it applied strictly to companies with more than fifteen employees.[7]

Considering how cruelly exploited women were before the war, small wonder that they eagerly embraced (and now are reluctant to let go of) the Labor Standards Laws of 1947, which prohibited night work and severely restricted overtime.

Factory women continued to add their muscle to the country's postwar rise from the ashes in the 50s, 60s, and 70s. Many photos illustrating Japan's economic miracle show spic-and-span factories filled with row after row of white-smocked women assembling TVs, cameras, and watches. Increasingly replaced in the 80s by "steel-collar workers"—the robots who can work twenty-four-hour days—many factory women have adopted a high-tech look themselves. These days, more and more photos show factory women, clad head-to-foot in space-age, dust-free white suits, peering into high-resolution microscopes at the IC chips that will launch Japan's next economic miracle.

Ironically, girls like high school graduate Hitomi Takahashi, still come from the farm to the factories in the big cities. Apple-cheeked Takahashi-san, twenty, works in a high-tech Toshiba plant that manufactures 64K and 256K RAM chips in Kawasaki, an industrial city outside Tokyo. Although I wanted to see her at work inspecting 256K RAM chips, I never got a look at her space-age suit. Japanese factories usually only allow guests to see last year's state-of-the-art technology, and since she worked in the R&D section, it was strictly off limits. We met instead in a guest room under the watchful eye of a company public relations man. In red sneakers, blue jeans, and a red-checked shirt covered by a white doctor's jacket, this lively girl sat at attention next to her girlfriend, another factory worker. Only once, when the public relations man left the room to make a phone call, did she admit that her job was monotonous, but she and her friend genuinely seemed to enjoy working, anyway. As my interpreter explained later, "It's their one chance to peek into the world. But their first goal is to marry someone."

At this plant, 80 percent of the 2,200 workers are men; only 400 are women. Ten percent are farmers working during their off-season. However, in young Takahashi-san's section of the plant, half of the workers are men and half are women. (All are high school grads.) Men can live in low-cost company housing or rent their own apartments. Girls must live in the company dormitories. That regulation supposedly protects them (and keeps their parents from worrying) and ensures that they arrive at work on time. Living conditions have certainly improved since the old days. Rather than having thirty or forty girls sleeping together in a large room, now three girls share an eighteen-square-meter tatami mat room. (They come from all over Japan: Okinawa, Tohoku, Kyushu, Niigata, Ibaraki, Nagano.) Takahashi-san says she has a big poster of pop

233

singer Momoe Yamaguchi (her hero) on her wall.

The day-shift workers have breakfast at the factory and the swing shift eat dinner there. The girls cook their other meals in the dorm's public kitchen. Takahashi-san likes instant noodles. Everyone has twenty minutes for lunch.

In this factory, only young, single women work shifts. If a married woman returns to work, she is rehired as a clerical worker with more regular hours (8:20 to 5:20). Takahashi-san says, "After raising my children, I want to come back as a clerical worker." Her more traditional friend disagrees. "I want to devote myself to my husband and children. I want him to lead me, and I want to follow him; I want to be his great support." She says, "I have no desire to come back."

With two bonuses a year and twenty hours of overtime a month, Takahashi-san makes about $9,400 a year working Monday through Friday. If she were at a smaller company, she'd probably work Saturdays, too.

HITOMI TAKAHASHI:

I was born in Showa 39 [1964] on January seventeenth in Yuzawa City [Akita Prefecture]. My father grows peaches, apples, pears, rice, and vegetables. My mother helps him during the planting and harvesting season. She works from 6:00 in the morning to 7:00 at night—dawn to dusk—in the fields. She's always very busy. And she helps my father by doing the housekeeping, too.

I told my mother that I'd like to send some of my salary home to her, but she told me save my money for my marriage instead, so that I can help pay for the wedding, furniture, and honeymoon. I really respect her. She works a lot harder than me. She does her job outside and the housekeeping, so she's really doing two jobs. In my job, the same work is repeated, so I gradually become more efficient. Then it's easier. But my mother—she's still working when everyone else is too exhausted to do anything. I wish I could be like her, but I wonder if I can.

My younger brother works for Nissan, and my younger sister is a third year junior high school student.

Before joining this company, I graduated from a girls' high school. About a third of the school's graduates went on to junior college or professional school, and two-thirds started to work like me. From the time I was a little girl, I wanted to work in a factory. I wanted to produce something. So I took the written test for Toshiba and had an interview. You don't need connections to work for this company. It was all my idea to work here. I'd always thought I'd like to work in the suburbs of Tokyo. Since I have an aunt in Kanagawa, my parents let me go, although they still worry about me. But now I'm worried about them, too. In March, my father became seriously ill—something to do with high blood pressure. He fell down, so now my mother has to take care of him. The doctor had told my father to stop drinking, but he didn't. So he ended up in a hospital in Saitama. The company would only let me have three days to visit him. I would have liked to have been with him longer, but we have our vacation twice a year when the plant closes for ten days around New Year's and in the summer.

This week I'm working the day shift from 6:00 A.M. to 2:15 P.M., and next week I work the swing shift from 2:15 P.M. to 10:30 P.M. So this week I'm up at 5:00 A.M. and in bed at 9:30. The dormitory, for 180 girls, is just a ten minute walk from here. [It costs only $7 a month, plus $8.25 for utilities.] It gets kind of noisy with all those girls, but it can be fun, too. I'm the head of the dorm committee, so I have to make sure everyone gets along. I also make plans for our disco party. It doesn't happen very often. Just once a year. That's for girls only. And I also make plans for doll's day [a national holiday also known as Girls' Day] on March 3. There's another party, too, a social dance once a year, for both the boys and girls working here.

235

I've worked at the Tamagawa plant of Toshiba for three years now. Every day I do the same thing. Looking through the microscope, I check the silicon wafers for imperfections. I have three minutes to check one lot of twenty-four wafers. Then I make some notes on my checklist. My first year, it was hard for me to find any tiny dirt or imperfections, but the other older workers could do it, and now I can, too. It's not hard once you get the hang of it.

We get about a week's training, but mostly we learn by doing. We always wear white body suits that cover everything but our faces, and we wear a mask over our mouths and noses. Work does get monotonous. I do the same thing every day, over and over again. Sometimes I wonder why.

I don't think so much about the possibility of promotion, because I don't know how long I will be here. When I was in high school, I wanted to be a leader. But now that I've entered this factory and the working world, I know that in this world, I want to be what I am—a tiny drop of water in the ocean.

In my free time, I do my washing and cleaning. I like to take a nap. Once in a while, I go to Tokyo to see the rock 'n' rollers dancing in Yoyogi Park, but I usually go to Yokohama with my friends to do my shopping because it's closer. Actually I have no desire to go anyplace. I only want to be with my boyfriend. He's nineteen, and he works in the same section as I do. Our section has already had one company marriage, a couple a year younger than I am. My boyfriend and I like to go the park together. We go to movies, and we both like to watch volleyball.

I hope I marry someone who will point out right and wrong to me. An able man, who'll say, "You should do this. You should do that." Sometimes I can be very selfish, even though I don't mean to be. In some cases, I can't control myself. So I want him to tell me what to do.

I want to have a love marriage. A cousin of mine,

thinking I was the right age for marriage, once gave me an *omiai* photo of a boy. I don't know why, but I felt that I never wanted to marry that way.

I know I'll never marry a guy with a lot of money. So I think I'll keep working if I marry someone here. But I'm not sure. It depends on his economic situation. When I have a baby, I'll quit temporarily, but I'd like to come back after the child is one or three years old.

From the time I was a kid, I saw both of my parents working very hard. And that kind of attitude is catching. I have to admit that sometimes I felt sorry for my mother out in the fields. I don't want to make my child sad by leaving it. A small child needs its mother. On the other hand, I do want my child to see me working, too.

My goal is have a family, and I want it to be a good family. I want it to be a family full of laughing voices. And I want to be with my child.

Are men superior to women? Well, men are men and women are women. A man who comes from an upper class has a lot of family responsibility. Now that I'm head of the dormitory committee and responsible for the girls, I have to be a leader. I feel a lot of responsibility. When I was just a member of the dorm, I didn't have the heart to make difficult decisions. But now I have to come to grips with problems. So now I realize that the working man has a lot, a real lot more, responsibility than women. Women are better at small things though. They are more conscious of little things. What I mean is, let's say some people have a conference. The men smoke and leave their dirty ashtrays. It's the ladies who remember to clean up the ashtrays. And I think women are superior in working with these small electronic things.

I don't know if we can say that women have directly contributed to the economic miracle, but they certainly have indirectly. We can see it in each home. The woman supports the family. She takes care of the husband when he comes home. She tries to make a nice atmosphere

2 3 7

around the house, so when her husband comes home all nervous and full of stress, she can help him relax psychologically. And of course she takes care of the children, too. And makes sure the house is clean.

If I were born again, I'd still be a woman, because I want to have children. To me the ideal Japanese woman is the famous singer, Momoe Yamaguchi. She's very popular with all Japanese women because she quit her job to raise her family. She quit two years ago at about age twenty-two and had a baby boy last April, so she's concentrating on her family. I want to be just like her. I want to have a family and devote myself to my husband. Momoe-chan met her husband, Tomokazu Miura, on a movie set. I can't remember the exact name of the film, but it was romantic. Everyone said that once she met Miura-san, she became really beautiful. She started her career young—at age fifteen. And as the years have gone by, she has become more and more beautiful and ladylike. I read that one movie director said that, whenever she appears on screen, her beauty permeates the setting. You know, once a magazine made a list of playboys and playgirls among the actors and actresses. She was very upset about being included, so she filed a lawsuit. She's really devoted to her husband. She watches over him all the time. She really takes care of him. She walks a half step behind him.

Momoe Yamaguchi is the idol of many young Japanese women. When Robert Redford came to Japan in 1984, the newspapers measured his immense popularity in terms of how many photographers and reporters he drew to his press conference, which was almost as many (although not quite) as Momoe-chan did before she retired at age twenty-three to marry her actor-husband. They were known as the *Goruden Combi* (Golden Combination). News of their marriage filled the air in the summer of 1980: TV specials, special issues of magazines, her numerous sayonara concerts. Arts critic Ian Buruma suggests that the media, acting as the "Confucian guardian of the public status quo," adores her because she promotes reassuring traditional values.[8] She willingly sacrificed her highly successful career for her husband, because she wanted to be a good wife and mother. All she wants out of life is to look after her husband and baby boy (little Yutaro, born on April 30, 1984—as Takahashi-san and all other fans know well). Still a much-sought-after *talent-o*, she will no doubt make a comeback someday. As for now, though, her behavior is totally appropriate. Nothing could make her more popular with her fans. She is Takahashi-san's role model.

MOM-AND-POP BUSINESS

Thirty years ago more than 60 percent of employed women toiled for the family (mostly in agriculture); now only 23 percent do.[1] With the growth of supermarkets and department stores, the number of family businesses has been declining. Elderly stationery store owner Ayako Tanabe worries about competition from the big all-purpose supermarket going up across the street, but fewer mom-and-pop store owners feel threatened since the government passed the large-store control law in 1980. Japan still has an amazingly large number of small shops—nearly two million—almost as many as the United States, which has double the population.[2]

Family businesses dominate the Tokyo neighborhood in which we live—some in shops so small they give new meaning to the expression hole-in-the-wall. Husband-and-wife teams run our camera shop, stationery store, dry cleaner, Japanese shoe store, Western shoe store, and electrical appliances outlet (the latter two being barely big enough for two people to turn around in). Two brothers run our sushi shop. We have only two chain stores in the neighborhood—the corner bread shop, which employs local housewives, and the 7–11 convenience store, again owned by a husband-and-wife team, working side-by-side the husband's sister and a few part-timers.

Most of the shops are strictly two-person affairs, though, with the husband and wife taking turns behind the counter. If the store gets crowded, mom or pop just gives a little call, and the other spouse appears from behind the curtain separating the shop and their living quarters. Both sexes are very good at charming the customer, and my two-year-old often comes home with a small toy or a piece of candy.

Although Japanese like to pass on the family business from generation to generation, I haven't seen any sons apprenticing to take over the local stores in our neighborhood. A small jewelry shop owner in Hiroshima sounded sad when he told me that his thirty-three-year-old son hadn't married yet. The young man and his girlfriend broke up a few years ago because she didn't want to work in the family store.

Women do have a respected and important role in running the family businesses. When the tax man comes, aproned and slightly rounded Kazuko Takahashi, thirty-three—and not her husband—opens up the accounting book she keeps for the small eating place she and her husband own in the northern city of Sendai. Always on the run, Takahashi-san works either on the second floor, taking care of her two children (an eight-year-old girl and a two-year-old boy) and her mother-in-law, or on the first floor scurrying around the family's restaurant, serving customers and cleaning up after her husband, the cook. Although equally well-trained in cooking, she's more proud of her husband and his skills ("He's almighty," she says)—especially his *gyoza* (Chinese dumplings filled with finely minced meat, garlic, onion and chopped cabbage), which she insisted I sample. People come from miles around to eat his speciality, she boasts, and rightly so. I ate one and became a believer. Freshly made and hot from the stove top, these delicious morsels are well worth a special trip.

Her husband appreciates her as well, noting how lonely he was the two times she returned to her parents to give birth. "We are like one person," he says. "I miss her anytime we are apart."

Both husband and wife seem to work nonstop, he behind the eight-person counter, and she dashing back and forth from the four tables in the front and two low tables on tatami, in the back, where we sat. About the size of one large American dining room, the restaurant seats almost thirty people.

Although Takahashi-san lets her husband wear the pants in the family, she's clearly the one with the ambition. The city of Sendai (population, 700,000) seems saturated with hundreds of Chinese noodle shops (she prefers to call their place a "Chinese restaurant"), but already Takahashi-san is talking about having "three, four, maybe five restaurants." Her other dream is to have some quiet time alone, maybe once a week in a tranquil place, where she could take tea ceremony lessons.

KAZUKO TAKAHASHI:

I was born in Ishinomaki, one and a half hours from Sendai, in Showa 25 [1950] on May 11. My parents are both retired, but my father, now seventy-two, used to do paint work for a shipbuilding company, and my mother, sixty-four, was a nurse. I have an elder brother and a younger sister, too.

After high school, I went to professional cooking school for a year. About half my high school friends went on to school, and the other half began work, usually as clerks in stores or shops.

Next I spent three years working in a Japanese restaurant, where I met my husband. Ours was a company marriage [shokuba kekkon]. I was twenty-one and he was twenty-four. We have a saying that a three-year difference

241

makes the best couple. It's our custom that the men be
older than the women they marry. That way women can
depend on the men. I think a love marriage is better than
omiai, although I can't really say much about *omiai*, since
I never did it. I never even had a boyfriend before my husband.

My next job was with another Japanese-style restaurant where I worked for six years.

Eight years ago, we opened our own noodle shop in
front of Sendai station. Because we made a lot of money
during the first three years, we built this restaurant in the
suburbs. (That was five years ago.) We live above the shop
on the second floor, as many store owners do. We live
with my husband's mother. I can't say I have a mother-
in-law problem, because I'm so busy that we have very
little time together. So there's no time to quarrel. In a way
we're lucky to have her here. If we didn't have her to look
after my little boy while I work, then I'd have to send him
to a public childcare center near here, and that would cost
about $140 a month.

I've always wanted to work. I am a career woman,
not the type to stay in the house. Even when I get older,
I intend to work—at least until I'm sixty. I get up every
day at 7:00 A.M. to make breakfast for my daughter so she
can get to school on time. I make something like ham and
eggs or miso soup and rice. Then I do the wash and cook
our breakfast while my husband sleeps. While I'm hanging out the wash, I usually watch Oshin. We eat at 9:00,
and we have a big breakfast because by dinner time we're
so tired. Since our breakfast is our dinner, we even eat
things like hamburger or just about anything you can
think of.

The restaurant is open from 11:00 in the morning to
8:00 at night. We call it Imaizumi Hanten. *Hanten* means
restaurant in Chinese. *Imaizumi* is the name of this new
residential part of Sendai. Many farmers used to live here,
so this part of Imaizumi is called Monkure, which means

the gate is dark, because by the time the farmers returned home from the fields at night, the gate was dark.

We have two employees right now at this restaurant. One is my fifteen-year-old niece, a second-year high school student. She's just helping out during her spring vacation. The other is our twenty-year-old nephew who's been here for a year. He wants to have his own shop someday, so he's working here to learn how to cook.

Every morning, after I finish with the breakfast dishes, I come downstairs to help my husband. I cut onions, chop carrots, cabbage, and garlic. He does all the professional work; I just get everything ready. My husband has worked in every kind of restaurant—Western, Japanese, and Chinese—everything except a sushi shop. He's done everything. He's almighty.

Our nephew helps me with sweeping and cleaning, cutting and chopping. And we wash the dishes from the day before. I'm particularly glad to have him during our busiest times—from 11:00 to 2:00 for lunch and 5:00 to 7:00 for dinner. We deliver, too. Anyone who's free will do that.

During the slow times from 3:00 to 5:00, sometimes we can take a break and drink tea or have a snack. I like to watch the TV talk shows, especially the ones that gossip about the stars—you know, who's going to marry who and who's getting a divorce.

After we close at 8:00 P.M., we clean up. We end up sitting down to dinner about 9:00, usually something Japanese like sukiyaki, tofu, or fried fish. We couldn't stand to eat Chinese after serving and tasting it all day. I really don't mind cooking at the end of the day. I never get tired of cooking. I just worry, though, because my husband is so thin. Grandma and the kids have something to eat earlier. I throw together their dinner around 5:00. Only on Tuesday—our day off—can I sit down to eat with the kids, which I love to do. My son isn't in school yet, but my daughter is in second grade. My husband and

I don't ever want our daughter to feel any entrance exam pressure. My husband says, "We just don't want her to be the worst student in the class. It's better to be average." But I want my daughter to be better than average. So we disagree about that.

After dinner, we don't take the bath in any order. Just whoever is free. I usually take my bath around 10:00, after I finish the dinner dishes. My happiest part of the day is the quiet time I spend reading the newspaper in bed until I go to sleep around 11:00. It sounds as if I work really hard? No, I don't think I work that hard. The hardest time of day for me is getting up in the morning. Now that's hard.

And the happiest time of year comes after the *Obon* summer holidays. (We can't take the summer holidays off like everyone else because we're busiest when other people are on vacation. During that time you could say we work too hard. But we have many loans to pay back to the bank.) After the rush, we take four days off ourselves. Last year the whole family went north to Hokkaido. This year we're going to Tokyo Disneyland! My daughter wants to meet Mickey Mouse. We also take three days off around New Year's [December 31, January 1 and 2]. Grandma goes to her daughter's house, and we go to my parents' house, and our employee returns home.

On Tuesdays, our day off, I get up at the same time as my daughter, because she still has school on that day. That's the only day of the week we have breakfast together. After I clean the kitchen, I go shopping in town. I buy clothes or utensils for the shop. Often I just window-shop.

Sometimes we eat out on our day off. When we do, we like to go to Western-style restaurants. The children really like meat, especially steak. (Grandma's not with us. She goes to her younger sister's house on Tuesdays.)

I don't really have a hobby. My husband does: he loves audio equipment and drinking sake with his buddies. I guess you could say my hobby is cooking. And someday when I have time, I'd like to learn tea ceremony. I just know I'd love the calm and serene atmosphere.

I have no time for girlfriends either. When I go to the PTA, I come back as soon as possible. About once a month, mothers have to go to watch the children in class or talk to the teachers. I think women are inferior because they have other business than work to attend to, like childcare. The family comes first, so they can't put all their energy into one thing, the way a man can.

I know many married women would like to go back to work, but they can't find a good job. They tell me I am lucky. The best they can do is find a part-time job in a supermarket or at a restaurant. Maybe they sell cosmetics or life insurance. Both male and female, everyone always asks my husband and me if we get tired of working together, but we never do.

We hope to have a bigger restaurant someday. We already have two, but I want three, four, five, maybe six restaurants. Usually a single couple will run a restaurant like this, but now many big businesses are trying to get in the act by setting up chains. Our other shop is run by my husband's younger sister and her husband. In our place, I keep the shop accounts. I'm too busy to do the household accounting, so my husband takes care of it. I think of the shop money first and the family money second. This shop is run like a company. My husband is the president, and he gets a full salary. I am the vice-president, and I get a half-salary. I'd like to expand into a family restaurant that serves not only Chinese but also Japanese and Western-style meals.

Hardworking Takahashi-san has big dreams. But out of such dreams great empires occasionally come. Back in the seventeenth century, Shuho, the daughter of a merchant married Takatoshi Mitsui, a samurai's son, who although he owned a sake store and pawnshop, preferred to spend his time reading poetry and the classics. So his wife took over the reins of the business, provided a tenacious and frugal example to her four daughters and four sons, and today is widely credited with laying the foundation of the great House of Mitsui, a gigantic business conglomerate. Her youngest son, Hachirobei Takatoshi Mitsui, well-trained by his mother, started a Tokyo dry goods store that became the well-known Mitsukoshi Department Store.[3]

Entertainers

In feudal Tokugawa days, the strict government regulation of classes detailing appropriate dress and size of houses, among other things, also controlled the sex business by establishing and licensing gay quarters in Kyoto and the well-known Yoshiwara district in Edo (Tokyo), and those quarters exist even today. Prostitutes (*yujo*) and geisha were two distinct and separate categories of entertainers; geisha were banned from dispensing sexual favors.[1] Talented in the arts of music and conversation, they may well have been the most educated women in Edo days. They preferred long-term relationships with their customers, in hopes that some wealthy patron might pay the geisha house to free them from their indentured work and perhaps even marry them.

Even today, contrary to their image abroad as erotic and enticing courtesans, most geisha are not prostitutes, although some of their competitors, the hostesses, may disagree. Mistresses, maybe, but not prostitutes—with the possible exception of many so-called geisha at hot springs who cater to transient customers. Many Japanese look on the modern-day geisha as repositories of the arts.

At the other end of the respectability scale, in the notorious Turkish baths (*toruko*), scantily clad girls (*toruko jo*) minister to all bodily needs and desires, despite the Anti-Prostitution Act of 1956. Due to vigorous protest from the Turkish government, the name of these massage parlors will change (the favorite alternative name currently is "Soapland.") But the service they provide, no doubt, will not. Some of the "masseuses" cater to male fantasies by first dressing up as stewardesses or nuns. Some suds themselves up and act like a human washcloth. Others dispense with any fanfare and just get right to the point in little private cubicles.

Somewhere in between these two ends of the spectrum are the strippers, pink salon girls, cabaret girls, and hostesses. The foreign wife living in Japan can at least understand what a stripper is. But what do pink salon girls, cabaret girls, hostesses, and geisha do? All of them are part and parcel of the evening entertainment scene to which wives are cordially not invited. Foreign wives do not appreciate the temptation placed in their husbands' paths or (occasionally, more accurately) laps. But there's no need to worry (too much). Foreign men being entertained by Japanese on expense account—few people could afford this entertainment on their own—tend to meet hostesses and geisha at the upper end of the extensive nightlife world. After several high-priced nights at a *ryotei* (teahouse) or hostess bar, most of these men will concede that all the silly games, inane questions ("Can you use chopsticks? Ooooooh!"), subservient attentiveness, and occasionally boisterous singing is really rather boring. "A night of junior high school naughtiness," is how one American TV correspondent characterized it.

Inflating men's egos is their business. Strippers and pink-salon girls cater to their customers' more lascivious side, cabaret girls talk and dance with the men, hostesses tend just to talk and maybe sing, but there are all kinds of hostesses among the estimated 80,000 in Tokyo alone. The kimonoed hostesses who abound at the numerous early evening receptions (the streets roll up early, even in Tokyo, due to long commutes) and mince around the gathering serving hot hors d'oeuvres and cold drinks tend to be middle-aged and older. They are not sexual bait. Only a few guests of honor or corporate chieftains are assigned their own hostesses, who follow their charges around like little shadows and cater to their needs—from the waist up.

Hostesses in bars have a different reputation and higher price—about $100 per person just to sit down at a club in the Ginza. They cater to a man's psychic and physical needs from the waist up—whether it be for a drink, snack, or ashtray—but a stray hand placed on the girl's thigh (or on his thigh) is also part of the game. Some hostesses, quite frankly, are prostitutes, or as the Japanese more delicately call sex-for-pay, "one-night love." (After a few drinks together with a customer, hostess and customer agree to meet in a hotel for a quickie. That way, if caught in a police raid, the customer could claim that she was his girlfriend, and thus not violate the Anti-Prostitution Law.) More often a hostess has a patron (*danna*) or boyfriend (sometimes more than one), who helps defray the high cost of her stylish wardrobe and, if she's lucky, sets her up in her own condominium. But not before a proper, often lengthy, courtship takes place. Still other hostesses manage to make a fair amount of money (more than the average salaryman) even with a strictly hands-off approach.

When an American professor of management asked me once whether any Japanese women had realized that starting their own small businesses was a way around pouring tea in large corporations, a newspaper photo of a smiling Ginza mama-san behind the wheel of her Benz 540K instantly popped into my mind. The National Tax Administration Agency reports that Japanese spend $14 billion a year on entertainment—more than on defense. So entrepreneurial hostesses often open their own club or bar to get their fair share of the $39 million that nightly flows from company coffers to the bars, clubs, and cabarets around Japan. Although one highly successful Japanese woman who started her own advertising agency directs ambitious young women to what she calls the *kana* industries—*free-lan-sah, de-zai-nah, ko-pee-rai-tah*, (freelancer, designer, copywriter),[2] thus far, sad to say, women have had the most financial success in the lucrative night world known as the water business (*mizu shobai*).

HOSTESS

The precursors to today's hostesses, known as café girls, began to give geisha competition in the 1930s.[1] But today's hostess bars are a relatively new and growing phenomenon, sprouting up in the early 60s as a way to circumvent the 11:00 P.M. curfew on bars, nightclubs, and cabarets.[2] *Snakku Rei* (Rei's Snack Bar), for example, is open from 7:00 P.M. to 2:00 A.M. and run by owner and mama-san Reiko Tsujimura in the southern port city of Kagoshima. Her place seats about twenty people and looks part bachelor pad, part living room, with its velveteen green sofa, brown shag rug, and wooden tables. Nine high stools stand in front of the bar, and soft rock plays in the background. Behind the sofa, a rented fern and umbrella plant flank a fake orchid, which any new hostess invariably tries to water. "The club might be better if bigger," says Tsujimura-san, "but good girls are hard to find."

One hostess wears a demure, buttoned-up white blouse and a flower-patterned skirt. She brings her customer's whiskey bottle, a bucket of ice, tongs, and napkins to the table. She delicately places the ice cubes in his glass, adds whiskey and more ice. If he takes out a cigarette, she eagerly lights it and makes sure that a clean ashtray is handy. They make small talk about the weather, his job, and family.

Tsujimura-san's ample chest rounds out her black silk V-neck dress. She wears black nylons and pumps. She has a gold ring on her left hand and around her neck a gold necklace that spells "R-E-I." Although considerably more independent than the average Japanese woman, she struck me as an earth mother, an appropriate image for a woman whose sole work consists of mothering men.

REIKO TSUJIMURA:

Three hostesses, a bartender, and I work at my snack bar. I've owned this place for five years. It cost me 20 million yen [$85,000] to start the business, because Tenmonkan is the best street and the rent is very expensive. But I should get back my investment in about three more years.

My snack bar has a cover charge of 3,500 yen [$15], including snacks like seaweed, rice crackers, and chocolates. Not nearly as expensive as a snack bar in the Ginza. (About two years ago I went to one with two girls and a boy. The total charge was 16,000 yen [$68] for what would have cost 7,500 yen [$32] in Kagoshima.) My place is also less expensive than the snack bar downstairs, which is bigger and costs 6,000 yen [$25]. They pay their girls more, the space is double, and they use mineral water, but those are small differences. My place is brighter and quieter. At many snack bars, people like to sing, but here we just play music in the background. The men drink and talk with the girls. They don't attack them.

Each man has his own bottle of whiskey, labeled with his family name and company name, which we keep there on the shelf. He pays extra for a beer or other drinks, though. Usually he buys the girl a 500-yen [$2] glass of orange juice or a beer. I'd say half the men pay with their own money, and the other half are on expense account.

We refuse strangers here. Whenever we see new people at the door, we never say "Welcome." An introduction by one of our clients is necessary. Since Kagoshima has the biggest oil storage base in the Orient, many oil tankers come into port, and sometimes a Japanese oil company man will bring the captain, engineer, or first mate here. The oil man brings only high-class people, so there's no trouble and no misunderstandings. The customer doesn't misinterpret friendliness for sex. If a foreigner is not accompanied by a Japanese customer, I refuse him. A foreigner can come without his Japanese friend only if he has the Japanese man's name card. But without a name card, I won't let him in.

Many years ago, my first fiancé died just before our marriage. And my parents had already bought me new kimonos and everything a bride needs. Then I went to Tokyo, where I met a boy from Ishikawa Prefecture. I brought him to Kagoshima, where we were married for seven years. I got into this business because some friends who owned a club asked me to help out. I had some extra time, so I did. While I was working at their drinking place, my husband, who worked in a grocery store, found a girlfriend who was not a working girl. I felt sorry for my husband's girlfriend, so I withdrew and gave him a divorce. Whenever they have a quarrel, my husband comes by here. Sometimes they both come. Everyone comes here.

Hostesses are often divorced women. It's a good job, especially if a woman has children, because she can go to the school for PTA meetings, which she couldn't if she had a job during the day. Besides, pay for a daytime job is only 500 yen [$2] an hour. That's too little to support a mother and child. At a snack bar a woman can make an average of 8,000 yen [$34] an evening or double what she'd make for a daytime job. Have you heard of baby hotels? They take care of young babies for girls who work.

I also have many university students working here as pinch hitters. They can't work regularly, especially around exam time, but I understand. School comes first. Occasionally a young wife works as a hostess, too. Let's say a couple marry young and they want to buy a nice house with a little garden. Both husband and wife have to work. Actually I have two pinch hitters right now. One is a Kagoshima University student, and the other is a department store clerk.

A good hostess has a bright personality. There are three requirements, really: 1) she must always be smiling; 2) she must dress nicely; 3) she must wear good makeup. If a girl fulfills these three conditions, she can be a good hostess.

How are a geisha and a hostess different? Well, we have no geisha in the city of Kagoshima. But many of the hot springs around here do, and if there's a big party in Kagoshima, they'll come from the hot springs into town. A geisha has a Japanese hairdo, wears Japanese dress, and has to be able to do a Japanese dance or play a Japanese instrument like the *shamisen*. At a snack bar, we usually wear Western-style dress, although at some hostess clubs, half of the women wear kimono and the other half wear Western dress. If there's a big party at a hotel that needs girls to serve food and drinks, our hostesses usually wear kimono.

A geisha is a high-class prostitute. Most of them have a patron. Only one-third of them don't go to bed with men. The other two-thirds are prostitutes, of which only 20 percent have a nice, rich patron. Thirty percent have a not-so-rich patron and a lover on the side. Since Japanese kimonos cost more than a thousand dollars each, these women have to sleep with other boys to earn money to buy kimonos. The remaining 50 percent have no patron, so they sleep with anyone at all.

In most cases, there's no sex at all in a snack bar.

Of course, if a girl loves a customer, that's different. But she doesn't do it for money. Yet there are some girls who want to make money through quick love. I have to admit that not all snack bars are the same. The low-class ones may offer sex.

I'd say only 20 percent of snack bar hostesses have a patron. That is, out of ten girls, two will have one fixed patron; four will have a boyfriend, and four will not. You know, a boyfriend can mean someone the girl sleeps with or just a friend with whom she has a meal or goes out driving. It is true that if she gives more service or sleeps with the customer, he'll come more often. And if the customer spends more money, she will have more payback income. As for the remaining four girls without a boyfriend, it's their choice whether to go to bed with the customer or not.

The other places where a man can go to relax are hostess bars, cabarets, or pink salons [*pink-u salon*]. Hostess bars are similar to snack bars—the man has his own bottle, he drinks and talks with the girls—except the cover charge is more, about 10,000 yen [$43]. The most expensive one here is 15,000 yen [$64].

At a cabaret, a live band is a must, and a much larger space is needed for dancing. That kind of place has *osawari* (touching). The man has to pay extra if he wants to sit or dance with a particular girl. The basic cover charge is 7,000 yen [$30].

We say a pink salon has *double-osawari* [double touching]. Again, you pay more for a particular girl. Why, just to walk in costs 22,000 to 23,000 yen [$94–$98]. Then, after making some conversation, the hostess will say, "How about going to another seat, an enclosed seat?" Yes, that means for sex. And sex costs anywhere from 20,000 to 50,000 yen [$85–$213], depending on whether she thinks the guy is rich or not.

In a pink salon, the girls have a minimum guaranteed wage of 8,000 yen [$34] a night (5:00 P.M. to mid-

253

night). Of course if a girl has sex with the customer, she earns more. Plus she gets a kickback on the naming charge (when someone asks for her by name and says he wants to sit with her) and any drinks he buys her. The top salary for a pink salon lady is 1 million yen [$4,255] a month. The average is 500,000 yen [$2,128], which divided by twenty-five work days means 20,000 yen [$85] a night. (At a snack bar, in general, the average nightly pay is 8,000 yen [$34]. The highest is 14,000 to 15,000 yen [$60–64].)

Some girls who work in a pink salon save their money for two or three years in order to start their own snack bar or other business. Being a pink-u salon lady is a way to get quick money. I myself wouldn't want to own such a business. The owners usually come from other prefectures. You see, sometimes there are police raids, and this gets in the newspapers, which all the Kagoshima people see. And what if the owner has many relatives and friends here? It's a dirty business, so it's done by outsiders.

Although I have a grudging respect for these hardworking hostesses (inflating men's egos does take energy), and as much as I liked Tsujimura-san (a sharp businesswoman), I still wouldn't want my husband to frequent these hostess bars.

Japanese wives don't seem to have much choice, though. The double standard persists. For women, the societally sanctioned response is to endure. But that doesn't mean that they like it. "Of course Japanese wives mind," a female journalist told me, "but they'd rather their husbands have sex with a professional girl instead of getting emotionally involved with a secretary at work. As long as it doesn't challenge the family, that's what counts." She adds, "Lots of people say that the divorce rate is lower than in the U.S. because Japanese wives allow their men to indulge in physical satisfaction."

Japanese men insist that they go out to these bars for

"business reasons": to entertain a client, to talk over problems and ideas with colleagues, to build relationships. As one explained, "A Japanese man is quite closed during the day, but at night he is quite open when he's having a drink and facing a nice-looking woman."

"The hostesses do make stupid conversation," acknowledges a frank, fortyish Japanese banker, known as a rakish man-about-town. "They ask me my favorite sports and tell me how handsome I am."

"But do you enjoy it?" I asked.

"Of course." He grinned. "Everybody does."

This man entertains about five nights a week, Monday through Friday, and includes among his favorite photos a blown-up picture of him (in the foreground) in a bar where an X-rated movie of a bare-breasted girl dressed in flimsy lingerie was playing in the background. He was delighted to explain the fine points of entertaining to me as we bar-hopped around the Ginza. He knew how to acquire blondes in New York and Scandanavians in London. ("For traveling Japanese, this is the experience of a lifetime," he says.)

"But what about the hostesses back home in Japan?" I asked.

"About 20 percent of men get what they want," he says. "The other 80 percent go straight home."

I was beginning to realize that the businessman's late-night world of sex was more fantasy or bluff than follow-through. Actually according to a *Kyodo News* sex survey, only one in five men had extramarital sex in the last year. (A miniscule 2.5 percent of wives were unfaithful.) Some men might like to participate in extracurricular nighttime revelry but physically don't have the energy for a long commute, a long day at work, and a night of whoopee. Most don't have an expense account or sufficient extra income, considering education costs and housing loans, except perhaps for a beer with the boys before heading home. Only wealthy entrepreneurs, company presidents, politicians, doctors, and dentists seem to be able to afford mistresses. Others just dream about it. Many more would just rather be home with their kids.

GEISHA

Geisha have been around for centuries. The first geisha appeared at parties in the 1600s, and surprisingly they were men. Beating drums and making jokes, they entertained the guests. Nevertheless, from 1780 on, female geisha out-numbered men and inspired countless artists, writers, and musicians with their exotic lives in the flower and willow world.[1]

On the west coast of Japan, graceful Michiko Uchiki, fifty, better known simply as Michiyakko, has a reputation as the best performer of Japanese dancing in the area. As was common for the well-educated young ladies of her day, this elegant woman with swept-up hair graduated from elementary school and *jogakko* [a five-year combination junior high and high school]. She lives in the traditional town of Kanazawa, where geisha are called *geiko*. Although these entertainers once flourished in all four sections of Kanazawa (north, south, east, west), now only three districts and 100 geisha remain—one third their number forty years ago. All around Japan, the number of geisha has rapidly dwindled—from a prewar high of 80,000 to 17,000 today.[2]

"I am a third-generation *geiko*," she says proudly. Both her grandmother and her mother were *geiko*. When Michiyakko was a baby, the law required that an only daughter of the geisha house could not marry without leaving someone behind to carry on her family name. Soon after Michiyakko was born, her mother married her father, and the little girl was left with her grandmother. Thus she grew up in a geisha house and began training in the traditional arts at the age of six. Her grandmother's advice was: "Keep your pride high and your head low."

Feminine is the atmosphere geisha cultivate, and feminine is the word for Michiyakko. Wrapped in a kimono that doubtless cost thousands of dollars, with her legs gracefully tucked under the layers of silk, this wrinkle-free older woman has an air of confidence, an aura of contentment. My image of geisha as husband-stealers substantially softened; this woman is clearly an artist, adept at both dancing and conversation. Lack of understanding of the Japanese language means that the geisha's verbal wit and charm are wasted on Western men (hence their one-sided image of geisha). Lack of appreciation for the traditional arts by younger Japanese men, and smaller expense accounts than those of their seniors—an evening of geisha entertainment can cost several hundred dollars per man— means that the true geisha's audience has been reduced to men in their forties and older. The geisha are a dying breed. Michiyakko is an elegant anachronism.

MICHIKO UCHIKI:

We are working women. Each woman is master of herself. You have to be strong. You can't be your own master if you are weak. There are some weak men who come here, and we have to be protective toward them. This is the world where men show their other side, their back side. We see the side not usually shown. I'm sure all men want to show the side that is liked by *geiko*. We like men who have a warm heart and are kind, but not those who spend money to show off or those who are stingy.

In my grandmother's day, we used to entertain guests in this house. We had several registered *geiko* here. These days, most of our entertaining is done at a certain kind of restaurant called *ryotei*. I also do formal dancing at a hotel. After that I may drop into houses near here to do informal dances. The atmosphere is always intimate and fun.

I don't think wives are jealous of us. But there are those people who misunderstand us and don't know the reality of our art. They think we are people who just want to seduce men. I'm glad that in the last five or six years more women are coming to our place. More and more husbands are bringing their wives to see our art.

I am a third-generation *geiko.* I haven't ever married. Will it sound strange to you if I tell you I have a child? She is twenty-five and not training to be a *geiko,* because she would like to marry. Although a family like this needs a successor, I won't object to her marrying. Times have changed. There was a time when I wanted to marry myself. But to be a real *geiko,* you can't marry. The working hours are too late. You are on a different schedule than a salaryman working in a large company. I know two or three *geiko* who are married, but their husbands are sushi shop owners or restaurant workers.

When I was a girl, a *geiko* started to learn the traditional arts on the sixth month, the sixth day at the age of six. (Age five by the way we count now.) Three sixes. That's still considered the best day to start training. There is no end to the training. You never quite learn everything. Even now I go to my dancing teacher's place at least once a month. And my teacher has her own teacher. There are always new dances to be learned—some three hours long, others last just three minutes. I watch other people and learn from them, too.

When I was little, I also learned how to bow and how to open *shoji* [sliding screen door]. I took lessons in Japanese dancing, tea ceremony, *shamisen* [a stringed instrument], and chanting, because sometimes you have to chant while dancing. My grandmother said, "If you learn too many arts, you won't be the best." She advised me to pick one and be the very best. So I did. (I've never wanted to be a loser.) I picked dancing. When I am dancing, I forget everything—whether I am very sad or very happy. I don't have to get drunk to forget my sorrow. And when I'm happy, dancing doubles my happiness.

At a certain stage in your training, you have to take a test. About ten teachers who have special certificates

2 5 8

give the test. If you pass this exam, you are given a name and make your debut.

I made my debut in Showa 23 [1948]. I was sixteen by the new way of counting (seventeen by the old system). That year a new labor law was going into effect that a girl or boy younger than eighteen could not work, so they hurried my debut. It was a hot summer. I did my hair myself, and I can remember the sweat dripping down my neck. There was no air conditioning.

Each new *geiko* has to give small presents to all the other geisha houses and to Japanese restaurants. I visited each house, gave my small present and said, *"Yoroshiku,"* which means "Please treat me well, as you see fit. Remember me." The kind of present varies according to the status of the *geiko.* If you are a real daughter of the house, you rank very high and must give very good presents. If you are just hired by a house, the presents don't have to be so valuable. I gave a set of Japanese sake cups made by a famous Japanese potter, Ohi-san. The youngest and newest *geiko* are called *shinbana,* meaning new flower. On the day of her debut, a new *geiko* becomes *shinbana* and keeps that name for about a year. I can remember that two of us made our debuts the same day. On our first night of entertaining, the other girl said, "Oh, I'm not tense," but when she poured the sake, her hand shook. She held her head so low that her chin touched her kimono and left white powder. Since I was brought up in such a place, I'd gotten used to carrying dishes to the table. When I served sake, I did it naturally. I just sat up straight. Since I could behave so naturally, I felt, "Oh, I am too bold."

A geisha's job is to entertain guests and show them her arts. The *"gei"* [pronounced "gay"] in geisha or *geiko* means art, you know. A geisha who does not have an art is not a geisha. Sometimes you hear stories of geisha girls who go to bed with their customers. But in my opinion they are not geisha. They are just selling their bodies.

If you want to be a first-rate *geiko,* you must behave all the time. If you have a patron, you must be faithful to him. If you have love affairs, that's not behaving, and that doesn't make for a first-rate *geiko.* You know, it's such a small society, everyone knows what you do.

There are some geisha who just clap their hands in time to the Japanese stringed instruments. But the customers look down on a girl who can only clap. They call those girls a name that means "Shinto priests," because the priests clap their hands to summon the gods.

Human relations are very important in a *geiko*'s world. These concerns are very complicated. They involve things like younger people paying respect to their elders. We try to bring up the younger ones that way. Let's say two *geiko* are entertaining and a bottle becomes empty. If the elder one goes to get more sake while the younger one remains to chat, it throws a wet blanket over the atmosphere. Even customers say it spoils the atmosphere. They call the elder *geiko* "elder sister." Whereas if the bottle is empty and the younger one says, "I'll go get it," that warms the customers' hearts. Without concern for human relations, the *geiko* will lose their charm, our customers say.

We also play games with the customer. Let's say we have two people standing face to face with a drum between them. First, they play *janken pon* [scissors, rock, paper]. The winner beats the drum, and the loser must turn around. They do this more and more quickly. Then if you lose three times in a row, another person takes your place.

A good geisha can't be sad. She must be gay and bright. She must be a person who likes learning the arts. A good geisha has to be able to drink in order to create a good atmosphere, and she must be able to stay up late. She can't become sleepy because there is no time limit. If the customers want to stay until 2:00 A.M., we can't tell them to go home.

We never accept strangers in our house. Even if they are millionaires, they must be introduced by other clients. We are never paid cash. We always send the bill later. Of course, the money we are paid and the money we can keep are different because the house gets a share. Many factors are involved in the cost really, such as how beautiful the kimonos are.

There are three geisha districts in the town of Kanazawa now. Mine, *Higashi* [east] is the most prestigious. Until recently a young woman had to take certain tests proving her artistic ability in dancing or on instruments. In some other districts though, if you were a hostess yesterday and want to be a geisha today, it's okay. Our district has about thirty-five or thirty-six *geiko,* out of a little more than a hundred total in Kanazawa.

In the old days the emphasis was on creating a nice, warm atmosphere through art, not just service. It's sad to say but these days the emphasis is on service. The customer seems to be more pleased with a beautiful, young girl than one with an art. Not many young girls these days want to be *geiko.* They can make money so easily at a bar or cabaret, while *geiko* have to spend so much time and money learning to play *shamisen* or whatever.

I'd say I've been very happy in my life. When I was young and wanted to marry, I thought, "Well in my next life, I'll marry." Now if I were reborn again tomorrow, I'd want to be a *geiko.*

To me, my art is my life. My happiest moments are when I am performing my best and dancing very well. To do my best, I need the cooperation of the *geiko* who sing and play *shamisen.* When our guests appreciate my dancing, I am almost in tears, I am so happy.

高年管理職

Older White-
Collar Workers

Twenty or thirty years ago, most young Japanese women followed the good-wife-wise-mother route prescribed by society. Now that they are in their forties and fifties, and their children are either grown-up or in school, these mothers are free to do as they please for most of the day. But for many it's an unexpected freedom that they don't know how to handle. One Sapporo housewife, at her twenty-fifth college reunion, compared notes with her classmates on their children and the empty nest. The big question on everyone's mind was "What's next?" After two decades or more of doing everything that everyone expected of them, suddenly society has no more guidelines for these devoted housewives to follow. Instead of having a few restful years before they die, as in prewar days, Japanese middle-aged women are faced with a yawning chasm of a second forty years that they don't know how to fill. After years at home diapering babies and washing dishes, they lack both self-confidence and marketable skills.

When a middle-aged woman scans the age-specific sex-specific ads of the help-wanted section of the newspaper in Japan, she is often disappointed. Regarded as unskilled labor, her choices are very limited. The ads for clerks, cashiers or secretaries in small companies generally request girls under thirty. Mothers pay a big penalty for interrupting their jobs to take care of their children and husbands. With few exceptions, they can never reenter a large company.

262

So middle age is a time of crisis for many a Japanese woman. Lacking *ikigai* [a sense of purpose], she begins the search for something else, something to give meaning to her life. Fearful of rejection, depressed and bored, some women turn to drinking. Most Japanese women who do drink start after age thirty-five. Experts note with alarm that the number of female alcoholics has been increasing in the forty- to fifty-nine-year-old age group. Drug use has increased among housewives, too. And divorce among middle-aged housewives is also growing.

Many middle-aged women opt for the safe alternatives of volunteer work with the elderly or handicapped or they attend culture *(bunka)* centers sponsored by newspapers *(Asahi, Mainichi)*, TV *(NHK)*, or department stores *(Sogo, Mitsukoshi, Tokyu)*. These big corporations offer courses ranging from the traditional (cooking, sewing, kimono dressing) to the more up-to-date (jazz dancing, English, microcomputers). "I fill my free time with lessons," says one *bunka* center maven. "Japanese women take many courses to find something worthwhile, something worth living for. Being busy is a national virtue."

Despite the low level of jobs available and the worry about neglecting family duties, every year more and more middle-aged women find *ikigai* in work. Today, they are the fastest growing group in the labor force.[1] More married women thirty-five and older work than young single women do.[2] Six out of ten forty-year-olds already hold jobs, an unthinkable number not so long ago, and a figure that would probably surprise the average Japanese on the street.[3]

Why this flood back into the job market? Money is one reason, whether for education, housing, savings for old age, or just plain day-to-day purchasing power. But some husbands resist the idea of their wives going back to work, taking it as an insult to their own earning ability. Their wives never make it out of the house. Some of those husbands do relent, on the condition that no one knows that the wife works. Each morning more than one Japanese wife dresses as if she's on her way to the *bunka* center or going shopping, when in reality she's off to work. (Many of these women willingly participate in this subterfuge fearing that their neighbors or children's teachers might think less of them for working.)

An increasing number of women rejoin the work force for psychological reasons (other than *ikigai*) as well. They complain "there's no excitement at home" and that they no longer want to be known just as Tanaka-san's wife or Hiro-kun's mother. They want to broaden their horizons and meet new people. As one housewife of thirteen years, who recently started work in an ad agency, graphically noted, "I just got tired of sitting at home in my own pickle juice."

RETURNING TO WORK

Teiko Sato, forty-eight, the mother of two and a housewife for twenty years, was asked to return to her old bank, where she had worked in her twenties. That was unusual. Most women have to gather up every ounce of their courage to answer a newspaper ad or to apply at an employment agency or company office.

Although on the job more than a year already, Sato-san still sounds a bit giddy about her triumphal return to the workplace. "All the neighbors envy me," she says. Sato-san is very proud of her bank and work (selling time deposits), and of her violet designer uniform (jacket, vest, and skirt) by top designer Nobuo Nakamura, which tells the world she is part of the bank she's so pleased and grateful to work for.

She wears very little makeup, only neatly placed lipstick. We talked in a coffee shop near her bank. I brought a small gift of chocolates for her, and she brought a small gift for me, a kewpie doll, which the bank gives away.

TEIKO SATO:

My husband is a research scientist at Tohoku University, the section chief of the low-temperature lab. I graduated from mission junior high school and public high school, the best woman's high school in Sendai. My father is a Shinto priest at Aoba Shrine, which was founded in memory of the feudal lord, Masamune Date.

I was born in Sendai on January 30, 1936. I started work as a clerk at the Industrial Bank of Japan (IBJ) at age eighteen. My bank has branches in New York, Atlanta, Los Angeles, Toronto, all over the world. I worked there for eight years and eight months before quitting at age twenty-seven, to take care of my mother-in-law, who had a stroke. Half of her body was paralyzed. Since my husband (whom I married at age twenty-four) was *chonan* [the eldest son] and we lived with his parents, I had to quit my job to take care of her. She couldn't even go to the toilet by herself. So I stayed home with her for four years and one month before she died. During that time I had two children—a son, now nineteen, and a daughter, now sixteen.

Then in February of last year I got back a job at my bank selling *saiken* (one- and five-year bonds). After twenty years' absence, I was fortunate to be asked back. My former employer telephoned me and said that a certain fifty-five-year-old woman was going to retire and would I like to take her place. He said, "You know a lot about the banking business already." But I was undecided because I had been a housewife for a long time. And even though my mother-in-law had passed away, I still had my eighty-five-year-old father-in-law to watch over. He's in the hospital now, but he was really fine then. During my many years at home, I had taken tea ceremony, flower-arranging, and how-to-wear-kimono classes. I'd joined a singing chorus and taken English lessons. I had many hobbies, yet deep in my heart I thought this is not what I want out of life. I didn't think of working, because my father-in-law is old, but when I received the phone call from my old bank, I thought, "Ahh, this is a good opportunity."

Since my father-in-law had been an elementary school principal and his wife a teacher, he approved of women working. After all, his wife did. And all my family agreed. Well, actually the children and my husband both said, "If it's O.K. with grandpa, it's O.K. with us." And they added, "You know if you stay home for a long time, your brain will get rusty." I'll only be able to work until age fifty-five, then I'll have to retire on the first of my birth month, as did the woman I replaced. Recently the bank decided to extend the retirement age to sixty, but in those last few years the employee receives only 60 to 70 percent of his previous income. So it's more like doing the work for your own pleasure, even though the amount of work is the same.

I'm very happy to be working after a twenty-year absence. I'm the oldest of the three women salespeople. They are ex-bank employees, too, who've come back after a ten- or fifteen-year absence. We also have four salesmen but they are retired workers who came from other companies.

I get my customers by calling on the phone or sending a letter to people who write to us for information. Sometimes I go to their house or company to give them the information. But I never go door-to-door to strangers' houses.

I work from 10:00 A.M. to 4:00 P.M., have both Saturday and Sunday off, plus I receive many benefits. We get lots of vacation—twelve days off the first year and thirteen days off the second. Of course we get a bonus twice a year, too. Our busiest seasons are June and December, when I often have to work until 6:00 or 7:00 P.M., but I don't mind, because my salary is better than it would be at other banks.

Many of my friends envy me and say I have a very

good job. I think it's an important one. I'm dealing with a lot of money, so I can't make the tiniest of mistakes. I'm happy that these people trust me with their precious money. And it's a lot of money.

Last year when my old boss called me, I thought it was too important a job to take and said I couldn't. But he called back another day when I wasn't home. My father-in-law took the call. And when I came back, he said, "You know, it's very kind of them to ask you back to work. A woman your age never gets such an important job. The best someone your age can do is to get a part-time job as a cashier at a supermarket or as a cleaning lady. So you'd better take it."

He's right, you know. I have some friends who sell Tupperware at house parties. Another friend returned to her old bank but she's only counting money. She doesn't even do any accounting work. I think that would be very tiresome. I know other women my age who are selling fish or arranging merchandise in their local supermarkets. Some of them work at home, making leather crafts or sewing embroidery on sweaters.

I have one friend who tutors math at home. She has a little *juku* at her house. A year before I returned to the bank I helped her by marking papers and telling the children the answers. I worked as her assistant from 2:00 to 6:00 in the afternoon three times a week for 500 yen [$2.22] an hour.

I don't want to say exactly how much I make—what will my colleagues think, you know—but my base salary is 90,000 yen [$400] a month plus commissions. And I'm far happier doing bank business than staying at home.

Now I am so trusted. Can you imagine, these people trust me with all of their money! Many of my friends telephone me to say, "I haven't seen you in a long time." Then they come in and buy *saiken*. That's helped me a lot because I get 20 yen [8 cents] for each 10,000 yen [$44] that I sell. (The one-year notes pay 6.382 percent interest, and the five-year ones pay 8.624 percent). Some intend to live on the interest of the money, and they ask me which is better, one- or five-year notes. Oh, I'm asked many things, and I advise them, including how to pay the lowest tax, of course. Many of my relatives, including my own mother and father, trust me! So I think last year when I started my job was a very special year for me.

Why am I surprised that they trust me? Oh, that's an American question. You have to understand that it's different for women here. When my cousin Kadowaki-san asked me if I would be interviewed, I thought back over my life. My first thoughts were that I had been buried in home life for twenty years. But those years weren't useless. On the contrary, all the lessons I learned help me a lot. (My, how I've changed since the days before I married!) Now I can listen to other people's stories with a lot of sympathy. I myself had a hard time taking care of my mother-in-law. I raised my children. I made friends with other housewives. All these experiences help me understand others. I'm definitely more thoughtful now than I was when I was younger. All of my old experiences are helpful when talking to my customers because they not only consult me about money, they complain about their frustrations with their mothers-in-law or about their problems with the children's education. I certainly know how they feel about the exams. I'm so nervous today because my son took the entrance exam to Tohoku University—for the second time—and we get the results tomorrow, so I listen well to these people since I've had similar experiences. I can sympathize with their troubles. And they in turn identify with me, because they see me as a housewife—the same kind of person as they are. Often those who complain and get my sympathy remember me. Oh, it may be a month or six months or even a year later, but all of a sudden they telephone me and ask me to come get their money.

So I go see them, the way I go to see those who want

me to pick up their monthly deposits, and we chat over tea. We just talk about the weather. They say, "Today is hot or cold," and I say, "Ah yes, isn't it?" I like to stress that I'm not just collecting their money. To those women who are taking care of their elderly or ailing parents, I tell them how to cure a stiff back or what to do about knee troubles. From my long experience, I can advise them about the best way to do diapers for elderly people. Or we talk about mother-in-law or daughter-in-law troubles. Whatever the customer wants to talk about, I often have similar experiences.

Actually, I do most of my business by phone. When I send letters, I write, "I was introduced to you by Mr. and Mrs. So-and-So, who is the friend or son of So-and-So. I'm glad to know you. Please come visit me at the bank, and I'm looking forward to hearing from you."

I don't make that much money, but half of it I save and deposit in my bank—in *saiken,* of course—and the other half I use for the children's allowance, birthday presents, or a family trip. Maybe the children want money to buy records, or on my husband's birthday, I get him a belt or a bottle of whiskey—he likes that—or a sweater, not very expensive things. Since my father-in-law was well last year, we went to a hot spring in the Tohoku area. We aren't taking a trip this year because my father-in-law is hospitalized with lung trouble. And the neighbors would say we were thoughtless if we went on a trip and left the old man in the hospital.

I believe more companies should employ women between the ages of thirty-five and fifty. These women have a lot of experience. Yet there are not many jobs for married women, particularly women over forty. When we moved to the newly developed area where we built our own house, I noticed that many, many housewives were doing piecework in their homes. Since their children are small and they live far from the city center, they can't go out to work, but they must have money to pay back the huge loan on their new houses. When I visited the home of one woman, I saw quite a few sweaters on her desk, and I complimented her saying, "You have lots of nice sweaters," but she answered, "They're not mine." I also saw many papers spread around and those were the accounting work she does for a credit card company. I was really surprised. My guess is that she makes 50,000 to 60,000 yen [$222 to $266] a month maximum.

And I know an old woman more than fifty years old who washes dishes in a restaurant. At my own bank, the cleaning woman is about fifty years old, too. I regret to say that in Japan many companies don't want to recognize the abilities women have. They decide that women from ages thirty-five to forty can do one job, and that women from forty to forty-five can do another. They decide by age.

When I read the newspaper recently, I saw an advertisement: Wanted, woman who can drive a car, real estate business, taking customers to houses for sale. Another ad wanted women to deliver ready-to-eat lunches and dinners. Such jobs are open to women. Not very good jobs, are they? A person without a brain could do them, although I have to admit I can't drive, so I couldn't do them. I was very lucky to get this job in the bank, wasn't I?

When I was growing up, I was the fourth child of five brothers and two sisters. I saw how busy my mother was. Most of the time my father was away. He stayed on Kinkazan Island, where nobody lives except Shinto priests. Once a month he came home with his many, many white robes, which my mother had to handwash. All in all, we had nine people in the family. That's why my mother was so busy. But I only have two children. It's much easier than in my mother's day.

My sixteen-year-old daughter has her own definite ideas about her future. She wants to enter the agricultural division of Tohoku University to become a researcher and find a way to raise enough food and enough plants inside Japan so that the country can be self-sufficient. Japan depends too much on imported foods for its people.

But in Japan career women tend to be single. And I'm against her (or my son) remaining single. I want them to marry and have a broad view of life. I told my daughter, "You can keep working as long as you want, on condition that you get married." And she said, "O.K., Mom." I don't mind what age she marries—no *tekireiki*—as long as she marries. That's my only condition. I do want her to be well-mannered and attractive to others, too. But I'll let her choose her own life.

This past year my son went to *yobiko* (full-time prep school) because he was *ichiro* (a first-year *ronin*). I'm not a *kyoiku mama*. I let my children study voluntarily. When my daughter has finals, she usually gets up at 3:30 A.M. to study until 6:30 A.M. I don't force her.

At first my own parents were surprised when they heard about my chance to return to the bank, then they were very glad for me. Still, they worried, "What will you do when your father-in-law gets older? What if he gets sick?"

What mattered more, though, was the opinion of everyone living in our house. My own parents' opinion doesn't matter so much now. Since I got married, I think more about the well-being of my father-in-law than of my own parents. That's the Japanese way of thinking. I have to. Fortunately my parents live in Sendai, so I can visit them during the New Year's and summer's holidays, ancestors' memorial day, my parents' birthday, and Christmas. But, even if they fell sick, I couldn't take care of them full-time. Maybe for a few days at most. That's the responsibility of the *chonan* and his wife. That's the Japanese way.

We take care of my father-in-law because my husband is *chonan*. Besides, his brothers and sisters are all in Tokyo. I go to the hospital every night after work and all day Sunday to see him. Since my husband works until 9:00 or 10:00 every night, he's too busy to go. Since my brothers, sisters, and parents all live here in Sendai, they go to visit him, too. You know, my father-in-law wasn't sick last February when I took this job. He was fine then. I didn't quit my job because I'd already taken care of my mother-in-law for four years, and my husband said he doesn't want me to lead a life just taking care of old people. He told me I should have my own life.

I'm not a career woman, just a working woman as well as a housewife. Now that I am a working woman, I get back home late sometimes. My husband doesn't complain, but I can tell he is not pleased with me, since I can't give him as much time as I used to. He often works late, and I have to admit I can't always wait up for my husband to come home, but I try. My friends do, too—although I hear the younger ones don't. (I don't know what they do.) If I don't feel ill or tired, I stay up to serve him whiskey. I try to let him relax, let him feel at home before serving him his dinner at nine or ten o'clock. And then after dinner I get his bath ready.

I envy the American woman because her husband washes dishes and helps around the house. Now that I'm working, my husband helps me fold and put away the *futon*. The children help too, because they know I'm so busy. My daughter gets up at 6:30 A.M. to turn on the heater and the rice cooker. I get up at 7:00. My son puts oil in the heater or cleans the bathtub or walks the dogs. Depending on who's going to be home late, my daughter and I take turns shopping and cooking. If she gets home early, she does it. If I get home early, I do—especially now that she has ballet lessons twice a week.

Before I went back to work, I baked cakes and took time to cook. Now there are no more homemade cakes. And only on Saturdays and Sundays can I make time-consuming dishes. Japanese traditional foods take time. So during the week, I sauté or fry foods or make *sukiyaki* or *shabu-shabu*—things that don't take much time.

Who is the ideal Japanese woman? That's a difficult question. . . . The ideal Japanese woman doesn't show off. She helps men to stand out. She does her duties as a wife and mother. I don't think it's necessary for a woman to stand out. Although I don't think this world is only for men, it is better for women to help men accomplish many important things. There are certain special fields for women such as volunteer work or juvenile delinquency. In those fields, women play an important part. But politics is male-centered. And in the family, men come first and women come second. I believe women should play their own part in society as in family life.

I can't really say I'm a modern woman, although my friends say I'm modern and active. I just think I'm busy and use my days efficiently. Every morning the children see me doing housework and cleaning the kitchen. Once I change out of my apron into my work clothes and start thinking, "Now I'm going to the bank," the kids tell me, "You look so different, Mom. Your face shines."

Another woman in banking, a twenty-eight-year-old OL, chose that job because her father told her that "a bank is a nice place to spend time before you marry." Men have a lot of fixed ideas about what is and what is not "appropriate" work for Japanese women. Woman are pegged as being good in jobs that require sensitivity, a delicate touch, and concern for human relations. Many of these jobs are in the service industry, a fitting role since women have for centuries served their fathers and husbands. Increasingly, many forward-thinking companies are moving women into sales where women can use their "personal touch." The insurance companies of Japan can certainly testify to women's skills in sales, since Japan is the best insured country in the world, and 80 percent of the sales staff are women.[1]

Surprisingly, many successful working women also perpetuate the sex-segregated myth of what work is "appropriate" for women to do and what is not. Although policewomen in Tokyo receive the same salary as men, they are confined to jobs in the traffic and juvenile divisions. Policewoman Michiko Tominaga, fifty-one, explains, "There are jobs that only women can do, like arresting pickpockets—women are better at that. And the traffic section—men like to move around, they aren't interested in cars that aren't moving. Women can do it."[2] Toshiba's Kyoko Sawai, a team leader in the computer and OA systems division—the only female team leader in all of the company—said, "My secret belief is that the software business is *better suited* [my italics] for women than men."[3] She, no doubt, meant that statement as a compliment to women, but as long as not just men but even women themselves feel that some jobs are more "appropriate" than others according to sex and not individual ability, fundamental change for working women in Japan will be difficult.

Japan proudly touts the increasing number of all-women teams of computer programmers and all-women personnel groups. The government was very pleased to send an all-women buying mission (household goods, furniture, and fashion) to the United States to help right the trade imbalance, if only in some small way. The kinds of work that are "appropriate" for women are at least expanding. In some companies women can do marketing and designing for other women; in other companies women are being given a chance in sales. What's not yet appropriate, however, is promoting women to management. As long as jobs and teams remain sex-segregated, women are unlikely to change men's opinion of their ability, and the equal-pay-for-equal-work law (Article 4) will continue to be as ineffective as Japan's constitutionally guaranteed Equal Rights Amendment.

At least, married women returning to work is becoming more "appropriate" behavior. The decision to go back is often driven by economics—money for the children's education, family housing loan, or increased living expenses. Already 45 percent of all married couples depend on two incomes.[4] These are not just low-income families either: 42 percent of these women had husbands who earned more than 5 million yen ($20,000) a year.[5] These days, as all Japanese know, it takes more money to keep up with the Tanakas.

WOMAN EXECUTIVE

Although the barriers to success remain high, a handful of Japanese women have taken to heart the title of a book, *Think Like a Man, Act Like a Lady and Work Like a Dog*, translated into Japanese by the country's first woman executive in a major Japanese company, Ichiko Ishihara. Successful Japanese professional women work hard and long. They are patient. They are serious about their work. They don't listen to their neighbor's disapproving whispers. They ignore society's message that a woman's place is in the home. If they have talent, luck, and perseverance, they build a solid career at a price—no family, or so I assumed.

The Japanese have a saying that "The man who chases two rabbits loses both." So I surprised myself when I began thinking of the names of successful Japanese executive women and realized that the majority of them are married. Actually, it makes sense, for in Japanese society, marriage gives a woman a certain legitimacy. Japanese consider anyone—male or female—who doesn't marry "odd," as do many of the unmarried themselves. One fortyish bond salesman, quoting prices to my husband, qualified his views by apologetically noting, "but, of course, I'm not married." The company gives men the message that it's good to marry; as the head of a household, they receive extra housing and family allowances. However, marriage has the opposite effect for a woman. It makes her seem less dependable to a company. The manager looks at her and wonders, "Is she thinking about making dinner? What if she gets pregnant? What if there's a family crisis? Will she quit?" The successful career woman disregards these suspicions on the part of

275

management and continues working anyway. Marriage can have its career advantages for her too. Many a career woman told me that she counts her supportive and understanding husband as "one of my secrets of success." Indeed, that kind of man is a prerequisite, according to a Saitama Prefectural Government study that showed that the number-one factor affecting whether women continue their work or not is the "understanding and cooperation of the family and men." It helps to have an understanding father too, who, if he is not actively encouraging his daughter, at least does not bind her with negative expectations.

Japan's best-known woman executive, Ichiko Ishihara, fifty-nine, has both—an understanding husband and a loving father who had high expectations of her.

Fashionably dressed in her beige-and-creme-striped jacket with rolled-up sleeves, trendy plain white T-shirt and simple black skirt, only her old-fashioned black schoolmarm shoes with their practical square, squat heels belie her age.

In 1979, she became a managing director of Takashimaya, the largest department store chain in Japan, and bold headlines read, "Mother Named Director of Takashimaya Store" and "Woman Attains Top Male Post."[1] Only twelve Japanese women are top-level executives (managing director, president, chairman) in companies listed on the Tokyo Stock Exchange. That means that out of 27,000 executives, only 0.05 percent are women. Ishihara is the only one who climbed the company ladder from the bottom, selling ladies shoes, to the top, as a member of the board of directors. Another successful woman executive worked for years as a magazine editor at a publishing company before joining Daiei (another retail firm) where after five years she became a member of the board. The other ten of the top twelve women took over the family business or are the wives of the ex-chairmen or the mothers of the present presidents. In other words, ten out of twelve are executives because of family ties.[2]

My twenty-five-year-old interpreter (whom, it turned out, I didn't need because Ishihara-san speaks perfect English) summed up her opinion of Ichiko Ishihara in one word—overwhelming. To me, Ishihara-san seemed not so much overwhelming—a lot of presence, yes—but rather like a take-charge manager with a dash of old-fashioned chutzpah. No false modesty and no lack of self-confidence. She gives out a name card with square rather than the more feminine, rounded corners. Needless to say, the word chutzpah has no Japanese equivalent. It is a trait that's in short supply in Japan—neither valued nor encouraged in men, and certainly not in women.

My interpreter also observed: "Ishihara-san's so articulate. That's why I think she's really somebody." She explained, "Most Japanese women are not expected to say clearly what they're thinking. For that matter they aren't even supposed to think so hard that they have their own ideas and opinions."

Being a rare commodity, Ishihara-san is much in demand to serve on government committees. She is currently or has been on committees of nearly all the ministries (MITI, Ministry of Finance, National Land Agency, etc.) "They need ladies' ideas," she insists. "All the other members are men, so when I speak, they listen."

ICHIKO ISHIHARA:

I was born on October twenty-second, Taisho 13 [1923] in Dairen, Manchuria [China]. My father worked for the Manchurian Railway Company, and my mother was a housewife.

I think the kind of Japanese who went to Manchuria were different. Like your pioneers. Manchurian Japanese became richer than ordinary Japanese because companies paid high salaries. My parents had gone there because they didn't want to spend their whole lives in a rainy

277

place like Toyama Prefecture, where they were born and grew up.

My father had a lot of influence on me. He never said, "Women should obey others. You should be a good housewife." In fact he didn't expect me to become a housewife at all. He had high expectations. My mother was a good influence, too. I like her very much. She didn't insist that I be a housewife either. I could always choose what I wanted to do. She has a very open mind and is very tender. Actually, she's a typical Japanese housewife, but she never tried to make me one by forcing me to take bridal training lessons. No, I never did that. She really thinks young, my mother. She's still going out to the movies.

I'm the eldest of six children—three boys and three girls in all. My two sisters are both housewives. They help me a lot. Sometimes they clean my house or do the cooking. My brothers are all salarymen. And their wives help me around the house sometimes, too. None of them is envious. They are all proud of me.

I went to a public elementary, junior high, and high school in Manchuria. One-third of all the graduates of our Japanese girls' high school went to work, one-third started university, and only one-third stayed home to prepare to marry. Young girls grew up differently in Manchuria than in Japan. We had more freedom. We were more independent, something like American women.

I had never seen Japan before I came back at age eighteen to enter Tokyo Women's College, which was a three-year mission school and teacher's training school. At that time, it was the most education a woman could get. Fortunately, back then, the entrance exam pressure wasn't nearly as bad as now, and even though it was wartime, the school had a very free atmosphere. Only during the last year of college (1945) was I mobilized to work in one of the armaments factories.

278

I majored in Japanese literature and lived in a dormitory since my parents were still in Manchuria. Whenever one of those big B-29s came and started dropping bombs, we all ran into an air raid shelter. I was so young that I had no fear. I wasn't worried. Like everyone else, we suffered from the food shortages. We survived on sweet potatoes and noodles. I can't remember what else, it was so long ago. I only remember that I was always hungry. But in 1946, the Americans gave us rescue food—lots of canned vegetables and meats.

Everything really changed dramatically after the war. I had always thought the Emperor was a god, but he became a human being. I was shocked. And the American Army came. The election system changed—women got the vote. The educational system changed—universities opened their doors to women. Before the war, we couldn't go to Todai or Hitotsubashi or other elite national universities. Only a few private universities admitted women.

The end of the war meant the return of my parents to Japan, too. It took them forty-five days by boat from Harbin to our native prefecture of Toyama. They arrived with only one suitcase. They had lost everything else. My mother didn't want to come back, but they had no choice. I had never lived in Toyama myself. But now I understand why it is called the back side of Japan. It's a very old-fashioned, rainy place. Toyama has only about a month of sunshine in a whole year. The rest of the time it's cold, windy, or rainy. Anyway, I met my family there and ended up teaching junior high school English. But I wanted to come back to Tokyo.

And the next year (1946) we did. The eight of us— six children and two parents—worked hard to help each other. I was the eldest child, so of course I had to work. I got a job in a photo lab working for the American Army for the aerial photography team. It didn't help my English, though, since everyone in the lab was Japanese. But

I worked there all day, then at night I studied hard for the entrance exam to Hitotsubashi. I really wanted to go to a coed university.

The war had a great influence on my philosophy of life. Before the war, I wanted to attend a women's college. All I wanted was an intellectual experience. That was it. So if the war had never happened, I might very well be a housewife in Manchuria today. But after the war I saw people returning to Japan with no possessions at all, people like my parents. About one in three of my friends in Manchuria ended up missing, and we still don't know where they are. All this really affected me. At the age of twenty, I realized that what you learn will always be with you, but what you possess can sometimes just disappear.

It was a very difficult exam for Hitotsubashi, but I was determined to become a businesswoman. Many graduates of Hitotsubashi are businessmen in Japan. Since my family lost a lot of things during the war, I realized the importance of money. And I resolved always to be self-supporting.

Students in those days didn't play for four years. They were quite serious. Many had just returned from the Army or the Navy. I was very poor, but I studied hard and worked hard. I got a scholarship, of course. And I worked part-time as a tutor of English to junior high school students.

I majored in economics, and when I graduated I applied to Takashimaya Department Store, which believed in equal opportunity for men and women. I learned about their policies from a Mr. Yashima who graduated from my university. Takashimaya had a very open and free atmosphere. That's why I applied here. I also applied to the Bank of Tokyo and Kanematsu Trading Company. But those two companies said they couldn't treat me as a man's equal, so I chose Takashimaya.

I was very excited about getting a job there. What a rare chance I had, to enter under the same conditions as

280

men! It's rare even today. In 1952, Takashimaya hired fifteen female university graduates. All the rest were high school graduates. Part of the woman's problem today is that she quits once she marries and has children. So she has no chance to move up the ladder.

I started as a salesgirl in the ladies' shoe department. I made 10,000 yen [$40] a month, which wasn't such a low salary at that time, and I really enjoyed selling ladies shoes. I loved being in direct contact with the customers. I still don't like desk work; it's more exciting to be out there dealing with people. After a year in ladies' shoes, I spent two and a half years in the planning section. That was a very important section since at the time we had only three stores, but many plans to expand. (Today we have eighteen stores.) Then I spent two years as a junior buyer of ladies' sweaters. After that, three years in housewares and four years in children's clothing. Then I became a submanager of the whole fifth floor—from baby clothes to boys' and girls' clothes to stationery. Next came five years as the sub-store manager in charge of planning and advertising. And finally in 1979, I became the director of public relations and a member of the board of directors. That was what made the news.

Public relations is very important to us. We take care of all our stores from our headquarters in Tokyo. We announce new store openings and this year's policy, but we also try to keep up to date on what's happening in the business world and other stores outside of Takashimaya. For example, when Isetan Department Store had a problem with their shareholders, we made a report about the situation for our president. We're always collecting information. So I spend a lot of time reading and keeping in close touch with journalists. I take someone out almost every night. But I don't go to bars. It's usually a nice Japanese or French restaurant.

Two years ago we opened a department store for working women, called Sesabi (from C'est Sa Vie) in

Tachikawa, and I'm the president. We realize that working women need a lot of convenience items like instant foods or toaster ovens and that they can afford leisure goods like skis and tennis rackets. We have almost all lady buyers, because it's a store of the women, by the women, and for the women. To us, women buyers are very important. But in other department stores, the buyers are almost all men. We believe that women know how a mother feels and what she wants to buy. It's been very successful. Sales have been up 10 percent every year.

I go there twice a month, usually on Sunday morning, since I live in Kunitachi, the next station. Yes, of course I work on Sunday. That's our busiest day.

Naturally, I continued to work after having our first baby, Keiko, in 1956. (We were married in 1954.) Japanese companies have the lifetime employment system, so if I stopped, I couldn't go back. Each company gives three months maternity leave—six weeks before the birth and six weeks after. I breastfed my little girl because I was very healthy. When it came time to go back to work, my mother, who lived next door, took care of her. The same with my son Akira, who was born in 1962. You see, we have no babysitter system. American working women are very fortunate that way. I've heard that daycare is very poor in Japan. That's the number-one problem of working women in Japan. We need help.

Takashimaya had no system for married women to come back to work. (It was six weeks after the baby was born or not at all.) Seibu Department Store tried to rehire their retired women, but I heard only 2 percent came back. There's another problem, too. Once a woman marries, her husband is sometimes transferred, and we only have eighteen locations. We don't have stores everywhere. So a lot of the married women work part-time in the supermarket or for us. We have 800 temporary workers in this store. They are paid less than the regular workers but the benefits are the same, except there's no retirement allowance. They usually work from 12:00 P.M. to 4:00 P.M. four days a week. It's a very good deal from their point of view because they have the morning hours free to clean house and get the children off to school, and they get home in time to make the husband's dinner.

I met my husband in an economics seminar at Hitotsubashi. Of course, it was a love marriage. I don't like *omiai*. I don't want someone introducing me to someone else. I believe that independent people should be independent. I don't need other people helping me to find someone. I can find my own husband. I think if you use your own common sense, you'll be happy living with the person you choose. Don't marry a person because someone else thinks you should. Marry for love, and you won't regret it. You'll be more committed. You'll have more of a direct link with that person.

Back then, though, most of my friends did *omiai*. I guess they thought it was the safest way. I don't know.

Of course, whoever my son, Akira (twenty-two, an economics major at Meiji University), marries is up to him. But I hope he gets a girl who is independent and smart. I don't like dependent girls. My daughter, Keiko, twenty-eight, should make her own decision too, whether she wants an arranged marriage or a love marriage. She went to Tokyo Women's College. It's a four-year school now. She wants a job like mine, but I don't think it's possible. She has ambition so she chose to work at AGF, a joint venture between Ajinomoto, the well-known Japanese seasonings company, and General Foods, the American food company. (American companies usually give the girls more of a chance.) But even though AGF has a good international and Westernized image, it's still typically Japanese. It's an old-fashioned kind of manufacturing company, where Japanese men don't want to promote women. As in most Japanese companies, the system is made up of men, so I think my daughter has no future there.

In a retail operation like ours, women's ideas are im-

283

portant. We have 200 female university graduates working here now out of 10,000 employees, half of whom are
women. Most of the 5,000 women are high school graduates. They are the girls at the elevators and the girls at
the counters, who work to make money for their weddings and to see what the outside world is like. They tend
to leave after three or four years to marry and have children. As for the university graduates, we have them work
as clerks for the first year. Then after two years they move
up to the planning and advertising section. Then it's up
to submanager. Many of them say they want to become a
director like me. So only a few retire—in the past five years,
only one or two percent have left.

Sometimes men have preconceptions about working
with women, but once they work with me, they have no
problem and they change their minds.

Only once did I worry about being discriminated
against in this company. As I said, I started at the same
level as the male college graduates, so when one of my
male colleagues was promoted to submanager and I was
not, I was upset. I was still a buyer, but he became a
submanager! So I complained to the personnel director. I
said, "Please tell me what's going on here. Is it that I'm
a woman or that I have no talent?" And he explained, "Mrs.
Ishihara, you have two children, and for each one you took
a three-month maternity leave, so after six months you,
too, will be promoted." I was, and after that I had no
problem. Most Japanese women wouldn't have complained in this situation, though. I was told that I'm unusual. But I firmly believe that a department store needs
ladies' ideas. Just look at our restaurant—80 percent of
the people eating are women. Look at the rest of the
store—80 percent of our customers are women. If department stores don't recognize women's ideas, I think they
will fail.

I think working in a department store is a good job
for women. They say government work is good, too. If a

woman can pass the exam, she gets the same pay and same promotions as a man. Law is also a good field for women, if they can pass the exam. Teaching and nursing, they're good, too. The bad jobs are in manufacturing, securities, and banks. And journalism has the problem of overtime and overnight work. I can't say that, if I had been a man, I would have risen higher and faster in my company. But if I were reborn tomorrow, I think I'd rather be a man. They have life easy.

We Japanese women want to be like American women. I like America very much. The women there are so independent. The feminist movement here is almost nothing, though. That's the Confucian influence.

The Japanese housewife depends on her husband and often complains about her job in the house. I am often told that they are envious of me. Well, if so, they should set their own goal and work toward it. Partly because the Japanese business world is a closed system, it's difficult and frustrating for them to reenter the working world. But all this complaining is no good either.

The big problem for the Japanese housewife is that she has no plans. And she always worries about what the neighbors and her friends will think. She's always comparing herself to them. I don't know, and I don't care, what my neighbors think. I've always been so busy, I couldn't see beyond my family and work. I work from 9:40 A.M. to 7:00 P.M. six days a week. And every night I entertain customers, colleagues, or journalists. I guess you could say I'm a workaholic. I do love working hard, and I love working for Takashimaya. It's like a second family to me. Every night, I get back home about 9:00 or 9:30. Before 10:00 P.M. anyway, so I can see my daughter and son. Then it's off to bed at 11:30 or 12:00. When the children were growing up, I did sometimes feel guilty about working, especially when they were sick. But now that they are grown-up, I seldom feel guilty.

My husband—he's a journalist for *Asahi Shim-*

bun—used to work in a building near here, so sometimes we could have lunch together. But now he lives in Kyushu. That's good for me, in that I can work after-hours and get home late. What I don't like is that, when I want to talk to him about something that happened at work, I can't. Or I have to use the phone. At least he comes back to Tokyo twice a month, and I can go down there once a month.

When the four of us are together, those are our happiest times. Whether it's for a simple meal or a few days spent at a hotel resort like Kawana in Shizuoka, which has a nice golf course (that's my hobby) and super restaurants. Of course that's a rare occasion, but . . .

My husband is an open-minded and fair man. He's a good journalist, too. He knew about my ambition before we married. I'd say he's unusual, different from the average Japanese man. A working woman should marry someone who has no prejudice against women. It's true my husband doesn't do any cooking or cleaning (he only cooks when we go hiking). Men don't want to be housewives. So I don't get any physical help, but he helps me a great deal mentally. I can talk about anything with him.

The average Japanese man, however, does look down on women. He thinks of them as weak and poor. You see, Japan is a male-dominated country, which has always maintained this order, this hierarchy. I don't think it will change. Men don't want ladies to be first here. I want ladies to be equal, but men don't like this idea. I think the new Equal Employment Opportunity Law may change things slightly. A lot of women are entering business and other fields now, and as more and more do, the sheer quantity of them will change the quality of how they are perceived and treated, don't you think? I think women have the same potential as men, but they aren't given a chance to show what they can do. I've been very lucky, and I know it. In most companies I'd be only an assistant manager by now and not a member of the board of directors. Two big things are holding back women: men don't want to work with them; and women don't want to continue their jobs for a long time after they marry and have children.

There are other factors as well. Japan as a nation has always had a tendency to maintain the existing order. Class has been abolished, but a certain social order exists, nonetheless. And any disturbance to this order is likely to be eliminated. Japanese feel that keeping order is more important than each person displaying his own character. Part of this order is an image of women or housewives known as *onna rashii* or feminine—how women are supposed to be. They should not be outspoken, and they should not stand out. This image has been held by society for a long time. If a woman is called *onna rashikunai,* that means she is not feminine. Similarly *okusan rashikunai* means a woman who is not suitable to be a housewife. Those expressions are insults.

But those of us in the business community are trying to create a new image of women. I want us to be like American working women, but I think we are twenty years behind you. Last week I was named head of a government-sponsored mission, a ladies' mission, that will go to the United States to buy American merchandise. I think something in Japan is changing when they start sending a ladies' mission abroad. In your country, it's natural. But in Japan, it's unusual.

I've been told I'm a symbol for Japanese working women. Every time I'm on TV, I get fan letters from young women. You know, in 1976, half of all Japanese were born after the war—it was a turning point in generations. Now, almost ten years later, 60 percent of the population was born after the war. These 60 percent have received co-educational schooling, a different type of education than the prewar generation. Less than 50 percent of businesses are run by the prewar generation. And in ten years a new postwar generation will be on top. Then maybe the situation will change. I hope.

Will the social order change in the next generation?

Access, certainly, is one of the keys to success. And the good news is that more and more male-only fields are opening up to women. In the early 1980s, the first women became air traffic controllers, police detectives, immigration officers. The prime minister named the first woman cabinet member in twenty-two years.

Rather than stand behind a Xerox machine for five years and wait to be noticed, more women are starting their own businesses. They have opened a temporary employment agency (Tempstaff), an advertising agency (Nippo Marketing and Advertising) and an all-woman software company (Modern Information Research Institute).

Every year growth industries such as information services and retailing absorb more and more young women. However, the best opportunities for young women in the future may well be with computers and microelectronics. Many female college graduates who would routinely end up in dead-end OL jobs are already opting to become "techno ladies" instead. With the shortage of qualified male university graduates, more and more companies are willing to give young women a chance. In 1984, IBM Japan hired sixty-nine new female graduates as systems engineers; in 1985 the number soared to 250. Hitachi upped the number of female computer programmers from forty in 1979 to 150 in 1984. With the skyrocketing demand for new computer software, women have a chance to break down old biases and prove themselves in a new sex-blind profession.

Every generation of Japanese women contributes to the economic miracle in a different way: today's grandmothers stayed home and worked for free in the family business or on the family farm; today's mothers focus on family, too, although after the children enter school, many of them reenter the work force. And the young women? They could be the fuel for what computer experts are calling Japan's next economic miracle—microelectronics.

Politics played a large part in improving business opportunities for women in the United States through Title VII of the Civil Rights Act and affirmative action programs. Yet in Japan, few women have chosen politics as a way to improve women's working conditions and women's status in society. Only on one issue—passage of the Equal Employment Opportunity Law—did forty-eight women's organizations join forces to support the bill. Antiwar feelings spawn only sporadic demonstrations. The abortion issue brings out women on both sides. But other than these three concerns, women have been remarkably quiescent in the 1980s. Gone are the student demonstrators of the 1960s and the political activists of the 1970s, who staged consumer boycotts and antipollution demonstrations.

Every major political party in Japan has a women's division, yet only nineteen women sit in the Diet's 252-member Upper House, the House of Councillors, and many of them are former TV talents urged to run because of their high visibility. Where the real power lies, in the Diet's 511-member Lower House, only eight women hold seats. All in all, they make up a paltry 3 percent of the Diet. Even fewer women are elected to seats in prefecture, city, town, and village assemblies.[3] Lacking political funds, strong party backing, and solid local organizations, "they [women] know the odds and don't even try," says Diet Member Mayumi Moriyama, fifty-six.[4]

Qualities essential to achievement—attitude, a strong will, and a willingness to make a commitment—are attributes all successful Japanese working women have. Yet historically Japanese women have been educated to be self-denying rather than self-assertive. That's why Raicho Hiratsuka, the founder of the first feminist group, noted, "The most significant barriers lie within ourselves."[5] At present only 61 percent of Japanese working women believe in equal pay for equal work; only 64 percent oppose any kind of sex discrimination in hiring or employment. At least figures

289

were higher among Japanese college women, at 77 percent and 78 percent, respectively. On all questions in this 1984 Tokyo Junior Chamber of Commerce survey, the attitude of Japanese working women and Japanese college women differed by at least ten points or more, indicating there is a change in attitude among the younger generation.

I had hoped that young men had a higher consciousness these days, as well. After all, more and more young fathers shop in the supermarket. A few even take a turn cooking at home, "appalling the older generation," as one working woman said, "who consider the kitchen a woman-only place." A young bachelor said, "We tell the girls we'll help around the house when we get married, but deep down we don't really want to." Evidently they don't. A 1984 survey by Chiba University polled young men at such elite Japanese universities as Waseda and Keio. The study revealed that 66 percent of these young men still believe a woman's place is in the home; 65 percent would rather not marry a woman majoring in a field that leads to a profession; 69 percent would rather marry a girl who studied tea ceremony and flower-arranging. "We are all equal in college," says a matter-of-fact, twenty-seven-year-old banker, "but once we graduate, women have to rely on men to survive. So women have to change."

Old attitudes die hard. But progress has been made since the days when their mothers married. There is increasing acceptance of women working once they marry, and of women returning to work. More college women work; and they want more challenging jobs. More women continue working even after childbirth. Women are working longer, and more aim to work until retirement.

Whether their husbands like it or not, whether society likes it or not, indeed whether some of them like it or not, the majority of Japanese women are working.

But what will happen in the future to women in the labor force if Japan encounters a recession? That will mean that jobs will be harder to get. But the women's husbands will be earning less overtime; salary increases will slow. So women will have to find work to supplement the family income. If, on the other hand, Japan should enter a period of high growth, the resulting labor shortage will force employers to encourage women to work. So, whether forced into the workplace by slow economic growth or encouraged by high economic growth, even more Japanese women will be working in the future.

Part IV

MOUNTAIN-MOVING DAY

Japanese women are hardly as restricted as the veiled women in Islamic societies, but their status is by far the lowest of women in advanced industrial societies, at least to Western eyes. "To Western eyes" is a key phrase. As former Ambassador to Japan Edwin Reischauer noted, the position of women in Japan "stirs indignation among Western women, particularly Americans."[1]

American women in Japan are not accustomed to being jostled in the elevator or to having their opinions only begrudgingly listened to. The number-one complaint of American women living in Japan is that they are not taken seriously.

But Japanese women have never been first off the elevator. They are accustomed to deferring to men and keeping their opinion to themselves. In one survey of women in six countries, Japanese women topped the list in believing in separate roles for women and men (71 percent); putting one's husband and family first (72 percent); and affirming that housework is the woman's responsibility (89 percent).[2] Another survey revealed that most Japanese men and women were content with their lives, and at 80 percent, compared to 74 percent, women scored even higher than men.[3]

The majority of Japanese women are, in short, satisfied with their lot in life. They speak of a web of circumstances, obligations and events that have made their role what it is. Although some talk as if they were indeed caught in a web, others see societal restrictions as a warm and protective cocoon.

And why would any right-thinking Japanese woman want to imitate Americans? Our image in Japan is not an enviable one. The male-dominated media of Japan, when not covering government, business, or trade, focuses on violence and sex in the States. *Violence U.S.A.*, a movie that detailed all the assassinations, multiple murders, and random acts of violence in America in the last twenty years, was big box office in Tokyo. A recent TV show covered what the *Japan Times* listing described as "the boom in centers teaching striptease to American housewives who want to lure their husbands back into the bedroom." One former Japanese newspaperman, in an unguarded moment induced by several beers, confided to me that he himself thought American women were self-centered, materialistic, aggressive, independent, loud, out for fun, and insufficiently concerned with taking proper care of their children. "Of course, you, Jane-san, are different," he added with some embarrassment. (Japanese are nothing if not polite.)

For any woman who lived through the war, or who has heard her mother's and grandmother's stories about B-29s dropping fire bombs that made night into day, and century-old family kimonos being traded for handfuls of rice, just being alive today seems like good fortune. And compared to the prewar days, when women had five children and no washing machines or electric rice cookers, their life in today's affluent Japan is positively luxurious. Many housewives even have time for a tennis game, a French lesson or lunch with the girls.

"Change is slow to come," says Mariko Fujiwara, research director of the Hakuhodo Institute of Life and Living, "because Japanese women are not willing to give up anything. They're not willing to take risks. So they go for small pluses rather than big trade-offs."

Yet there are cracks in the contemporary Japanese woman's facade of contentment. An extensive Hakuhodo Institute of Life and Living study, focusing on the anxieties of Japanese women, found that some young housewives, ages twenty-five to thirty-four, are restless, but feel they can't change their situation because they are tied down by their children. Many middle-aged housewives, ages thirty-five to forty-four, feel that they have reached a turning point at which they would like to make changes, but they are afraid of jeopardizing the comfort and security of their present lives. Many of the older women, ages forty-five to fifty-four, have a feeling of pride and a sense of well-being, but some wonder why they devoted their entire lives to serving others and feel they must make up for lost time by devoting their remaining years to themselves. If these women could live their lives over again, they say they would take more control of their own fates.[4]

Those women who have in fact taken more control are the working wives. Yet they, too, have many reasons to be dissatisfied: low pay, low-level jobs, slim chances for promotion. Unlike men, they are accused of neglecting their families by working. They also carry the burden of a double day—when they finish work in the office, factory or store, they return home to start their cooking and cleaning. They have no role models, no old-girl network, and considerable childcare worries.

Yet their numbers are increasing. Why? The answer is an easing of the social pressure to stay at home and an increasing need for a second income.

More and more Japanese women are reaching the end of the era of living their lives solely through their husbands and children. Married women today have fewer family obligations and much more free time. They want to expand their house-bound horizons with hobbies, volunteer work, part-time jobs, or full-time work. Ironically enough, they are getting a boost from the mass media. Although Japanese newspapers and TV still link juvenile delinquency with working mothers, they also give the opposite message by noting that women who stay home have a "narrow outlook" and by providing the public with almost daily reports on each and every woman to enter any male-dominated field.

Although young Japanese women are still renowned for being *yasashii* (tender, kind, gentle), the days of total obedience are over. Young wives are less disposed to being nurses and maids at home. They want their husbands to help around the house, at least a little. They want the whole family to go out to eat at least once a month, if not once a week (hence the rise in the number of family restaurants). They are less likely to pack away their high fashion Japanese clothes when they marry. They buy new clothes less often, but they still want to look as nice as they did when they were *dokushin kazoku* (single aristocrats). They insist that their husbands talk with them more. And although young husbands may still be number one in the family, the idea of walking behind them strikes young wives as absurd.

These increasingly well-educated young women have never known the hardships of war, only lives of material comfort and success. But they sense something is missing. Now they are searching for spiritual fulfillment for both their families and themselves. They encourage their husbands to put the family first and work second. In their own words, they want to "humanize" Japan. One seldom articulated aspect of that humanization is the changing role of women. Maybe the status of women is not rising as quickly as many women would hope. But as one housewife noted, "We say we are happy and content because we *are*—as long as the situation keeps improving."

Even the most traditional man I know, an executive at one of Japan's most old-line companies, acknowledges that change is coming. "It may be fifty or one hundred years," he says, giving a more conservative estimate than anyone else I talked with, "but it will happen."

He sighs. Many Japanese men, while recognizing that

298

change is on the horizon, long for the old days, before the time when the oft-quoted saying became popular that "After the war, women and nylons both became stronger."

Successful career woman Ichiko Ishihara believes that significant change will come within only twenty years. The most optimistic estimate of all comes from Ginko Sato, a Ministry of Labor official who for many years has been professionally concerned with the role of women in Japanese society. She predicts great changes within the next decade.

Whatever the timing, change will come. I think of it in terms of the erosion of a mountain or the movement of a glacier—barely perceptible, but steady, strong, and inexorable.

The words of the well-loved poet Akiko Yosano seem even more appropriate today than when she first wrote them in 1911:

> The mountain-moving day is coming
> I say so yet others may doubt it
> Only a while the mountain sleeps
> In the past all mountains moved in fire
> Yet you may not believe it
> But oh this believe
> All sleeping women now awake and move
> All sleeping women now awake and move.

Japanese women are beginning to awake and move, forging quiet paths toward equality. As sure as cherry blossoms bloom in the spring and typhoons rage in the fall, there's a quiet revolution going on in Japan. Yet some Japanese men seem to think that the changing role of women is temporary. Many feel that the problem will blow away if they just ignore it long enough—a very Japanese way of looking at things. One university professor described today's growing number of working women as simply the crest of a wave. "Those women have illusory power, but these things are cyclical," he assured me. A banker said simply, "It's like the swing of a pendulum. That's all. They'll go back home."

I don't think so.

The momentum is building. Millions of underemployed and overeducated women are sitting at home, bowing beside the escalators, serving tea, or greeting customers—just waiting for their talent to be tapped, ready to contribute to the next economic miracle.

Mountain-moving day is coming. In fact, it may already be here.

Notes

Introduction

1. Robins-Mowry, Dorothy. *The Hidden Sun: Women of Modern Japan* (Boulder, Colorado: Westview Press, 1983), pp. 6–11.
2. *Labor Force Survey*, Ministry of Labor, 1984.
3. Ibid.

PART I FAMILY

1. *Basic Administrative Survey*, Ministry of Health and Welfare, June 1984.
2. *Trend in Household Composition*, Statistics Bureau, Prime Minister's Office, 1982.
3. Chie Nakane, *Japanese Society* (Middlesex, England: Penguin, 1970), pp. 132–33.
4. Ruth Benedict, *The Chrysanthemum and the Sword* (New York: New American Library, 1974), p. 254. (Originally published by Houghton Mifflin in 1946.)
5. Ian Buruma, *Behind the Mask* (New York: Pantheon, 1984), p. 25.
6. Nakane, op. cit., p. 132.
7. Takie Sugiyama Lebra, "Autonomy for the Japanese Housewife in Her Later Years," Asiatic Society of Japan lecture, Tokyo, September 10, 1984.

Marriage

1. Statistics Bureau, Management and Coordination Agency, 1980.
2. "Japanese Women and Marriage," *Tokyo Newsletter*, Mitsubishi Corporation, January 1983, p. 10.
3. Edwin O. Reischauer, *The Japanese* (Cambridge: Belknap Press of the Harvard University Press, 1977), p. 205.

Divorce

1. Basil Hall Chamberlain, *Japanese Things* (Tokyo: Charles E. Tuttle Company, 1971), pp. 503–4. (Originally published as *Things Japanese* in 1904.)
2. Kimpei Shiba, "Women Growing Bolder," *Asahi Evening News*, May 30, 1984.
3. Yoshiya Ariyoshi, "Tokeiji," *Shipping and Trade News*, February 3, 1981.
4. *Present Status of Women and Policies, Third Report on the National Action Program*, Prime Minister's Office, April 1983, p. 9.
5. *Survey of Single Mother Families*, Ministry of Health and Welfare, May 1984.
6. Ibid.
7. Ibid.
8. "Singer, Actress Announce Divorce," *Japan Times*, June 19, 1984, p. 2.
9. Sadako Ogata, "Women of Japan," Harvard Club of Japan lecture, Tokyo, November 23, 1983.

Feminism

1. "The Women of Japan," *About Japan Series* (Tokyo: Foreign Press Center, July 1977), p. 25.
2. Y. Nishimura, "The Intimately Oppressed," *Japan Times*, January 9, 1985, p. 7.

SEX AND PORNOGRAPHY

1. Terry Trucco, "Why Does Japan Love Lolita?", *The International Herald Tribune*, December 3, 1982, p. 9.
2. Robert Whymant, "Dietmen Bank on Miss Instant Noodle 1983," *No. 1 Shimbun*, May 15, 1984, p. 8.
3. Wendy Cole, "Rape Crisis Center Opens in Tokyo," *Tokyo Journal*, November 1983, pp. 7–8.

BIRTH CONTROL AND ABORTION

1. "Population Vital Statistics," Ministry of Health and Welfare, 1984.
2. "Japanese Couples Make Love Less: Survey," Kyodo News Service, *Japan Times*, April 3, 1983.

3. "Teen-age Abortions Jump Over 10% in Japan," *Asahi Evening News*, June 3, 1983.

OLD AGE

1. *Statistical Analysis of Elderly Population of Japan*, Prime Minister's Office, September 1983, p. 2.
2. Ibid., p. 5.
3. Ibid., p. 1.
4. Yoshie Yamaguchi, "Coping With the Aging of Society," *Japan Times Weekly*, September 10, 1983, p. 7.

PART II   EDUCATION

1. Yukiko Maki, "What Meiji Meant to Japanese Women," College Women's Association of Japan lecture, February 27, 1984.
2. Arthur Waley, introduction to Lady Murasaki's *The Tale of Genji* (New York: Doubleday Anchor, 1955), p. ix.
3. Basil Hall Chamberlain, op. cit., p. 597.
4. *Basic Survey of Schools*, Ministry of Education, March 1984.

Education Mama (Kyoiku Mama)

1. *Basic Survey of Schools*, op. cit., March 1984 and Statistical Abstract of the U.S. 1984, U.S. Department of Commerce, p. 160.
2. Edward B. Fiske, "U.S. Pupils Lag from Grade 1, Study Finds," *The New York Times*, June 17, 1984, p. 30.
3. Edward B. Fiske, "Japan's Schools: Intent About the Basics," *The New York Times*, July 10, 1983, pp. 1, 28.
4. "Higher Education May Not Lead to Higher Income," *Japan Times*, September 28, 1984, p. 3.
5. Fiske, "U.S. Pupils Lag From Grade 1, Study Finds," loc. cit.
6. "Tokyo Bay Crash Victim," *Japan Times*, February 12, 1982, p. 2.
7. "Youth Electrocutes Himself Over Tests," Kyodo, *Japan Times*, January 18, 1982, p. 2.

SCHOOLS AND TEACHERS

1. Fiske, "U.S. Pupils Lag From Grade 1, Study Finds," loc. cit.
2. *Stride by Stride, Women's Issues in Tokyo: The Current Situation*, Tokyo Metropolitan Government, December 1983, p. 25.

303

Three Students

1. *Basic Survey of Schools*, p. 160.
2. "Education in Japan," *About Japan Series*, (Tokyo: Foreign Press Center, May 1978), p. 25.
3. *Stride By Stride*, p. 23.
4. *Basic Survey of Schools*, Ministry of Education, July 1983, p. 26.
5. Ryoko Akamatsu, "Changing Trends For Women in the Japanese Work Force," American Chamber of Commerce (in Japan) lecture, October 16, 1984.

JUNIOR COLLEGE STUDENT

1. Sally Solo, "Students Are Learning About Sex, But Not at School," Associated Press, September 25, 1984.
2. "Feminization of Boys," *Mainichi Daily News*, May 5, 1982.

RONIN

1. *Basic Survey of Schools*, May 1984.

THE CHALLENGE AHEAD

1. *White Paper on Youth*, Prime Minister's Office, December, 1981.
2. "Slight Crime Drop Noted By Teachers," *The New York Times*, September 27, 1984, p. B4.

PART III   WORK

Career Woman

1. *Present Status of Women and Policies, Third Report on the National Action Program*, Prime Minister's Office, April 1983.
2. *Labor Force Survey*, Ministry of Labor, 1984.

Job-Hunter

1. *Survey on Corporate Hiring Plans*, Ministry of Labor, 1981.
2. *Labor Force Survey*, Prime Minister's Office, 1981.
3. Deborah Smith, "Satisfaction of Life in Japan Prevents Challenge By Women," Associated Press, *The Daily Yomiuri*, January 26, 1981, p. 5.

4. Hiroshi Takeuchi, "Working Women in Business Corporations—The Management Viewpoint," *Japan Quarterly*, July–September 1982, pp. 319–23.

Part-Timer

1. *Female Part-Time Employees*, Labor Force Survey, Prime Minister's Office, 1984.
2. *Part-Timers By Company Scale*, Prime Minister's Office, March 1981.
3. *Present Status of Women and Policies, Third Report on the National Action Program*, Prime Minister's Office, April 1983, p. 7.
4. Special Report on Women, *U.S. News & World Report*, August 6, 1984, p. 46.

OL (Office Lady)

1. Ian Buruma, "Young Japanese Bow to an Old Tradition—and Keep Bowing," *Far Eastern Economic Review*, December 8, 1983, p. 52.
2. Kimpei Shiba, "Enviable Office Ladies," Japan Yesterday and Today, column 341, *Asahi Evening News*, March 31, 1982.
3. Mayo Issobe, "Office Ladies' List Beefs, Boss's Faults, Work Goals, Interests," *Japan Times*, November 22, 1984, p. 10.
4. "Poll Finds 'Office Ladies' Are Rich, Independent and Sneaky," Associated Press, *Asahi Evening News*, July 10, 1984, p. 3.
5. "OL: The Female Office Workers," *Sumitomo Quarterly*, Autumn 1983, p. 28.
6. "College Coeds See Jobs As Marriage Maneuvers," *Japan Times*, October 6, 1982, p. 2.
7. *Annual Labor Force Survey Report*, Statistics Bureau, Prime Minister's Office, 1983.
8. *Basic Survey of Social Life*, Statistics Bureau, Prime Minister's Office, 1981.
9. *Stride by Stride*, p. 45.
10. Ibid., p. 45.
11. "3 Infants Die at Unlicensed Day Centers," *Japan Times*, March 12, 1981, p. 2.
12. Haruko Watanabe, "Added Incentives for Working Mamas," *Mainichi Daily News*, June 19, 1984.
13. Tomiko Shirakigawa, "Talking Shop," *Japan Times*, December 23, 1983, p. 13.

Blue-Collar Worker

FARMER

1. "Census of Agriculture and Forestry 1980," Statistical Information Department, Ministry of Agriculture, Forestry and Fisheries.
2. Masako Ozawa, "Sharpening Distinctions Dissolving the Classless Myth," *Japan Times*, November 28, 1984, p. 11.
3. Nicholas Valery, "What Makes Yoshio Run? Japan: A Survey," *The Economist*, July 9, 1983, p. 13.

FACTORY WORKER

1. Sharon L. Sievers, *Flowers In Salt* (Stanford, CA: Stanford University Press, 1983), p. 55.
2. Ross Mouer, "Women in the Labor Force, From the Meiji Period through World War II," *Kodansha Encyclopedia of Japan* (Tokyo: Kodansha International, 1983), p. 264.
3. Sievers, op. cit. pp. 56–57.
4. Ibid. pp. 54–78.
5. Ann Nakano, "Voices From Within—Mina Yamanouchi," *Mainichi Daily News*, August 13, 1984, p. 4.
6. Sievers, op. cit. pp. 81–83.
7. Mouer, op. cit. pp. 264–66.
8. Buruma, op. cit. pp. 42–46.

MOM-AND-POP BUSINESS

1. Toshiko Fujii, "Women in the Labor Force, Women Workers Today," *Kodansha Encyclopedia of Japan* (Tokyo: Kodansha International, 1983), p. 265.
2. Valery, op. cit. p. 13.
3. Mary R. Beard, *The Force of Women in Japanese History* (Washington, D.C.: Public Affairs Press, 1953), pp. 109–10.

ENTERTAINERS

1. Liza Dalby, *Geisha* (Tokyo: Kodansha International, 1983) p. 54.
2. Kathy Pearsal and Hiroko Asami, "Working Women in Japan: Help Needed," *Tokyo Journal*, April 1, 1982, pp. 4–5.

HOSTESS

1. Dalby, op. cit. p. 80.
2. Bob Horiguchi, "Inside the Weeklies," from *Shukan Shincho, Japan Times*, December 21, 1982, p. 7.

GEISHA

1. Dalby, op. cit. p. 56.
2. Ibid. p. 80.

OLDER WHITE-COLLAR WORKERS

1. *Present Status of Women and Policies, Third Report on the National Action Program*, Prime Minister's Office, April 1983.
2. "Married Women Are Growing As Major Force in Job Market," *Japan Economic Journal*, December 7, 1982, p. 8.
3. "Japanese Perspectives: Impact of Working Women," *Japan Times*, January 30, 1984, p. 5.

Older White-Collar Workers

RETURNING TO WORK

1. Masayoshi Kanabayashi, "In Japan, Most Guys Pestering You To Buy Insurance Are Gals," *The Wall Street Journal*, March 25, 1981, pp. 1, 18.
2. "Same Pay, But Assignments Limited to 'Appropriate Areas' ", *Asahi Evening News*, August 25, 1984, p. 3.
3. "Women Are Rising Force in Program Development Jobs," *Japan Economic Journal*, August 14, 1984.
4. *Percentage of Dual-Career Families*, Statistics Bureau, Prime Minister's Office, 1983.
5. "Long Recession Driving More Housewives To Work Outside," *Japan Times*, July 11, 1983, p. 2.

WOMAN EXECUTIVE

1. "Mother Named Director of Takashimaya Store," *Asahi Evening News*, March 14, 1979 and "Woman Attains Top Male Post," *Mainichi Daily News*, March 15, 1979.
2. *Kaika Suru Ka? Josei Juyaku Jidai* (Opening Up? The Female Executive Age) *Nihon Keizai Shimbun*, July 2, 1984, p. 9.

3. *The Women of Japan*, Prime Minister's Office, March 1984, p. 15.
4. Steve Vogel, "Competing With 'Pushy, Ambitious' Men in Politics," *Japan Times*, March 28, 1984, p. 11.
5. Sievers, op. cit. p. 164.

PART IV   MOUNTAIN-MOVING DAY

1. Edwin O. Reischauer, *The Japanese* (Cambridge: Belknap Press of the Harvard University Press, 1977), p. 204.
2. "Traditional Roles Accepted By Most Women: Survey," *Japan Times*, April 5, 1983, p. 2.
3. *Japanese Women In Turmoil* (Tokyo: Hakuhodo Institute of Life and Living, 1984), p. 22.
4. Ibid. pp. 136–40.

Bibliography

Ariyoshi, Sawako. *The Twilight Years*, Trans. Mildred Tahara. Tokyo: Kodansha International, 1984.

Beard, Mary R. *The Force of Women in Japanese History*. Washington, D.C.: Public Affairs Press, 1953.

Benedict, Ruth. *The Chrysanthemum and the Sword: Patterns of Japanese Culture*. Boston: Houghton Mifflin, 1946.

Buruma, Ian. *Behind the Mask*. New York: Pantheon Books, 1984.

Chamberlain, Basil Hall. *Japanese Things*. Tokyo: Charles E. Tuttle, 1971. Originally published in 1904 as *Things Japanese*.

Christopher, Robert C. *The Japanese Mind*. New York: Linden Press, 1983.

Cook, Alice H., and Hiroko Hayashi. "Working Women in Japan, Discrimination, Resistance and Reform." *Cornell International Industrial and Labor Relations Report*, No. 10. Ithaca, N.Y., 1980.

Dalby, Liza. *Geisha*. Tokyo: Kodansha International, 1983.

Doi, Takeo. *The Anatomy of Dependence*. Trans. John Bester. Tokyo: Kodansha International, 1973.

Fields, George. *From Bonsai to Levi's*. New York: Macmillan, 1983.

Frédéric, Louis. *Daily Life in Japan at the Time of the Samurai, 1185–1603*. Trans. Eileen M. Lowe. Tokyo: Charles E. Tuttle, 1973.

Japanese Women in Turmoil. Tokyo: Hakuhodo Institute of Life and Living, 1984.

Halloran, Richard. *Japan: Images and Realities*. Tokyo: Charles E. Tuttle, 1969.

Hearn, Lafcadio. *Japan: An Interpretation*. Tokyo: Charles E. Tuttle Company, 1959.

Ishimoto, Baroness Shidtue. *Facing Two Ways, The Story of My Life*. Stanford: Stanford University Press, 1984.

Kodansha Encyclopedia of Japan. Tokyo: Kodansha International, 1983.

Kuroyanagi, Tetsuko, *Totto-chan, the Little Girl at the Window*. Trans. Dorothy Britton. Tokyo: Kodansha International, 1982.

Lebra, Joyce, Joy Paulson, and Elizabeth Powers, eds. *Women In Changing Japan*. Stanford: Stanford University Press, 1978.

Lebra, Takie Sugiyama. *Japanese Women, Constraint and Fulfillment*. Honolulu: University of Hawaii Press, 1984.

Nakane, Chie. *Japanese Society*. Middlesex, England: Penguin, 1970.

Reischauer, Edwin O. *The Japanese*. Cambridge: Harvard University Press, 1977.

Robins-Mowry, Dorothy. *The Hidden Sun: Women of Modern Japan*. Boulder, Colorado: Westview Press, 1983.

Shiba, Kimpei. *Oh, Japan!* Kent, England: Paul Norbury Publications, 1979.

Sievers, Sharon L. *Flowers In Salt: The Beginnings of Feminist Consciousness in Modern Japan*. Stanford: Stanford University Press, 1983.

Taylor, Jared. *Shadows of the Rising Sun*. New York: William Morrow, 1983.

Trager, James. *Letters From Sachiko*. New York: Atheneum, 1983.

Vogel, Ezra F. *Japan as Number One: Lessons for America*. Cambridge: Harvard University Press, 1979.

Waley, Arthur, trans. Lady Murasaki's *The Tale of Genji*. Garden City, N.Y.: Doubleday Anchor, 1955.

Index